Wiley Global Finance is a market-leading provider of over 400 annual books, mobile applications, elearning products, workflow training tools, newsletters and websites for both professionals and consumers in institutional finance, trading, corporate accounting, exam preparation, investing, and performance management.

Trade the Congressional Effect

Trade the Congressional Effect

How to Profit from Congress's Impact on the Stock Market

ERIC T. SINGER

WILEY

John Wiley & Sons, Inc.

Published by John Wiley & Sons, Inc., Hoboken, New Jersey.

Published simultaneously in Canada.

For general information on our other products and services or for technical support, please contact our Customer Care Department within the United States at (800) 762-2974, outside the United States at (317) 572-3993 or fax (317) 572-4002.

Wiley also publishes its books in a variety of electronic formats. Some content that appears in print may not be available in electronic books. For more information about Wiley products, visit our website at *www.wiley.com*.

Library of Congress Cataloging-in-Publication Data:
Singer, Eric.
  Trade the Congressional effect : how to profit from Congress's impact on the stock market / Eric Singer.
     p. cm. – (Wiley trading series)
  Includes bibliographical references and index.
  ISBN 978-1-118-36243-3 (cloth); ISBN 978-1-118-42046-1 (ebk);
ISBN 978-1-118-43436-9 (ebk); ISBN 978-1-118-41709-6 (ebk)
 1. Stocks–Prices–United States. 2. Investments–United States.
3. Portfolio management–United States. 4. United States. Congress. I. Title.
  HG4915.S56 2012
  332.63′220973–dc23

                                                        2012022655

Printed in the United States of America

10 9 8 7 6 5 4 3 2 1

To my loving wife, Aet, so beautiful, so patient, so wise.

Contents

Acknowledgments

I want to thank everyone who encouraged me and helped make this book a reality. To my son Brett for his day-to-day help, thank you. To my daughter Jamie for her encouragement, thank you as well. Carol Mann heard about this book for years and represented me well when the time came. But for Amity Shlaes's encouragement and suggestions, I probably would not have started. Robert Asahina helped me to frame the project and take the critical first steps. To Joe Steinberg, thank you for being a true friend. That goes for you, too, Robert Harow. Many friends and colleagues read it and/or generously shared their thoughts or help on the project, including Charles Pradilla, Brett Joshpe, Chris Anci, David Berkowitz, Adam Steinberg, Clyde White, Ira Stoll, Tresa Veitia, Diego Veitia, Ted Weisberg, Jon Frank, Morgan Frank, Matt Pilkington, Dana Rubin, Walter Molofsky, Shane Burn, John Regan, Brian Saroken, Jeff Skinner, Matt Chambers, Dave Ganley, Eric Frenchman, Bob Cresci, Sam Solomon, Dan Ripp, Andrew Gundlach, Paul Zaykowski, Joe Ancona, Elisabeth Richter, Walter Robertson, Joe Plummer, Sterling Terrell, Matt Pilkington, and Wes Mann. I'd also like to thank my interns for their help on this project. I hope they choose America over Singapore. No acknowledgment would be complete without thanking my father and mother, who gave me a great education. Finally, I would like to thank Pamela van Giessen, Evan Burton, and Emilie Herman for believing in this book, and giving me the chance to publish it through John Wiley & Sons, Inc.

Introduction

"Government is not reason, it is not eloquence. It is a force. Like fire it is a ... dangerous servant and a fearful master, never for a moment should it be left to irresponsible action."

— George Washington

"Government is not the solution to our problem ... Government is the problem."

— Ronald Reagan

Who would have thought in the 1990s that by the end of 2011 we Americans would have had a lost decade in which our investments were shattered, our equity in homes would disappear, our 401(k)s would be cut in half, and our stature as the preeminent economy of the world would increasingly be called into doubt? The convulsions of the past decade have resulted in economic and social setbacks of epic proportions. Our standard economic remedies have been tried and tried again, but now seem impotent against the giant new challenges facing us.

We have arrived at this surprisingly desperate moment after 100 years of slow but relentless growth in—and dysfunctionality of—government in general, and Congress in particular. Our politicians have engaged in magical thinking for so long that the magic is gone. They actually believe they can, like Harry Potter, speak incantations and create jobs and prosperity for everyone. But unlike Hollywood special effects, there are no economic or political spells that can dispel our troubles. We are in a mess caused by our own willful abandonment of our core principles. The remedies we used to believe in no longer work.

The public already knows something is very wrong but can't quite put its finger on what it is or, especially, what to do about it. As of February 2012, Congress's approval rating is 10 percent, according a Gallup survey,[1]

1

below its former all-time low in the crisis of October 2008, when the equity markets were plunging, on their way to a frighteningly sudden 50 percent loss in less than nine months. In fact, out of 16 major institutions, such as the military, the police, and so on, Congress now ranks dead last.

Congress would have us believe that every little morsel and crumb we receive is dispensed to us by a gracious government that has changed the social safety net into a pampering spa, and that if we don't let Congress continue to dispense us goodies, we will have nothing. But we should not want the government to do us any favors. When it looks into our wallet and finds a 10-dollar bill, it immediately takes credit for those 10 dollars. But government can only subtract value, it cannot create value. This subtraction of value is what I call the Congressional Effect.

This book provides a new, empirically objective way to understand day by day what our government takes away from all of us. It shows in hard numbers what we lose out of our wallet when Congress acts. Knowing exactly how much poorer we are because of relentless government bloat, this book suggests concrete investing strategies to make Congress's systemic dysfunction work for you, and to hedge the risk and the damage that Congress so casually and relentlessly inflicts on your life savings as represented by your portfolio and your house.

OUR DAMAGED ECONOMY

In the past 10 years, the U.S. economy has suffered one disaster after another, all of which were predictable and many of which were avoidable. In the 1990s it would have been inconceivable to think the following would have occurred by the end of 2011:

- That the government, in the name of "affordable housing," would use Fannie Mae and Freddie Mac to force banks to lend to a wider pool of people, thus creating a giant credit bubble.
- That the credit bubble would in turn inflate housing prices to unsustainable levels, which in turn set up the housing collapse.
- That the housing collapse would be so massive that it would wipe out a third of the average net worth of every American household, with the value of the housing stock falling on average by 33 percent from its peak,[2] and with roughly 29 percent of homes with mortgages upside down[3] (where the balance owed exceeds the value of the home).
- That the collapse of housing prices would end housing's role as a store of value.

- That families would move in with each other out of economic necessity, ending 200 years of household dispersion and threatening 20 million houses (and their associated mortgages) with abandonment.[4]
- That there would be a record 12 percent of all mortgages in default or in foreclosure in 2009,[5] representing over 5,400,000 homes.[6]
- That Fannie Mae and Freddie Mac—notwithstanding their role in all of the above—would be the *only* financial entities to escape significant reform in the comprehensive Dodd-Frank reform law.
- That Lehman Brothers, Goldman Sachs, Morgan Stanley, Citibank, Merrill Lynch, and other major investment banks would be allowed to leverage their debt to over 30 times their equity by 2007, up from 12 times in 1999, setting them up for having their equity wiped out when the market experienced an epic collapse in 2008, and requiring massive bailouts from the government in 2008 to stay in business.[7]
- That the collapse of these institutions would result in the Federal Reserve's accepting their mortgage paper, thus finding itself with $2.8 trillion in questionable assets and liabilities by the end of 2010,[8] against equity of $50 billion, resulting in leverage of over 56 times by the end of 2011, just when the economy looked like it might reenter recession.
- That the Fed would begin to print money like crazy, euphemistically calling its program "quantitative easing" (that is, the nominally independent Federal Reserve, which has its top executive appointed by the president and is subject to congressional review, buys Treasury bills and bonds from the United States Treasury, but insists that no money has been printed, even though there has been a tripling of the money supply).
- That the Federal Reserve would, as Bill Gross of PIMCO puts it, "financially repress the savers of this country"[9] by effectively offering no return on their capital in order to keep short-term interest rates fixed at zero.
- That the Federal Reserve would use the moment when our credit rating was deteriorating to shorten rather than lengthen our liabilities, giving us less room for error should the other nations decide they no longer want to purchase our debt.
- That a return to the prevailing interest rates of five years ago of 5 percent[10] would require the United States to pay $750 billion per year[11] just to service our debt, an amount equal to 27.5 percent of our 2007 budget.[12]
- That we would be borrowing 43 cents out of every dollar spent by the federal government in 2011.[13]

- That the exploding regulatory regime would create a drag of $2 trillion[14] on our economy and enormous destabilizing forces in each sector of the economy.

- That the government would put both enormous deflationary and inflationary forces into the economy at the same time, without any understanding of how much they could undermine faith in the future and job and new business creation and with no concrete understanding of which force would prevail.

- That the government would ignore two centuries of established bankruptcy law in the GM and Chrysler bankruptcies to favor unions over creditors, a high-profile example of the ongoing erosion of the rule of law, which in turn would cause consumers, investors, banks, and business to freeze at the switch in a deflationary offset to all that money we have created.

- That the Congressional Budget Office would maintain a nominally cash-based, time-limited, formalistic analysis of our budget as the basis for discussing our future, when such accounting would be outlawed in the private sector.

- That the American consumer would be retrained to consider strategic default on debt a viable option.

- That the median household would lose half its retirement savings.

- That by 2011, the average U.S. household real income would fall to levels below those of 1996,[15] wiping out 15 years of financial progress.

- That we could have a several-year period when the official unemployment rate could stay at what was once considered European levels of about 10 percent, and that more than half those laid off would be out of work over a year, with their jobs skills and careers irreparably damaged.

- That the number of people on food stamps would reach 46 million.[16]

- That enormous amounts of additional transfer payments would be orchestrated, including a vast food stamp program, free health insurance for the poor, extending unemployment benefits to 99 weeks, expanding Medicaid and Medicare eligibility,[17] all with the perverse effect of reducing confidence in the economy, not enhancing it.

- That the amount of transfer payments each year would exceed all the money raised from income taxes—leaving no way to pay for defense or interest on the national debt without borrowing heavily from our potential enemies abroad.

- That Congressional innumeracy and unrestrained profligacy would strongly contribute to gold's rising from $290 per ounce in 2000 to a high of over $1,900 an ounce during 2011 and 10% deficit spending.[18]

- That the U.S. government would resort to serial staggering but impotent stimulus efforts, adding over $5 trillion of unnecessary and unusually unproductive excess spending, and as result borrowing an extra $5 trillion, which was in turn added to the national debt,[19] all in the name of creating jobs, but in fact having the exact opposite effect of destroying jobs.[20]

- That the General Accountability Office would not be able to issue an audit opinion on the 2010 financial statements of the federal government "because of widespread material internal control weaknesses."

- That as a result of this excess spending, the debt of the United States would be downgraded for the first time since formal credit ratings began in 1917. Not all of these disasters were the direct fault of Congress. But by the summer of 2011, it had become clear that the governance of our nation had unalterably changed.

For three years in a row, the Senate ignored the 1974 Budget Act and did not even pass a budget, ashamed of the scrutiny it would bring. But that shame did not translate into slowing down the legislative process when Congress wanted to be reckless. For example, the Senate and the House both were able to pass two laws: health care reform and Dodd-Frank, each with over 2,000 pages and less than 72 hours to read them before passage. The 2010 House of Representatives did not pass a budget either.

In 2011, instead of long-term planning, Congress passed a series of continuing resolutions, kicking the budget can down the road. No material progress was made as the United States approached its self-imposed deadline of August 2, 2011, to raise the budget ceiling. Although the debt ceiling had been raised 74 times since 1952, this was the first time it was to be raised without a formal budget process.

And that budget process clearly has become more of a farce. All the time that might have been used to reach an orderly reduction of spending was squandered in what got labeled by the mainstream media as bipartisan grandstanding. Unable to do its actual job of compromising, Congress delegated its responsibility to a "super-committee" of a dozen senators and congressmen charged with finding more budget cuts or disarming America. This is somewhere between taking yourself hostage and asking for money, on the one hand, and simply telling your mom that you are going to hold your breath until you turn blue on the other. Grownups (i.e., people over the age of five) don't act this way.

Seeing this tantrum, Standard & Poor's and the Secretary of the Treasury, Timothy Geithner, both cited a dysfunctional Congress as an important factor in the decision to downgrade the U.S. debt because "the effectiveness, stability and predictability of American policy making and political institutions have weakened."[21]

Compounding our domestic problems, the rest of the world has engaged in much of the same profligacy, creating ominous international threats:

- The euro is on the brink of failing as a currency, which will throw international trade into turmoil.
- The developed nations of the world are spending $4 trillion more than they take in, putting incredible pressure on all Organisation for Economic Co-operation and Development (OECD) currencies as a store of value.
- Our Pax Americana, which has prevailed since World War II, is coming apart at the seams, with our allies increasingly unable or unwilling to support us, and increasingly louder domestic voices in both political parties in favor of isolation, which is called "standing down" when used to describe our military alliances, and "fair trade" when used to describe the desire for more protectionism in our international trade relations.
- We are dismantling our military at the same time our rivals are increasing their commitment to new weapons systems.
- Our traditional allies, the Europeans, have so burdened their people that Europe's population is now shrinking at a faster rate than the Soviet Union's did just before its collapse, bringing into question how long we can rely on any of the Europeans as reliable allies in a world with rising unaligned powers like China, India, and Brazil, and the newly destabilized Arab countries.

So our domestic economy is on the brink, U.S. debt has been downgraded, the dollar is increasingly suspect as a store of value, the worldwide economy is teetering, and the Pax Americana is eroding. Millions and millions of Americans have lost their jobs and much of their life savings. And what does the public hear about Congress making tough choices? That if we don't increase overall domestic spending by 5 percent from 2010 to 2011, the Cowboy Poetry Festival in Nevada may be in jeopardy.

It is one thing to have a bad Congress when it has little impact on the economy. After the Civil War in the late 1800s, Congress was notoriously corrupt, and the public largely laughed it off. Mark Twain said: "It could probably be proved by facts, statistics and otherwise that there is no distinctly native American criminal class except for Congress." But it is one thing to laugh off Congress when the federal budget accounts for 3 percent of the economy, and quite another when it accounts for 25 percent of our national economy.

The Federal Reserve, acting under its two sometimes conflicting mandates from Congress of price stability and full employment, controls the money supply and sets short-term interest rates. Almost every instance of a troubled industry is troubled because Congress—either directly or through the Federal Reserve or other government entities—has stepped in to change the pricing of that industry:

- In housing, at Congress's insistence, mortgages changed from 20 percent down payments with 30-year fixed rates to as little as 3 percent down with variable rates backed by government guarantees—and people got way over their heads in debt.
- Government stepped into the health care industry and, within one year, the average family's insurance premium increased by 9 percent to $15,073, 5.8 percent above the nominal increase in CPI of 3.2 percent for 2011.
- In the auto industry, the government mandated fleetwide fuel efficiency standards, and GM and Chrysler became uncompetitive without government support.
- Even in the case of debit cards, the government stepped in and ordered the banks to charge $0.24 per transaction instead of $0.44 per transaction, with the result that the banks have started to raise other fees they charge.

The list of industries where Congress has forced new pricing or terms on previously established, freely negotiated commercial relations is endless. This book will examine several industries in detail, with an eye toward understanding how Congress interfered and made things worse for everyone.

In each case, Congress's new pricing enabled a particular congressman or group of congressmen to get more power or more donations, or both. But most of the time, when Congress changes—or even merely threatens to change—the rules for an industry, stocks of the companies in that industry suffer. This is the Congressional Effect at work.

When Congress sets prices, they are always wrong. When the free market discovers prices, they are at least occasionally right. Without the feedback created by knowing the right price, we will always misallocate capital. The financial benefits to us all of getting Congress to stand down from price fixing are enormous and will be spelled out in detail. What's true for physics is true for Congress. Heisenberg showed us that the measurer affects what is being measured, and this became a key aspect of quantum theory. While we may think we have a Newtonian model of how government works, with simple cause and effect between legislative intent and positive economic effect, every government action in fact has unintended consequences. The mere act of having the government look in your wallet to allocate resources decreases what's in your wallet. But what is predictable is Congress's persistent dysfunction, so investors can learn from this book how to systematically avoid legislative risk in the stock market.

CONGRESS'S ROLE IN WEALTH DESTRUCTION

In William Bernstein's magnificent book *The Birth of Plenty* (McGraw-Hill, 2004), he summarizes what he thinks are the four conditions for a civilization to build true prosperity: property rights, rationality, efficient capital markets, and a good communications and transportation infrastructure. The material progress we have had since the Industrial Revolution has flowed from America's having these four attributes in abundance. But with the accelerating growth of government, particularly during the past 10 years, property rights, rationality, and efficient capital markets have all been sharply eroded in America.

Our progress since the Industrial Revolution has been reflected in our wealth growing at a rate of 2 percent in real returns per capita, per year, since about 1800. That may not sound like a lot, but this seemingly small but relentless improvement was enough to change us from an agrarian society to the modern economy of the twenty-first century. You can think of it this way: Living 2 percent better each year is like getting an extra week of vacation for each year you are working. It is this small but steady rate of improvement that is at the heart of the American Dream: that the next generation will live better than this one.

But lately, government has impoverished all of us compared to what we would have today if it were smaller. For example, deficit spending of nearly 10 percent of our economy on mostly wasteful and inefficient projects is a manifest travesty. What's worse is that the political debate, at least as portrayed by the mainstream media, is typically framed as being about Congress getting the price right, about properly allocating between competing interests, with the government acting as disinterested referee. But the government is *never* a disinterested referee. Today's government is just as interested in controlling as much property as possible as King George was in 1776. We have arrived at a moment in time where Congress has practically lost its ability to function, to be a serious steward of our nation. Our planning horizon has shrunk from decades to months, and our current solutions are panicky and short term. The increasing rapidity of the news cycle has made political responses all the more volatile and short term. As the media have become more fractured, Congress feels more in jeopardy, and has in turn become more dysfunctional. The ever more granular self-sorting of America into polarized, partisan pockets increasingly threatens politicians across the political spectrum, forcing them to spend political capital to avoid challenges from the more radical elements of their base, whether on the left or the right.

Having said all this, I do not want to leave the reader with impression that all our troubles are always and in every case Congress's fault, especially when it comes to investments. Many forces outside the control of Congress and the United States are rapidly increasing and creating both risks and opportunities. The breakdown of Europe, the rise of the East, and the tech revolution and its implications for productivity and mobility of people and capital are enormous factors for investors that have little to do with Congress but strongly affect your investment returns. But these risks and opportunities are both knowable and much more fairly presented to us by the popular business media every day. In contrast, for over 100 years, the popular press has painted a picture of our government as mostly benevolent when in fact it is mostly the opposite with respect to investments. The goal of this book is to help you recognize, from an investing point of view, why President Reagan's quip that the nine most terrifying words in the English language are, "I'm from the government and I'm here to help."

Are there ways to make Congress's relentless dysfunction work for you as an investor? Fortunately, there are. As an investor, you do not have to take it on the chin from Congress all the time. Instead, you can follow Congress's intentions, assess where they will do the most damage, and set up your investments to avoid the risk and damage they inflict.

This book shows you how to use Congress's short-term horizon to enhance your performance relative to the risk you take, and how to use the long term to take your investments safely past each crisis du jour, especially the ones created by Congress for Congress's benefit. You will learn Congress's historically overwhelming and persistent impact on the short-term direction of the market. You will be given investing approaches to make Congress's relentless dysfunction reliably work for you and not against you in figuring out what to do in these manic and unprecedented investment times.

SUMMARY

Ken Fisher once referred to the stock market as "the Great Humiliator." All honest market participants have been humbled many times by the stock market, and have had their expectations crushed, along with their portfolios. It is the nature of investing that it is difficult to be consistently smarter than the stock market, which represents the second-by-second collective calculation of billions of people with vast distributed and expert knowledge. However, once you understand the nature of the incentives that each politician has that collectively result in Congress's relentlessly working against your portfolio, you will be more easily able to recognize when to use their efforts to your advantage. After all, in the February 2012 Gallup survey mentioned earlier, Congress ranks dead last in respect among all 16 institutions, including the public schools, banks, big business, organized labor, and health maintenance organizations (HMOs).

If you've ever looked at any of these institutions and thought you could do a better job on something, there is no reason to think that you can't do a better job on your own life savings by avoiding some of the mistakes created by Congress. It turns out that once you see the stock market from their perspective, you will have a better idea of what to expect and how to reduce the casual, relentless damage they inflict on your portfolio every day. As the size of the government has expanded relative to the overall economy, a great deal of damage has been to done to the wealth of our nation, particularly over the past decade. While there is always a natural ebb and flow to the business cycle, there is something fundamentally flawed with a political system with so many policies that helped to wipe out a decade of economic progress. Much of this recent and terrible damage is attributable to flawed government policies, many of which come to pass because of the perverse incentives our leaders have to interfere in our lives. In fact, one section this book describes how Congress uses behavioral finance principles to consistently get the *worst* process and corresponding results available when "solving" problems.

We see the impact of these policies in all of our popular measures of well-being—employment and housing statistics, the size of our debt relative to the economy, economic growth and gross domestic product (GDP) statistics, and so on, and almost everyone understands that the economy is in trouble. Not as well understood is the generally negative impact that Congress has on our stock market—both daily and over the long term. This book will help you specifically understand that impact and how to use it to get better results in your own investing, and give a glimpse of how much wealthier we could all be if we could systematically reduce the negative impact of Congress on our wealth.

NOTES

1. www.realclearpolitics.com/epolls/other/congressional_job_approval-903.html

2. S&P Press release, "Home Prices Continued to Decline in November 2011 According to the S&P/Case-Shiller Home Price Indices," January, 31, 2012, www.standardandpoors.com/spf/docs/case-shiller/CSHomePrice_Release_013118.pdf

3. http://bottomline.msnbc.msn.com/_news/2011/11/08/8687925-nearly-29-of-mortgaged-homes-underwater-report-finds?lite

4. Jia Lyn Yang, "How Bad Is the Mortgage Crisis Going to Get?," CNNMoney, March 17, 2008, http://money.cnn.com/2008/03/14/news/ economy/krugman_subprime.fortune/index.htm

5. David Kirkpatrick, "Mortgage Default Rates Stunning," March 6, 2009, http://davidkirkpatrick.wordpress.com/2009/03/06/mortgage-default-rates-stunning/

6. Bill McBride, "Report: Record 5.4 Million U.S. Homeowners Delinquent or in Foreclosure," March 5, 2009, www.calculatedriskblog .com/2009/03/report-record-54-million-us-homeowners.html

7. Dealbook, "As Goldman and Morgan Shift, a Wall St. Era Ends," September 21, 2008, http://dealbook.nytimes.com/2008/09/21/goldman-morgan-to-become-bank-holding-companies/ and Bethany McLean, "The Meltdown Explanation that Melts Away," March 19, 2012, http:// blogs.reuters.com/bethany-mclean/2012/03/19/the-meltdown-explanation-that-melts-away/

8. CrisisSite.com, "Impact of Debt Crisis on Financial Institutions," www.crisissite.com/an-insight-on-impact-of-debt.html

9. www.bloomberg.com/news/2012-03-01/gross-says-savers-face-lengthy-financial-repression-video-.html

10. www.treasurydirect.gov/govt/rates/pd/avg/2007/2007.htm

11. Chris Arnold, "Debt's Impact Could Be Worse if Interest Rates Rise," July 22, 2011, www.npr.org/2011/07/22/138590769/debts-impact-could-be-worse-if-interest-rates-rise

12. www.whitehouse.gov/sites/default/files/omb/budget/fy2013/assets/hist .pdf

13. Veronique de Rugy, "How Much of Federal Spending Is Borrowed for Every Dollar?," July 11, 2011, http://mercatus.org/publication/how-much-federal-spending-borrowed-every-dollar

14. Mike, Tighe, "'Hidden Tax': Govt Rules Cost Economy Nearly $2 Trillion," April 19, 2011, www.newsmax.com/InsideCover/government-regulations-economy-trillion/2011/04/19/id/393329

15. Conor Dougherty, "Income Slides to 1996 Levels," September 14, 2011, http://online.wsj.com/article/SB100014240531119042655045765685439 68213896.html

16. S. L. Carroll, "46 Million People on Food Stamps, and the Economy is Improving?," February 16, 2012, http://news.yahoo.com/46-million-people-food-stamps-economy-improving-001800201.html

17. Employment Development Department, "New Developments on Federal Unemployment Extensions," May 8, 2012, http://edd.ca.gov/ Unemployment/Federal_Unemployment_Insurance_Extensions.htm

18. Hibah Yousuf, "Gold Tops $1,900, Looking 'a bit bubbly'," August 23, 2011, http://money.cnn.com/2011/08/22/markets/gold_prices/index .htm

19. http://townhall.com/tipsheet/guybenson/2012/04/19/obamas_5_trillion_ moment

20. Matt Cover, "1.9 Million Fewer Americans Have Jobs Today Than When Obama Signed Stimulus," July 14, 2011, http://cnsnews.com/news/ article/19-million-fewer-americans-have-jobs-today-when-obama-signed-stimulus

21. S&P statement: www.standardandpoors.com/ratings/articles/en/us/? articleType=HTML&assetID=1245327305715 and Geithner, http:// video.msnbc.msn.com/nightly-news/44052329#44052329

CHAPTER 1

What Is the Congressional Effect?

C ongressional talk is not cheap. In the summer of 2011, the awful spectacle of Congress's inability to timely resolve the budgetary issues regarding our debt cap and the resulting downgrade of United States debt took a heavy toll on the stock market. What is so disturbing is that in their brinksmanship, our lawmakers never seem to consider just how much their actions cost us. What is truly upsetting is the amount of wealth destroyed merely by political talk, even when that talk doesn't lead to action. This wealth destruction is the *Congressional Effect*. It is empirically demonstrated in the aggregate by looking at how the stock market is affected on a daily basis by Congress. In turn, this broad Congressional Effect is generally comprised of a series of legislative impacts on sectors and, sometimes, individual companies.

From 1965 through 2011, measuring each of the 11,832 trading days during that period, the price of the Standard & Poor's (S&P) 500 Index rose at an annualized rate of less than 1 percent on days Congress was in session, but over 16 percent on days they were out of session. This enormous difference between in-session days and out-of-session days is not coincidental, but rather reflects the cumulative effect of unintended adverse consequences on the U.S. stock market from anticipated and actual congressional legislative initiatives. Whenever Congress focuses on an industry with the potential for changing the rules for that industry, investors have to discount what Congress may or may not do to change the business plan of the companies in that industry. Some investors wait for the final version of the new rules so they have more certainty about the business models of the companies before they buy. But sellers often have to sell for reasons having nothing to do with the latest news about an industry. When there are disproportionately more sellers than buyers, you have periods of underperformance, which happens much more frequently when Congress is in session.

All of this is aggravated by the sheer number of opportunities for Congress to make news. Since there are 535 members of the House of Representatives and the Senate, with 23 House committees and 104 House subcommittees, and 17 Senate committees with 70 subcommittees, there are many industries that Congress can affect on any given day.

This book looks at the Congressional Effect in depth, and offers several strategies for how to optimize your portfolio. Once you understand the nature of the incentives that each politician has that collectively result in Congress's relentlessly working against your portfolio, you can better use their efforts to your advantage. The rest of this chapter describes how the theory of Congressional Effect was discovered and the evidence supporting it.

HOW WAS THE CONGRESSIONAL EFFECT DISCOVERED?

For me, late Friday afternoon is the business equivalent of being in the shower: The pressure of the week is spent and it's OK to let your mind wander. I get lots of my ideas then. At these times, I am almost always tired from working my butt off, and the only people you can reach are your old friends and acquaintances, who don't mind having a little downtime to see the latest stuff you are mixed up in.

I remember the particular Friday afternoon in January 1992 that I discovered the Congressional Effect. The weather was freezing in New York City, in the 20s and windy. The sky was that clear, cold blue you get when the sun is bright and the day is short. I was head of investment banking at a scrappy, growing Wall Street research firm, but in those days we were quite small and could only afford offices in Manhattan's Garment District. (For those of you who know Manhattan, this is a little incongruous. It was almost the investment-banking equivalent of the set of Zero Mostel's version of *The Producers*.) My tiny office was about 50 square feet, the size of a cubicle, but in fact was a built-out room with 12-foot ceilings. Gary Glaser, perhaps the best analyst ever of the auto companies, had an office next to mine. In those days, Gary smoked four packs of cigarettes a day. If you ran your finger along the walls of his office, you could pick up the tar and nicotine. Things were grimy.

We didn't have much of a brand name in those days. We had to fight for every deal we did and for every dollar we raised for our clients. And at that moment in time, I was almost completely stalled. I had been trying to raise money for an industry that competed with cable TV. Over a year and a half, I had called on 200 banks and venture capital firms to raise money for terrestrial multichannel TV—a precursor of satellite TV using specialized frequencies—only to be told it would never work, the public didn't want competition, the banks would never lend to it, and so on. In many cases, I was calling on funds that had a vested interest in the cable industry, either through direct investments or by virtue of having investors connected to that industry. It was a brick wall. We needed to get to the wide public market and ask a broader array of buyers if they thought there was a need for competition for cable TV.

I had one client, ACS Enterprises, which had filed for a $10 million initial public offering (IPO). ACS provided cable TV programming to 30,000 paying customer households in Philadelphia and was trying to raise $10 million in a public offering. The Securities and Exchange Commission (SEC) was dead set against ACS at that time and just bombarded the company with a parade of never-ending comments that felt like they were designed to make the company throw in the towel on raising more money. For example, after the prospectus had been on file with the SEC for three months, they asked the company to specifically state as an emphasized warning that it "might face unforeseen obstacles" in competing with the cable TV companies. We dutifully amended the draft prospectus and resubmitted it to the SEC. After three more months—an eternity to a small company starved for cash—the SEC came back and asked us to "spell out and specify" the unforeseen obstacles we might anticipate. We replied that they had made us put this warning in to begin with, and that if we knew what they were, they would no longer be unforeseen. All these pettifogging, time-killing requests from the SEC occurred against a background of a company running out of money and staring at bankruptcy.

I reacted quite stubbornly to the idea that the industry was not finance-able and was racking my brain for ways to make my deals work in spite of the government and in spite of cable competition. I was stewing. It being Friday afternoon, I called a friend to complain about the horrid state of the world.

In the middle of my complaining about my deals, one of my friends, no doubt trying to cheer me up, told me they were probably stalled because the market in general feared the Buffalo Bills might win the 1992 Super Bowl. After all, this was their third consecutive trip to the big show, and it seemed this time they would finally get it done. There was then, and there still is, stock market folklore that when a team from the old American Football Conference wins the Super Bowl, the stock market will go down for the year. I told my friend not to worry, for sure Buffalo would lose, and even if they didn't, the January Effect would bail us out in the stock market. And if the January Effect didn't kick in, there would be a Summer Rally . . . and if not, the year would be saved by the Santa Claus Rally, and so on.

As it turned out, there was no need to worry, because the Dallas Cowboys crushed the Buffalo Bills 52–17, and the S&P 500 Index did indeed go up 10 percent that year. But the question did get me thinking about correlations. At that time, I was an investment banker raising money for small public companies, most of which competed with larger cable TV companies. I knew there was stock market folklore about seasonality and wondered if I could figure out a new way to play the stock market. There are hundreds of aphorisms about the stock market that pass for market wisdom in the same way campaign slogans are used by some voters to decide their election choices. The most famous is probably "Sell in May and go away." It's based on the idea that not much news happens in the summer, so there is nothing to drive stocks higher. A different version of this is "Buy bonds in May and go away," based, I suppose, on the good old days of yesteryear when bonds paid noticeable rates of interest and people led stable, dignified lives based on interest income. The underlying theory was that if there was going to be little market-moving news, it was better to be earning interest and have more fixed income exposure.

There were also other tactical timing phrases that suggested timing the market based on things like tax considerations and flows of funds. For example, there has long been the sense that there is a January Effect—that one can buy stocks in December and sell them higher in January. This is based on the idea that losing stocks are thought to be disproportionately sold at year end to get their losses realized for tax purposes, and repurchased in the new year. This fact, coupled with some increase in fund flows into retirement accounts in the new year as the result of year-end bonuses being paid, has made the logical case for the January Effect. Objectively, the data support that there has been a January Effect but to the extent it had a bigger benefit when capital gains taxes were higher and more of the market was in taxable funds, it has apparently subsided a lot since 1990. Then, too, there were the feel-good moments often associated with a rally—there is stock market folklore about a Santa Claus Rally and a Thanksgiving Rally and an Easter Rally, all supposedly coinciding with these holidays.

But at the time, while there were, and are, very sophisticated seasonality analyses that large firms use to inform their trading of every class of securities, there was to my knowledge no "Unified Theory" of market timing except that it was in general a bad idea. I had heard that Einstein was searching for a "Unified Field Theory" to explain the four physical forces of gravity, electromagnetism, and strong and weak nuclear forces with one common explanation. I asked myself if there might be one "Unified

Field Theory of Tactical Market Timing"—a single overriding explanation for how stocks traded with respect to seasonality.

At this time in the early 1990s, my clients were all competitors of cable companies, but they had been adversely affected by new complicated rules the government had imposed recently on cable companies. The government had put a cap on the prices charged by cable TV companies, and as a result everyone in that business was struggling to stay afloat, even with apparent local monopolies. While this sounded like it was a good deal for consumers, it was actually a terrible deal for everyone: cable TV companies, their would-be competitors, and ultimately, consumers. Having thought the rules wouldn't change, many cable TV companies had borrowed to the hilt. Once the rules changed, cable TV companies and their lenders often found themselves in the twilight zone. Because they had local monopolies, the banks often lent to them at high multiples of cash flow. Once their rates were capped, the cable TV companies often would find themselves current on the interest they had to pay on their loans, but in violation of some of the covenants of their bank loans. In the aftermath of the savings and loan (S&L) crisis, these loans became known as "performing nonperforming" loans. Think about that term for a moment and you will begin to understand what happens when government intervenes.

These "performing nonperforming" loans became problem loans for the banks, which in turn had to reduce lending to the cable TV industry to satisfy the bank regulators. Cable TV expansion was halted. Since the cable TV industry was sick, raising money to compete with cable was even harder. The banks thought that if cable's loans were in trouble, creating new competition would only make things worse, and they mostly refused to finance any cable competitors. Consumers were worse off because although in the short term their prices were fixed, new entrants were prevented from entering competition and then offering more choices. When the government fixed prices, it did so at a time when offering 24 channels or 36 channels sounded like an incredible array of offerings. Just 20 years later, we know how feeble that offering is in hindsight. Imagine having the exact same 36 channels today.

The threat of government action hurt all cable TV stocks during that period. Even Comcast, which we now know was perhaps the best cable TV company of its time, had its stock price stay virtually stalled from November 15, 1989, when the Cable Consumer Protection and Competition Act was first proposed, until it passed over the veto of President George H. W. Bush in October 1992. In that period in the aftermath of the law, its stock declined over 6 percent from $2.87 per share to $2.69 per share. In comparison, the S&P 500 Index rose almost 30 percent during the same period, so Comcast investors really suffered underperformance for becoming a government scapegoat. It is very bad for a stock to be demonstrably "dead money" while other stocks are participating in the greatest bull market in three generations. What made it worse was that during this time period Comcast grew its business from two million subscribers in 1988 to almost three million in 1994, mostly through organic growth, and increased revenues per subscriber, so it was growing its top line at over 15 percent per year and entering into the cellular phone business, but its stock went nowhere in those two and a half years[1] (see Figure 1.1).

So there I was on that cold January afternoon. My clients were all competitors of cable companies, and the government was making it difficult for my first cable competitor client trying to get public money. All of the wireless cable TV companies had been swept up in the complicated rules the government had imposed recently on cable companies, and both cable and wireless cable companies were all struggling to stay afloat mostly because of government interference. The main reason was that the government had stepped in and told the cable TV companies they could not raise their prices. In turn, their stocks suffered and their would-be competitors suffered. Of course, with more competition, cable rates were likely to go down in real terms over time. And then it struck me: What if government action was the single explanation for the stock market folklore of the January Effect *and* the Summer Rally *and* the Christmas Rally *and* so on.... If government interference could lower the prices of cable TV companies and their shares prices, maybe it had the same impact on other industries,

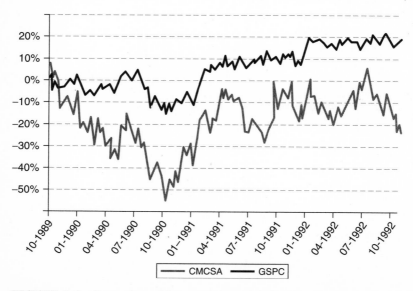

FIGURE 1.1   Comcast vs. S&P. Data source: Yahoo! Finance

and maybe that was a factor, or even *the* factor, in the seasonality of stock prices. My firm was a well-respected institutional research firm (even if, or perhaps because, we were in the Garment District). Every morning, research analysts for specific industries would analyze the news and explain to our equity salesmen how it affected the companies they followed. Half the time, the news was about new threatened government initiatives. When it was, institutional buyers of the stocks in that industry would buy less in that industry while they waited for clarity on what might happen.

Knowing that Comcast had unfairly suffered along with the entire flock of would-be cable TV competitors, that almost every industry suffered when there was news from the government, that the government was stopping a perfectly good competitor from getting to market, and that seasonality folklore seemed to coincide with Congress's schedule, I decided to at least see the data.

EARLY RETURNS SHOWING THE CONGRESSIONAL EFFECT

I called in my assistant and asked her to look up the days when Congress had been in session and when they had not, and to compare S&P 500 prices on the in-session days and the out-of-session days for the past year. Just for kicks, I looked at how the S&P 500 (without taking dividends into account) performed on a daily basis over the past year (1991) whenever the Senate was shut. Allowing for some nuances of taking daily averages, the S&P was up about .00012 percent when the Senate was open and .0025 percent when it was closed, a difference on the order of 20 times! Moreover, the Senate was open twice as much as it was closed, so most of the gain for the year occurred only when the Senate was closed. The data were very compelling. The market did incredibly better when Congress was out of session. This seemed too good to be true. Certainly, 1991 must be an aberration. And maybe using the Senate alone was misleading. So, I needed more research.

I then asked her to go back five years. What I found surprised me. When I looked at the 1,261 trading days from 1987 through 1991, the market did five times better per day when Congress was not in session. From 1987 through 1991, the S&P 500 rose about .0010% on business days when Congress was closed, and just about .0002% when the legislators were in action. Now, this was a more modest difference, but over many more observations. The folklore surrounding the Super Bowl at that time was based on the correlations of 25 Super Bowls with the year-end results for 25 years. The very first thing financial advisers are taught is that "correlation is not causation." While this is true for relatively small samples and modest correlations, there is a point at which overwhelming correlation demonstrates causation. I believe the Congressional Effect has such overwhelming correlation that it demonstrates causation. Even the first five-year test, which was based on 1,261 observations, had a much greater source of statistical proof than most common stock market folklore.

The other incredibly important point that came to light from this first study was that not only did the Congressional Effect identify a way to make money in the stock market, it was also less risky. When I discussed this phenomenon with financial advisers I knew, they confirmed that the risk-adjusted returns were stunning. Not only did the market do five times better per day, but in this five-year period it had less daily volatility and it outperformed the overall market. This seemed like the holy grail of investing. Less volatility *and* higher returns. The standard deviation of returns was significantly greater when Congress was open than when it was closed.

Let's put this into perspective. If, say, stock A pays twice as much as stock B and has a greater certainty of returns, you'd probably pay a lot more for stock A, right? Which suggests that the stock market would go up a lot more and be a safer place if the members of Congress would simply have the good sense to stay home. Well, the implied returns of using the Congressional Effect approach were less volatile, too. I then went back 15 years. At this request, my assistant pointed out in those pre–desktop computer days that the little model I asked for involved 25,000 entries. I encouraged her to be vigilant for typos. The data were still compelling, with out-of-session days giving about twice the return of in-session over an aggregate observation of 3,784 trading days.

Inspired by the data, I wrote an article on the subject for *Barron's*, which introduced the Congressional Effect. My key conclusion at the time was

> "... *our nation earns less on its equity when Congress is open, and much of its returns when Congress is closed. We all know the evil Eighties plunged the country into too much debt, and took away too much equity. Now, if that equity was higher, we'd all be better off. If Congress stayed home, we'd have calmer markets with improved chances for higher returns and higher stock prices.*" [2]

I went on to allude to that famous quote sometimes attributed to Mark Twain and sometimes to Judge Gideon Tucker that "no man's life, liberty, or property is safe while the legislature is in session." And I couldn't resist pointing out that "the Founding Fathers apparently felt much the same thing about lawmakers in general, summed up in the statement by Tom Paine: 'That government governs best that governs least.'"

The *Barron's* article was well received by everyone except my boss. Over lunch we talked about it. Our conversation, which I recall verbatim to this day, was brief:

Boss: I don't want you to spend a single minute more on this Congress stuff. I want you to focus on raising money for the wireless cable industry. Exclusively.

Me: And what's in it for me if I don't spend any time at all on this idea?

Boss: Your continued employment.

My cranky boss had a flair for the dramatic. But he had a point. I was being paid a salary to be an investment banker raising money for firm clients, not an investment manager. Besides, I was still seeing red because of the 200 banking and venture professionals who had told me the industry was simply not financeable. I went back to focusing exclusively on raising money for the wireless cable industry. We eventually raised over $1.5 billion for small public companies that competed with cable TV companies. The wireless cable industry grew and grew. By 1994, the industry had a convention with over 3,000 people attending, and I was named the industry's "Man of the Year" for showing up with so much money. The frequencies controlled by those companies attracted the attention of the major telephone companies and eventually became a core part of their data offerings. When our clients graduated to larger investment-banking firms or were merged, or in some cases, failed, I moved on to raise money for other small companies. The 1990s were great times in the stock market, and great times to be an agent raising money.

The more I thought about the Congressional Effect, the more it made sense to me. Having taken the data back, by hand, by 15 years in 1992, I decided to take it all the way back to 1965.

The dataset that I used as my proprietary set confirmed that since 1965 there was definitely a full-blown Congressional Effect. Ignoring dividends and transaction costs, and just focusing on the pure daily price action, from 1965 through 2011, measuring each of the 11,832 trading days during that period, the price of the S&P 500 Index rose at an annualized rate of 0.72 percent on days Congress was in session, but 16.60 percent on days they were out of session, a difference of over 20 times per day (see Figure 1.2).

Expressed differently, a dollar invested in 1965 just on the 7,767 in-session days would have compounded into $1.25, while the same dollar invested on just the 4,065 out-of-session days would have compounded into $11.91 compounded over 47 years. As government has gotten bigger over the past 10 years, and our federal deficits have gotten larger as a percentage of the national gross domestic product (GDP), this relationship has gotten more extreme. A dollar invested at the beginning of 2002 through the end of 2011 just on in-session days would have turned into $0.61, while the

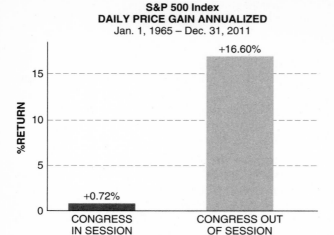

FIGURE 1.2   In-Session Days vs. Out-of-Session, 1965–2011.
Source: Congressional Effect Management, LLC

same dollar invested just on out-of-session days would have compounded into $1.56. In that same period, on days Congress was out of session, the market went up at an annualized rate of 14.80 percent, but went down at an annualized rate of −6.49 percent when it was in session, an annualized difference of 1.148/0.9351, or 22.76 percent (see Figure 1.3).

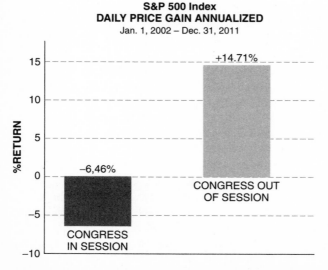

FIGURE 1.3   In-Session Days vs. Out-of-Session, 2002–2011.
Source: Congressional Effect Management, LLC

THE SMOOT-HAWLEY ACT: THE MOTHER OF ALL CONGRESSIONAL EFFECTS

At this point, I decided to look at the biggest historical legislative event—the Smoot-Hawley Tariff Act of 1930—to see if it had a Congressional Effect. This law sharply raised the most important tax of the day—tariffs—and is widely credited as the single most important cause of the Great Depression and the stock market crash associated with it. From its historic high of 384 in October 1929, the Dow Jones Industrial Average fell to a low of 41 in July 1932. President Hoover had campaigned on a platform of raising tariffs for farmers, and the Republicans controlled Congress as well as the presidency. The law was first presented to the House on May 9, 1929, when the Dow Jones Average had closed at 323.51 the day before. The House vote for it occurred on May 28, 1929, and the Dow closed at 298.87, a decline of 9.24 percent while the legislation was considered. However, there is little evidence that the stock market reacted harshly to the bill, and it went on to make new highs in September. The timeline of the Smoot-Hawley Act and the stock market is shown in Figure 1.4.

In "Log-Rolling and Economic Interests in the Passage of the Smoot-Hawley Tariff" (NBER Working Paper No. 5510, 1996), Douglas Irwin and Randall Kroszner show that the severity of the tax raise by the act was largely the result of log-rolling, or the trading of economic favors between legislators so that each one could go back to their specific constituencies and say they had delivered special favors. In fact, from the 1880s through the 1930s, the Republicans had run on platforms of raising tariff protection, and the Democrats had run on platforms of lowering tariff protection. The vote in the House was not the deciding factor for the legislation, and there

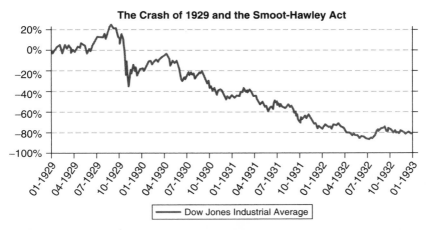

FIGURE 1.4 The Crash of 1929 and the Smoot-Hawley Act. Source: Bloomberg

was no roll call vote as to each tariff. However, the House Republicans, having won an unusually large majority, treated the legislation as a "done deal" that effectively prevented any Democratic amendments.

The legislation's main debate occurred in the Senate, where there was a lot more visibility to the trading of political favors to get specific tariffs raised. The Senate Finance Committee reduced more rates than it raised in deliberations ending in September, and, coincidentally, the stock market peaked in September 1929 at 384 on the Dow. Once into the Senate considerations there were multiple opportunities to renegotiate rates up by separate amendment votes, putting heat on individual Senators. The final law restored most of the higher tariffs that the House had wanted, and was passed by the Senate on March 24, 1930, by a vote of 53 to 31. The Dow was at 279.11. It went to a conference, where a final version was passed. President Hoover, calling the bill "vicious, extortionate, and obnoxious," signed it over the objections of 1,028 economists in a petition sent to him because he had campaigned on a platform of limited tariff increases, and Republican party leaders prevailed on him to follow through.[3]

Trade retaliation happened before the law was even signed. Our largest trading partner, Canada, raised retaliatory tariffs in May 1930. The Smoot-Hawley Tariff Act was signed into law on June 17, 1930, with the Dow at 228, 40 percent below its highs. Neither Smoot nor Hawley was reelected and the majority of historians agree today that raising the taxes of that day—tariffs—which invited retaliation from our trading partners, was the key policy error leading to the Great Depression.

THE CONGRESSIONAL EFFECT DATA AND LAUNCHING A MUTUAL FUND

Armed with these data, I had to do something more than just read about it. In 2006, I asked one of my closest friends to consider opening an institutional-size account that traded only to optimize for the Congressional Effect. It would invest in Spyders (S&P Depositary Receipts; SPDRs) when Congress was out of session, and the cash account at E*TRADE when they were in session. I told him that he would have made money the year before to whet his appetite. He looked at me and said, "You know, Eric, I could really care less about the short term. How did this compare with the S&P 500 going back many years?"

I did a back-test for him. It assumed that one knew every day at 4 p.m. Eastern Standard (New York) time whether Congress would have a legislative day the next day and that you could earn at least what Fed Funds paid every day on your idle cash. It also assumed that S&P dividends are smoothly distributed day by day over the 252.25 trading days in the average year, and it ignored any transaction costs associated with trading. Of course, in real life, Congress can change its schedule at the last second or after hours so that you might not know their schedule at 4:00 every day; specific dividends are paid on specific days by specific companies; and transaction costs and inefficiencies cut into returns when you're actually trading. But the back-test was designed to get a general picture of how the strategy would have done.

I presented my data to my friend. He said, "You know, Eric, matching the market with half the risk is a pretty good bet. I'll give you some money to invest." God bless him. Without his commitment, I would have never started at all.

Now I had a bigger decision to make. In the summer of 2007, my family visited some friends in France. They had a vineyard in the south of France. Their large stone house had a great view. From their pool you could see the vineyard spreading before you and the mountains rolling down to foothills as they sloped towards the plains of Provence. The air was fresh and beautiful, and every day we had a spectacular French meal of local foods and wine from the vineyard. It was a wonderful summer moment.

Thinking it over, I realized I had always been an agent for someone else but that I finally had an idea around which I could form a business of my own. It was a big change to take full responsibility. There were a lot of reasons not to do it. Starting a mutual fund would cost a lot of money, and there would be several years where it was likely that not only would I not have any income, I would have a lot of fund expenses to cover. And it was entirely possible that the fund would not succeed, and that I would have wasted precious savings, and have to start all over again.

But I thought there were two important reasons to launch a fund apart from the American dream of having your own company. First, I thought that if you could match the market over long periods of time in returns with half the risk, it would serve investors very well. Without that, there was no reason to start another mutual fund in a world where 26,000 funds already existed and 99 percent were bigger and stronger and had better distribution. And there is always a need for the reduction of risk for investors.

Second, I thought the fund would help people understand how much wealth Congress destroyed by its constant meddling, and contribute empirical support to the forces for a smaller government. So the Congressional Effect Fund was launched.

The prospectus was filed in October 2007. In our Investment Philosophy section, we quoted Thomas Paine: "That government is best that governs least." The investment corollary of that is that government that governs most governs worst. It was implicit in our announced philosophy that the more the government intervened in the market, the worse it would be for the stock market overall. In May 2008, the mutual fund went public.

SUMMARY

The Congressional Effect is the usually negative impact on the stock market that occurs when Congress considers legislation that may change the business model for a sector or even an individual company. Investors have to adjust their valuations to account for potential changes in business models. Since on most days Congress is considering some legislation, the Congressional Effect historically has occurred more often than not on a daily basis. From 1965 through 2011, the price of the S&P 500 Index rose at an annualized rate of less than 1 percent on days Congress was in session, but over 16 percent on days they were out of session.

I noticed this Congressional Effect as an investment banker in the 1990s when legislation capping the retail price of cable television service hurt that industry. Looking at the historical record, and considering the stock market impact of major legislation like the Smoot-Hawley Tariff Act, I launched a mutual fund seeking to take advantage of this data.

This book is designed to help you understand how the Congressional Effect works and what Congress's incentives are to continue it, and identifies sources that can be used to anticipate new sources of legislative risk. It also outlines ways that portfolios can be allocated to take advantage of the Congressional Effect and further protect your portfolio from ongoing legislative risk.

NOTES

1. www.pressnews.net/cmcsk/history.htm
2. Eric Singer, "Legislator Go Home," *Barron's*, March 2, 1992.
3. Amity Shlaes, *The Forgotten Man: A New History of the Great Depression* (New York: Harper, 2007), 96.

CHAPTER 2

The Congressional Effect and the Limits of Modern Portfolio Theory

Modern portfolio theory (MPT) is a theory of investment that attempts to maximize expected return for a given amount of risk, or equivalently minimize risk for a given level of expected return, by carefully choosing the proportions of various assets within a portfolio. It was first articulated by Harry Markowitz in a groundbreaking article in 1952 entitled "Portfolio Selection."[1]

To briefly summarize his findings, he focused on two kinds of risk, the first of which was "systematic" or "market," which related to the broad economy and included such factors as the overall economy, wars, crop failures, floods, the broad equity market, interest rates, and other macro factors that could not easily be reduced by diversification. The other risk in a portfolio was "unsystematic" or "specific" risk, which related to how an individual stock might perform in ways uncorrelated with the overall portfolio. He showed that by prudently diversifying a portfolio, the risks of individual stocks could be used to reduce the overall volatility of a portfolio and give it greater predictability.

This chapter is a brief overview of modern portfolio theory, which assumes that the market has fully digested all relevant information available at the time of investment. One corollary of this theory is that since the market has full access to data and is efficient, the short-term distribution of stock prices is likely to be so random that it does not make investment sense to ever try to time the market. The assumptions behind MPT are examined. This chapter then looks at the distribution of daily prices in connection with the Congressional Effect and finds that they are historically not random, and concludes that it can make investment sense to trade the Congressional Effect.

MPT is the foundational framework that has been used by most investment professionals as their starting point for constructing portfolios for over 50 years. It uses standard deviation to measure risk and develops for each stock a beta, or a measure of much of an individual stock's change in price, which can be attributed to the price movement of the overall market. Alpha is the return of one stock in excess of market returns.

A well-diversified portfolio allows investors to have confidence that the behavior of consistently saving is worthwhile and worth sticking to in order to create a lifetime habit of saving that enables a successful retirement. The single most valuable service a financial adviser can perform for clients is to reinforce this behavior so that they become successful, consistent long-term investors. While most investment professionals do their absolute best to provide good returns on a risk-adjusted basis, the key to successful investment advising has more to do with getting clients to adopt the behavior of consistent investing than it does with performance.

MPT has several core themes, the most important being that in order to get higher returns, an investor must suffer more exposure to risk. Of course, to relate risk to returns, one has to measure them. It is easy to measure returns: that's the return of principal plus excess returns, whether in the form of interest or dividends. And as to risk, we largely measure that by volatility and variability over time. The Holy Grail of investing is to find sustainable excess risk-adjusted returns, but the logic of MPT suggests that this is difficult to do in practice.

The key analysis of MPT is that the market is highly efficient and that all observed anomalies will not work over long periods of time to provide cost-effective ways to realize sustainable excess returns. This is called the efficient market hypothesis (EMH). One of the leading proponents of EMH is Princeton professor Burton Malkiel. In 1973, in his book entitled *A Random Walk Down Wall Street* (W. W. Norton, 1973), he argued that since most information is known and immediately, or rather efficiently, discounted by the market, investors would do just as well randomly diversifying as they could with active managers. He observed that on average active money managers underperformed the broad market over long periods of time, so an investor might as well take exposure to broad swaths of the market as a whole to achieve diversification. To emphatically make his point, he suggested using a monkey to throw darts at the stock pages of the *Wall Street Journal*, using the stocks the monkey hit.

The monkey with the dart image struck a sour note among most financial professionals, who pride themselves on being very intelligent and using their intelligence to impress their clients that great care and foresight is being used to manage their money. I can really sympathize with their dilemma. After all, when the first suborbital space flight was going to be made using a monkey, the astronauts who lost the competition to be the first American in space used to razz America's first astronaut, Alan Shepard, by reminding him "a monkey's gonna make the first flight." In fact, the first Mercury flights were completely controlled from Cape Canaveral (now Cape Kennedy) on the ground. How can you really be a hero when a monkey can do what you do?

Well, if you are an astronaut, you have at least one key advantage over a monkey: you can claim victory by telling them just how you did it, even if you were mostly just along for the ride. We humans are limited in our ability to understand monkeys—otherwise, Alan Shepard could have been upstaged. It is the communicating to clients that is a key part of the value added of a financial adviser, allowing him to lead his client through the dangers of the market. And as advisers realized they could spend more time on marketing, and gather more assets, and get similar results, they increasingly embraced indexing for a portion, or sometimes all, of their asset allocation. The key was they just had to talk about it, even if Cape Canaveral was almost completely in control.

In 2003, Professor Malkiel reviewed the critics of MPT and EMH and found them wanting. One of the core assertions of EMH is that over even very short-term horizons, stock prices are randomly distributed. If this is really the case, then the transaction costs of short-term momentum trading should exceed the excess returns that are available in theory, making momentum-based trading uneconomic. Professor Malkiel asserts that "many" of the patterns identified disappear once they are identified, citing as an example the "January Effect."[2]

The January Effect was based on the observation that small stocks that could be sold for tax losses tended to have a big bounce in January when the pressure to realize losses for tax purposes abated. It was present forcefully until about 1990, when it began to be less predictable as a factor. His stringent test of a predictable factor seems to be one that allows an investor to outperform the market over long periods of time and through all investment cycles, after everything—including transaction fees—has been included. He goes on to assert that momentum, growth, and value investing cannot beat the market over time.

The most difficult example of apparent consistent outperformance for Professor Malkiel to explain away was that of small stocks, which have outperformed the S&P by about 2 percent since 1926—an incredible sustained outperformance for an asset class. He disputes this result by touching on "survivor" bias, which is the idea that the small companies that fail are not kept in the small company indices. But he is troubled by the thought that a class of stocks with comparable beta to the S&P 500 could beat the S&P 500. To rationalize this outperformance, he cites Fama and French's work that when size is used as a proxy for beta and coupled with price-to-ratio, it does explain the higher long-term returns generated by small-cap and value investing. In that acknowledgment, he seems to be saying that beta may an imperfect measure of risk because it is an incomplete expression of market risk. He is certainly right that all theories are imperfect on some level.

His final attack on active management is that there are relatively few investors who have beaten the market throughout all investment cycles. I think that is an extreme test. There are in fact over 26,000 mutual funds, so that number is a pretty select group. He cites in particular evidence that 71 percent of all mutual funds failed to match the S&P 500 Index over a 10-year period ended 2001. First of all, this example ignores the manifest success of some of the greatest investors we have—the Jim Simons and Warren Buffetts and Ray Dalios of the world who have gathered enormous assets under management based on outperformance. Moreover, this period covered was one that had the most of a raging bull market. Anyone could index or buy and hold almost anything in that time frame and look and feel smart. In a secular bear market, 10 years of negligible returns is likely to make even those with the strongest stomach abandon their long-term plan, in which case the financial adviser would have failed.

It's true that only in Lake Wobegon can all the children be above average. To the extent that all mutual funds have transaction costs and management fees, they are always at a disadvantage on creating total return in excess of the market. But as I said earlier, for many people, the primary value of an adviser is his or her impact on securing sustained investing behavior. The Jim Simons and Warren Buffetts and Ray Dalios of the world are important not only for their actual success but for the inspiration they give all of us to persist. There is an adage in the mutual fund industry that mutual funds are sold, not bought. There is a satisfaction and psychic value to branding that funds create at a cost that adds value and commitment that are likely to create more successful, consistent investing behavior. Mutual funds spend large sums on branding and distribution, and it is money well spent for their investors because it reinforces optimal investing behavior. Not everyone can stand being a leaf floating down the river of life.

HOW MPT HAS BEEN USED BY FINANCIAL ADVISERS

How was the work of Markowitz and Malkiel distilled into practice for financial advisers? If all short-term returns of stocks are random, then it follows from MPT and EMH that investors will be net losers, after transaction costs are considered, from trying to time the market tactically. For advisers, this has been translated into "buy and hold," which is followed by "you don't want to be *out* of the market on any of the 10 biggest days of the year because you would then sharply underperform the market." To reinforce this observation, over the years, in response to most observed market correlations, financial advisers often have asserted that "correlation does not mean causation" as a sort of mantra to dispense with the need to examine any correlation in particular. This is important because when you are dealing with small sets of data, it is relatively easy to find overlays that match that may not have much, if any, discernible connection to the market theory being asserted. Small data sets are 20 or 30 or even 40 single data points. A good example is the Super Bowl indicator mentioned in Chapter 1, which has an 80 percent correlation with the S&P 500. Sounds like a lot, but it is not. Over the past 45 years since the Super Bowl started, there have been 34 years when the S&P 500 was up, a 75 percent chance of having an up year. Over that same time frame, a team from the NFC won 24 times, and the market was up 87 percent of those years. By comparison, 67 percent of the time an AFC team won, the market was up. Three games out of 45 with different results could just as easily have made the AFC indicator a featured bull market indicator. Moreover, it is difficult to conceive of any good explanation for why the Super Bowl Indicator would be predictive. It is exactly for these kinds of situations that the slogan "Correlation is not causation" is useful as a time-saving decision tool.

But MPT has its limits, and some of its corollaries are questionable. Matt Forester, CIO of Creative Financial Group, once described MPT to me as "GIGO"—code language for being susceptible to "garbage in, garbage out." If our Constitution gives us the right to "the pursuit of happiness" perhaps it's best to think about MPT as the "pursuit of rationality" to describe the market. And it is an imperfect pursuit at that.

However, while MPT can help us avoid obviously flawed theories, or investing in patterns, it is important to articulate the underlying assumptions of MPT and EMH.

Travis Morien, a financial adviser in Australia, has done a good job of summarizing what he perceives as the flawed assumptions of MPT. He lists them as follows[3]:

- There are no transaction costs in buying and selling securities. There is no brokerage, no spread between bidding and asking prices. You pay no taxes of any kind, and only "risk" plays a part in determining which securities an investor will buy.

- An investor can take any position of any size in any security he wishes. No one can move the market, and liquidity is infinite. You can buy a trillion dollars' worth of stock in a small speculative mining stock or buy one cent's worth of Berkshire Hathaway. Nothing stops you from taking positions of any size in any security.

- The investor does not consider taxes when making investment decisions and is indifferent to receiving dividends or capital gains.

- Investors are rational and risk averse. They are completely aware of all risk entailed in an investment and will take positions based on a determination of risk, demanding a higher return for accepting greater volatility.

- Investors, as a group, look at risk-return relationships over the same time horizon. A short-term speculator and a long-term investor have exactly the same motivations, time horizon, and profit target. Regardless of who you are, you will always give an investment the same amount of time to work out and volatility will be your only concern.

- Investors, as a group, have similar views on how they measure risk. All investors have the same information and will buy or sell based on an identical assessment of the investment and all expect the same thing from the investment. A seller will be motivated to sell only because another security has a level of volatility corresponding to their desired return. A buyer will make a purchase because this security has a level of risk corresponding to the return that he wants.

- Investors seek to control risk only by the diversification of their holdings.

- All assets, including human capital, can be bought and sold on the market.

- Investors can lend or borrow at the 91-day T-bill rate—the risk-free rate—and can also sell short without restriction.

- Politics and investor psychology have no effect on the markets.

I would add a key assumption not emphasized above: the markets are not rigged, and the key determinants of price, such as interest rates, are not fixed. That assumption is not valid today.

Perhaps the best way to think about MPT and its core assumptions is that MPT is like Newtonian physics. At normal speeds, it is a pretty good approximation of the physical universe. But when it approaches its boundaries, like the speed of light, things change. This is important because the relentless work of the market is to discover price by using all the measuring capability known to man. In the next few pages, I will highlight how some of these assumptions break down in practice as the markets approach limits that are the functional equivalent of the speed of light.

FORMULAS DISTORT VALUATION IF INPUTS ARE NOT FREE MARKET INPUTS

Some of our most basic equations for understanding stock values start to lose their grounding when you have a zero bound on interest rates. Let's start with the capital asset pricing model. It is usually expressed as follows:

$$\overline{r_a} = r_f + \beta_a(\overline{r_m} - r_f)$$

where r_f = Risk-free rate
β_a = Beta of the security
r_m = Expected market return
R (a) = Return on the asset

When the risk-free rate is zero, very low market returns will justify many stock purchases. When most stocks are good because they are on average yielding more than fixed income, very slight rates of growth can be used to justify very high stock valuations. This happened in 1929, and it was not good for investors. This is particularly true where real interest rates after inflation are negative. But negative real returns for fixed income signal an economy in distress. The world economy is very much in distress, with fixed income bouncing along at near deflationary prices. To buy time, the Fed and the European central banks have gone on a liquidity spree, lending freely to banks at nominal rates, and recently the Fed told us it would keep interest rates low through 2014. What happens when these low risk-free rates affect other rates used to understand value?

For example, the most frequently used calculation in discovering the value of a stock is Gordon's growth model for discounted dividends:

$$P = D \cdot \sum_{i=1}^{\infty} \left(\frac{1+g}{1+k}\right)^i = D \cdot \frac{1+g}{k-g}$$

where P = Price
D = Dividends
g = rate of growth
k = discount rate

When the risk-free interest rate is set at zero, as the Federal Reserve bank has done, this model can lose its integrity because the second expression of this equation has the term $k - g$ in the denominator, making it zero or negative for some inputs. In normal times, the risk-free rate is substantial, the discount rate is much higher, and good growth rates yield valuations that made sense historically, particularly for large slow-growth companies. But if the risk-free rate is very low, resulting in very low growth rates and discount rates being used, this equation suggests that very high-equity valuations can be sustained with very modest growth. But very modest growth—the kind you might have on the verge of a double-dip recession—is by definition fragile growth and causes our most basic equations to perhaps give off wrong signals about the value of the equity market. Just a few years ago, when interest rates were not as rigged by the Fed, some models used the risk-free rate or a rate very close to it as the discount rate to assess the highest upside of stocks. In a zero interest rate policy (or ZIRP) environment, using this equation, there is a chance that all growth stocks will grow to the moon. Unfortunately, with the financial repression of ZIRP, a lot of investors are chasing returns into the equity market as they in effect follow Gordon's growth model. This may not be sustainable even though it represents the core engine of individual stock selections that in turn drives the stock selection for many portfolios.

MPT relates to ZIRP by assuming all information is perfectly discounted in the market. But when the interest rates are set at a bound of zero, all portfolio managers are flying much more blindly. In effect, the mood of the market is much more subject to fashion swings because there are fewer grounded inputs. Hence, we wake up to find out "It's a risk-on day" or "It's a risk-off day." The job of the market as a whole is to discover price. When a key variable of each individual stock price is a rigged input, the MPT assumption that all information is known and properly discounted breaks down. Put differently, when the major asset choices are fixed-income securities or stocks with a yield significantly above that of fixed income, on the numbers there may be very little choice but to go into stocks. But that doesn't mean that stocks are accurately priced. It means only that the financial repression of ZIRP has largely forced investors into equities. It is hard to see how market information can be efficiently priced when the key variable for understanding prices—the risk-free rate—has been artificially set at zero.

In his defense of MPT and EMH, Malkiel assumes that there are no disparities in liquidity. But the daily commitment of funds to the market shows that there are enormous disparities. Some people estimate that over 60 percent of the daily volume in the market is now driven by high-frequency traders. It certainly is for stocks listed on the New York Stock Exchange. These are shops that locate as close as physically possible to the data feeds of the exchange networks so they can be one or two milliseconds faster that their competition when applying sophisticated algorithms to the proprietary trading strategies of the dominant traders in the markets. When, as stated in *Information Week* magazine, "a one (1) millisecond advantage in trading applications can be worth $100 million a year to a major brokerage firm" and the majority of the daily capital put to work in the market fights for that kind of advantage, it is no longer appropriate to think that all participants have equal access to information, execution, or liquidity, as MPT does.[4] Identifying MPT as the basic Newtonian approach also suggests that there are limits to thinking that what is measured in the stock market is unaffected by the measurer. The term reflexivity describes the feedback loop created by changing perceptions of market value and shows how measurement in the stock market is different from measuring an object in Newtonian physics.[5] For example, if a momentum stock rises quickly and the company raises more cash at higher equity values, having more cash gives the company more ability to compete, and it gives more investors a rooting interest in that stock. MPT has created its own feedback loop so that now, as indexing is more prevalent in the market, more of the market is correlated, giving rise to the contradiction that the more investors seek low correlated returns by indexing their portfolios, the more their portfolios have correlated returns.

The combination of fixed, short-term, risk-free rates of zero; widespread indexing; and high-frequency trading have created a shorter and shorter-term investing environment. If you listen to Bloomberg Radio, which I enjoy doing every trading day, you find that there are many days that are announced as "risk-on" days when the market is rallying and "risk-off" days when the market is falling, but every one of these days is deemed to be a good day for investing in the broad market. In fact, over the past year, the market has become much more volatile on a daily basis. For example, in 2011, there were 96 days with 1 percent swings. This compares to 57 such days on average in the previous 46 years.

Given the heightened overall volatility of the market due to structural forces such as high-frequency trading, fixed interest rates of zero, and the feedback loop of more indexing creating more correlated trading, it is time to turn to MPT's implicit assumption that stocks are not affected by political decisions. In his defense of MPT and EMH, Professor Malkiel noted that many people raise the Crash of 1987 as proof that the market is not efficient. He cites in his rebuttal example that using the discounted dividend equation with an interest rate that moved from 9.0 percent to 10.5 percent would be sufficient to explain what happened to stocks. The problem with his statement is that interest rates rose gradually, but all stocks were repriced by 22 percent in one day.

He acknowledges the political environment but really gives it too little weight. It's best to understand the Crash of 1987 as a giant traffic accident occurring in a fog bank on a California freeway, resulting in 100 cars being totaled before anyone knew there was even an accident ahead of them. The only *apolitical* aspects of the Crash were the high-interest-rate environment coupled with high stock valuations, which made for a fragile environment. The precipitating causes were not valuations by themselves but three separate destabilizing political actions by our government.

WHAT CAUSED THE CRASH OF 1987?

What really happened in the Crash of 1987 is that on the Wednesday before the crash, Congressman Dan Rostenkowski, chairman of the House Ways and Means Committee, passed committee votes to eliminate interest deductions on junk bonds (now known as high-yield bonds) if these bonds were used for acquisitions. Congress's motivation was to provide protection to the entrenched managers of companies that were potential takeover candidates. But the tax committee clearly did not have a clue as to the unintended consequence and cost of providing such protection. Every stock trades to a greater or lesser extent on its potential to be a takeover candidate. With one news release, the politicians forced the market to consider that there may no longer be any acquisitions involving junk bonds. The so-called "deal" stocks, such as United Airlines, those held by arbitrageurs, had their own Crash on the Wednesday, Thursday, and Friday before the crash. By Friday night, half the major houses on Wall Street knew that all their profits for 1987 had just been wiped out by three days of losses in the firm's proprietary arbitrage accounts.

This legislative action destabilized the market.

The second blow to the market was another political blow. Over that weekend before the crash, Secretary James Baker, trying to get the Germans to lower their interest rates, threatened to let the dollar go down in value. It was a glimpse of the fracturing of exchange rate accords. Coming as it did with Wall Street's profits for the year already wiped out, it set off a massive panic.

The third political blow was more like a pressurized altitude bomb that was set to go off if the markets moved too much. In those days, individual stocks could not be shorted unless the last price had been an "uptick." This rule, instituted in the 1930s to stop bear raids on stocks, slowed panic reactions. The regulators allowed the sellers of portfolio insurance to find a way around the "uptick" for selling short. However, portfolio insurance had become an institutionally popular way to try to reduce risk for investment managers. So some players in the market were regulated on pricing and others were not. This contribution to the crash was a third political contribution.

It is difficult to overstate that sense of panic that most market participants had on that Monday morning, October 19, 1987. Rather than cite dry statistics, I'd like to take a partial detour into that day for me. In those days, I was a mergers and acquisitions investment banker with PaineWebber. My personal memory is that I had worked for six months to get a meeting between Bill Bindley, who ran the pharmacy company Bindley Western and had flown in from Indiana, and a Dutchman (who shall be otherwise nameless), who had flown in from the Netherlands, to discuss the possible sale of the company. Dr. Joe Plummer had found the Dutchman, and I had found Bill. Joe and I worked together in those days, and being involved with him was like having Babe Ruth hitting behind you in a baseball line-up. At the close of business on Friday, Bindley Western's stock was $11 per share. The potential buyer and seller sat down to direct negotiations, with the buyer saying, "You know, we could do something for you at $15 per share." Bill Bindley countered with $17, and my hope was rising that both sides were signaling that a deal could be done in the middle of the bid/ask at about $16 per share.

At 9:30 a.m., Cliff Baxter entered the meeting and made a comment that the stock market was down an incredible amount. In fact, the Dow Jones Industrial Average (DJIA) was down 3.68 percent, (82.57 points) at the open. Seizing an opportunity, the Dutchman asked, where is Bindley Western stock? It opened at about $9 1/2 per share. Bill Bindley announced that he could see doing something at $16 1/2 per share. The Dutchman asked for coffee, and then food, and then went to the bathroom.

By 10 a.m., Bindley Western stock was at $8 per share, and the Dutchman was talking about the need to reexamine everything in the light of the new market valuations. He tried out $13 to $14 per share, saying it was an even higher percentage above the market than his original offer. Now it was Bill Bindley's turn to head out to the men's room and ask for more coffee. I was getting more and more depressed that my entire year was about to go bust.

At around 11 a.m., Cliff Baxter came back in the room. The Dutchman was now asking him for updates on Bindley Western stock prices about every three minutes. It hit $7 per share. The Dutchman said to Bill Bindley, "Your stock was $11 per share when you came in here, and now it's $7 per share. There must be something you are not telling me. The best I can do now is to give you Friday's closing price of $11 per share for the entire company." To his everlasting credit, Bill Bindley got up and said, "This business has been in my family for 100 years. I am not selling it on a day of panic." And off he went. He was absolutely right—he subsequently sold Bindley Western to Cardinal Health (NYSE: CAH) for $2.3 billion in February 2001. For me, it was a disaster. The merger and acquisition business had always been feast or famine, but the toll of going from feast to famine in two hours was especially hard that year.

This particular deal fell apart because of the Crash of 1987. In my opinion, the rise in interest rates and Secretary Baker's intervention in the currency markets had created an environment that was susceptible to panic, and the presence of portfolio insurance had created a potential for a panic, but none of these three inputs were the proximate cause of the Crash of 1987. Interest rates tended to move in an orderly way. Currencies, even with intervention, moved in an orderly way. And portfolio insurance needed a price trigger to become lethal. The proximate cause of the Crash of 1987 was the inexplicably casual trial balloon of eliminating interest deductions for junk bonds if they were used for acquisitions. With one news item, the market was forced to drastically reconsider value in a way that can happen only with a noneconomic actor. The price action of the deal stocks defied all expectation. I did not understand it at the time, but my lost deal was caused by the Congressional Effect. In the end, seeing the error of their ways, the politicians did not pass the tax bill. But for many market participants who were either wiped out or lost great sums in that one day, the fact that Congress ultimately never passed the law was little comfort. Just the market's flinch from this sudden and capricious suggestion was enough to wipe out 22 percent of the equity value in the U.S. market alone on that day. The Congressional Effect shows the impact of Congress on the reflexivity of a stock or an industry: legislatively imagined obstacles to an industry, created by government, can sharply depress a stock or a sector, even if they are merely proposed.

THE MAGNITUDE OF THE CRASH OF 1987 REFUTES MPT

I still think the magnitude of the 1987 crash alone refutes MPT. A 22 percent move in one day of the entire equity market is simply too big to consider the market as being efficient. One of MPT's key axioms is that the returns of an investment are normally or randomly distributed, so it makes little sense to try to time the market. In our financial culture, the vast majority of financial professionals embrace MPT to a greater or lesser extent. In a generally rising stock market with high transaction costs, as it was from Eisenhower through Clinton, it made historical and intellectual sense for brokers, financial advisers, and portfolio managers to use MPT as a justification for *never* timing the market. The popular thinking was that missing the handful of big up days could cause you to underperform the broad market. The episode of the Crash of 1987 invites the retort to MPT that if you can avoid the biggest down days in the market, you might do better. Congress was in session when it set in motion that crash.

MPT ASSUMES ALL DAILY PRICING IS RANDOM, BUT THE CONGRESSIONAL EFFECT SHOWS IT IS NOT

MPT, like most theories, is only as good as the assumptions behind it. The Congressional Effect shows that MPT's key assumption—that daily returns are randomly distributed—is wrong. The statistical data in support of this is overwhelming. Unlike the Super Bowl indicator, which involved 45 data points, the Congressional Effect is confirmed by 11,832 daily observations over 47 years. On the 7,767 days from 1965 through 2011 when Congress was in session, the stock market went up in price on days at the annual rate of 0.72 percent, whereas on the 4,065 days when Congress was out of session it went up at the annual rate of 16.60 percent. These figures ignore transaction costs, tax effects, and dividends.

These data were further confirmed by Lamb, Ma, Pace, and Kennedy in 1997. Their study, which covered the period from 1897 through 1993, found that "almost the entire advance in the market since 1897 corresponds to periods when Congress is in recess."[6] They looked at a total of 26,337 trading days, comprising 9,950 in recess days and 16,387 in session days. Using the DJIA, they found the average daily return on in-session days was .0042 percent and on in-recess days 0.0541 percent. This is a difference of over 13 times, over a period representing over 90 percent of the available meaningful data on the United States stock market. It is an extraordinary magnitude for an effect to be so consistent over such a long period. Even more interesting were their findings over two more recent time horizons, 1984 through 1993, and 1988 through 1993. Between 1984 and 1993, the DJIA increased 2672.74, of which 2346.92 points occurred on out-of-session days. The 87.8 percent of increases that occurred on closed days were significant to the 0.10 level. A staggering 95 percent of the DJIA increases were accounted for on closed days between 1988 and 1993, significant to the 0.05 level. The index shows that not only does a statistically significant level of returns coincide with out-of-session days over three time horizons but that the Congressional Effect is growing as government grows and investors become more wary about its impact on the market.

To otherwise rationalize this anomaly, Lamb and Ma examine the January Effect to account for some of the return disparities, since Congress is usually in recess in the beginning of the year. The January Effect refers to the price increase of small stocks in January, as individual investors sell their underperforming equities in December to claim capital losses for tax purposes. However, this notion is discounted as not contributory to the Congressional Effect, as the January Effect affects only small firms not indexed by the DJIA. Regression also supports that when the January Effect is isolated, it is not significant to the returns, and the Congressional Effect remains significant. They find the only other explanation (and in my opinion, the *best* explanation) is that Congress adds uncertainty to the market, as policies and bills are debated through unresolved legislation. Until final votes are cast, the market cannot resolve uncertainty on in-session days, leading to more stable positive returns on closed days.

Building on Lamb and Ma, in 2006, Professors Michael F. Ferguson and H. Douglas Witte conducted a massive study, also finding a "strong link between Congressional activity and stock market returns."[7] Taking the data back to 1897 day by day, they found (ignoring transaction costs and dividends, and giving a credit of one basis point per day for interest earned on cash balances) that a dollar invested in 1897 just on the in-session days would have compounded to $2 over 108 years. The same dollar, invested just on out-of-session days over the identical period would have compounded into $216.

To verify the statistical significance of returns on open and closed days, Ferguson and Witte used some very sophisticated techniques to try to eliminate the impact of other potential overlapping daily return anomalies such the Preholiday Effect, the January Effect, and the Turn of the Month Effect. Even with those anomalies neutralized, they still found that small daily increases on out-of-session days accumulated to an annual 3.3 percent to 6.5 percent outperformance of the broad stock market. In the time since their study, government has gotten bigger as a percentage of our economy, and the Congressional Effect has become greater on average on a daily basis.

Additionally, when daily returns are accounted for trading days of the week, trading days before holidays, and seasonality, there is still a significant three- to six-basis-point increase of the Congressional Effect per day. They also found public opinion of Congress also adds to the Congressional Effect, where returns are highest and risk is lowest when a relatively unpopular Congress is out of session, while returns are lowest and risk is highest when a relatively popular Congress is out of session. Akin to market influences, such as the Sunshine Effect that plays on investor mood (increasing valuation expectations), the general public disdain toward politicians and Congress dampens the market further when it is in session—to which I would say: almost every day Congress is in session is like a rainy day.

Ferguson and Witte saw the threat of increased regulation (as Congress could pass new legislation) affecting the market as creating investor uncertainty while Congress is in session; they even cited Malkiel as acknowledging this possibility. They found an increase in volatility when Congress was in session as well, which is consistent with heightened legislative risk. To the extent that they found an increased Congressional Effect when Congress is unpopular, I would add that the current Congress is the most unpopular ever measured since 1939 when pollsters began tracking Congress favorability levels. One would probably have to go to the Civil War in 1861 to find a less popular Congress, and even that would be subject to doubt. At that time, the Republicans were at least popular in the North. In today's partisan world, both self-identified Republicans and Democrats have utter disdain for Congressional leaders of their own parties. As a result, Congress has approval ratings at about 10 percent, and it can be reasonably be expected over long periods of time that this will translate into continued presence for the Congressional Effect.

One other confirmation of the Congressional Effect casts doubt on modern portfolio theory. If MPT is correct that all daily stock prices are randomly distributed, then there should be little confidence that one can observe a consistent difference between in-session days and out-of-session days. A statistical test called a t-test is what is used to test the significance of the correlation between such different classes of days. A t-test determines whether the means of two populations are statistically different from each other. Generally, in the social sciences, the goal is to have a 95 percent confidence factor that two data sets correspond to each other in order to determine that a relationship between two data sets is not random. In fact the data reflecting the Congressional Effect is overwhelming. By comparing the mean annualized returns of S&P 500 on Congress in session days with out-of-session days, it can be determined that there is 99.937 percent confidence that out-of-session days have a higher annualized return. Another t-test determines with 99.630 percent confidence that in-session days have a lower annualized mean return than the overall daily S&P 500. This represents several orders magnitude of higher confidence than supports most observable social science theories. While small set correlations like the Super Bowl indicator do not equal causation, I believe it is fair to say that 26,337 data set correlations with confidence factors in the high 99 percent levels in fact do indicate causation. In this regard, modern portfolio theory does fall short. To the extent MPT was typically used to persuade investors to adopt a buy and hold broadly diversified strategy, and therefore not miss any of the big up days, I believe the Congressional Effect observation can be used to structure a tactical approach that helps an investor disproportionately avoid the big down days over a long period of time.

SUMMARY

The limits of MPT are that short-term prices are not always randomly distributed, so it is possible to achieve market returns without taking full market risk over full investment cycles.

So the data are overwhelming. But what does the data really say? Modern portfolio theory assumes that reward is always commensurate with risk. But as we have seen, there are many assumptions built into MPT that are questionable. Historically, trading the Congressional Effect, over long periods of time, investors can capture returns that are comparable to the broad stock market, but have much less the risk. This is a big claim, but it is what happens when legislative risk is systematically reduced.

MPT says this should be impossible, because higher returns must be compensated for with higher risk, but in this case higher returns would have been achieved without higher risk. Now that we know the statistical evidence supports the existence of a Congressional Effect, it is time to turn to the cause of the Congressional Effect—Congress.

NOTES

1. Harry Markowitz, "Portfolio Selection," *Journal of Finance* 7(1), March 1952, 77–91.

2. Burton G. Malkiel, "The Efficient Market Hypothesis and Its Critics," *Journal of Economic Perspectives* 17(1), Winter 2003, 59–82.

3. www.travismorien.com/FAQ/portfolios/mptcriticism.htm

4. Richard Martin, "Wall Street's Quest to Process Data at the Speed of Light," *Information Week*, April 21, 2007.

5. The term *reflexivity* was coined by George Soros in *The Alchemy of Finance: Reading the Mind of the Market* (Wiley Investment Classics, 1987).

6. Reinhold P. Lamb, K. Ma, R. Daniel Pace, and William F. Kennedy, "The Congressional Calendar and Stock Market Performance," *Financial Services Review* 6(1), 1997, 19–25.

7. Michael F. Ferguson and Hugh Douglas Witte, "Congress and the Stock Market," March 13, 2006, http://ssrn.com/abstract=687211

CHAPTER 3

Congressmen as Issues Entrepreneurs

O ne reason I decided to investigate the Congressional Effect is that I have an abiding interest in politics. I watch lots of political news, and attend lots of gatherings where our leaders are speaking. One night, I had the chance to sit down after a long evening with a congressman who was wrapping an evening of campaigning. His train back to D.C. wasn't for a while and I was very happy to have some time with him one on one. Most of the time was spent on his views of the issues of the day. But I was really curious as to how he really saw his role. As we started to work on a second bottle of wine, he took a break from talking about his views to ask me what I did for a living. I told him I was an entrepreneur. In a moment of strenuous empathy, he told me, "I'm an entrepreneur, too!"

I said, "Really, I thought you worked for the government and got a fixed salary, full medical benefits, and a pension."

He said, "I am an issues entrepreneur!"

I asked, "How does that work?"

He said, "Well, as a legislator, I legislate. So I look for an industry that has something that needs fixing. Every industry needs some fixing. And then I see what kind of an impact that issue has, what the lobbyists have to say, and whether I pick up support or votes or both from pressing for or against a piece of legislation."

Every congressman has the opportunity to be an "issues entrepreneur," seeking rent, votes, personal profit, and/or attention. And because attention sometimes translates into higher office with more power, there is constant competitive pressure to find an issue that a congressman can use as leverage to gain campaign dollars and voter support.

THE TIME-MONEY-VOTE CONTINUUM: CONGRESS AS A BUSINESS

This chapter looks at the job of each congressman from his own self-interest, which usually but not always consists of getting reelected. Congressmen with longevity (and most of them achieve at least longevity) can get very wealthy over time, mostly from seeking rents and trading upon their influence, as opposed to their W-2 income as a congressman. It is not a new thought that Congress is often corrupt, but it is seldom thought of in the context of how it affects the stock market. I do not mean to suggest that congressmen never act in the interest of the country—but rather that the system as a whole provides them endless incentive to intervene in markets with predictably bad results. The business of each congressman is constantly to refresh their pool of supporters. To gain more votes, they can spend time or money with constituents and return favors. That is why there is a continuum: time equals money, and money equals votes, so the average congressman rightfully equates the two as he tries to guarantee his reelection. Once you see the forces that drive reelection, you will understand why there is a relentless Congressional Effect in the stock market. This chapter reviews the business dynamics of being an entrepreneurial congressman and the average economics of an election cycle.

Each election cycle, there are 435 members of the House of Representatives who have to be reelected. In 2010, the average winning House member spent $1.4 million on their reelection effort, with the average incumbent spending $1 million and their average challenger spending $166,000 (according to *Mother Jones*). Senate races in large states can cost 10 times as much or more. The average congressional district had about 700,000 people in 2010. The average district had a little over 200,000 voters in 2010, and a little over 280,000 in the presidential election year of 2008. So, on average, each congressman is looking for roughly somewhere between 110,000 and 150,000 voters and their votes to be reelected. Senate races on average cost several times more than a House race.

Just to paint the issue as an order of magnitude on an overall basis, the average winning House incumbent spent $1,400,000/110,000 votes or about $13 per vote in the last election to get elected or reelected, as the case may be. Of course, there were races that cost a lot less and a few that cost several times more. But the averages are useful for understanding what drives a congressman. And since most congressmen start with a base of loyal—or at least habitual—voters, it is probably better to think of each congressman as usually more worried about finding 25,000 to 50,000 new voters in his district than about his base. In big, round numbers, he is thinking that he has to spend $5 to $10 per base voter, and perhaps $20 to $30 for each new voter.

The key concept here is that fresh voters are the bone marrow of reelection. The base will vote out of conviction and habit, but, unfortunately, for most politicians the base constantly erodes. Fresh blood is required. And that is why as much as each congressman wants to be a figure on the national stage, every day there are handfuls of voters to meet in person, and every handful counts.

As an issues entrepreneur, he can theoretically get at least one or more of the following from every old and new issue:

- Campaign donations
- Votes (from the base and from new voters)
- Volunteers
- Endorsements
- Alliances
- Projects and jobs specifically for his district
- Projects and jobs specifically for supporters
- Opportunities for profitable trades and investments
- Groundwork laid for subsequent career as lobbyist

For each congressman, some of these represent simply a different means of gathering votes. For example, 100 volunteers may translate into an incremental 5,000 new votes just as well as $200,000 of TV advertising does. Similarly, a piece of pork-barrel legislation may create local jobs in the congressional district. For example, in Brooklyn Heights, where I used to live, there was a court building built with federal money, the Emanuel Celler Building, named after Congressman Emanuel Celler, which was then upgraded to be named after President Theodore Roosevelt. This complex cost $371 million to build, creating perhaps 3,000 jobs. Assuming every person attached to a job has a family, and everyone in that family reliably votes for the incumbent, a building like that can secure perhaps 5,000 votes, some of which count toward that goal of 25,000 to 50,000 new votes. Moreover, some of those people will become volunteers working on a campaign, and so have a multiplying effect.

In fact, in 2010, $16 billion was spent in earmarks across 435 congressional districts nationwide, for an average of $36 million per district. Assuming each of these translated into several dozen, or perhaps several hundred, jobs within a congressional district, every congressman voting for earmarks comes back to a portion of his constituents with the message, "Hey, I brought home the bacon." There is a direct relationship between the patronage created by earmarks and votes. That is why even though they are incredibly embarrassing as a whole, earmarks continue to have a place in our federal budget.

Of course, it sometimes happens that a congressman is sincerely interested in an issue, and his promotion of the issue attracts voters to his side, even without cash changing hands. In theory, this is how our democracy is supposed to work. The average congressman starts by figuring out who is in his district by profiling its various types of voters, inventorying the issues that are important to them, and conceiving of a winning coalition. In red states, for example, Second Amendment rights tend to attract voters, while in blue states, for example, expansion of government support programs often attracts voters. Many congressmen are happy just to be able to recite the party line and repeat it in a safe district. It is only the most successful issues entrepreneur congressmen who are able to "nationalize" (i.e., get nationwide attention) issues and gain attention beyond their districts. That doesn't necessarily mean that they always succeed in staying in office even if they successfully "nationalize" their issue. For example, Congresswoman Michelle Bachman ran for president and dramatically increased her fund raising as well as how much her opponents could raise against her. But with all that said, the checklist for each entrepreneurial congressman's assessment of each issue looks a little like this:

How many people care about this issue?

If I approve it, how many fresh votes do I gain?

How many base votes do I keep?

How many votes do I lose?

What competition do I create?

How much money can I raise based on this issue?

How much spending will apply to my district based on this issue?

Am I creating a vote I will regret in the future?

Can I look like I support this while actually not supporting it?

Does this issue give me campaign cash?

Does this issue get federal budget money to be spent in my district?

Is this an issue I can influence down the road if I leave Congress and become a lobbyist?

I admit that this list does not emphasize what is good for the country or the state or even the congressman's district. Of course, there are times when congressmen consider these issues as well. And there is a continuum in our congressmen from the most enlightened to the most venal. But as a practical matter, "the good of the country" is so far away in time compared to the demands of the next election that on many issues it is just a much lower priority question than many of the preceding ones for most congressmen on many issues.

What emerges from evaluating each of, say, 25 major issues and several hundred minor issues that might appear in front of a congressman in the course of a legislative term is that each one is viewed as an opportunity to raise campaign cash, votes, or both. Every legislative session literally has thousands of laws introduced. Some are of vast importance to the economy, and some just to a handful of people. But the overall take-away is the same: if every law could sway on average 1,000 new voters, repeated 25 times, that would result in 25,000 new voters, a practical margin of victory for most congressmen. Of course, there are not 1,000 issues of equal rank in terms of capturing the attention of the public. In that regard, there are perhaps 20 or 30 hot-button issues that at any given moment can even be really perceived as being active issues in a particular legislative session. Accordingly, the leverage associated with each issue trails off with issues of lesser importance. Nevertheless, our laws have become a gravy train for congressmen seeking rents for providing possible advantages to various companies and industries.

While these numbers are not exact, as an order of magnitude, they are very helpful for understanding the core dysfunctionality of Congress. A hundred votes in a district on one issue are probably enough to get a congressman's attention, and 1,000 votes are definitely enough if it is an additive to his base by virtue of being a new issue. As we saw earlier, if a new marginal voter costs on average $25 to reach by advertising and other campaign means, then $25,000 of donations completely gets the attention of a congressman.

So if $25,000 is important, then what can a congressman gain from a sustained seeking of rents on a big legislative issue? The answer is a lot. For example, in March 2012, a controversy erupted over the new guidelines for reimbursing health care expenses for contraception. A law student at Georgetown Law School, Sandra Fluke, appeared in testimony in front of House Democrats complaining of the burden of purchasing contraceptives. Under the new health care law, contraceptives are a reimbursed expense. This is a great example of an entrepreneurial issue because it had both vote counting and campaign finance associated with it. The issue was used by the Democrats to frame the health care debate as one over "reproductive rights," and as of this writing in March 2012 the issue apparently generated some additional polling support The Republicans preferred to portray the issue as a Freedom of Religion question, asking whether religious institutions should be required to fund practices repugnant to their core beliefs.

Of course, it would be wrong to assume that members of Congress are always the aggressors. Often, companies and industries make donations to influence Congress. Lost in the contraceptive debate was the real issue: the new health care act mandated that all contraceptive products be subsidized under the new law, and required "FDA Approved" (translation: "branded") products to be purchased with the mandated health care. In effect, the U.S. pharmaceutical industry had purchased monopoly status from the government in many areas where they had been subject to competition.

Since President Obama was elected, the pharmaceutical industry has been the largest lobbying force of any industry. Tim Carney of the *Washington Examiner* identified the drug industry as the largest lobbying force in the United States.[1] It spent $635 million in the last two election cycles. This is more than was spent on a combined basis by the oil and gas and Wall Street industries. By spending, they got to change the way the law affected them so that they received benefits as well as burdens from the new law. In particular, there were no price controls for drugs in general and no permission for foreign sourcing of drugs (reimportation), and, most important, at least 30 million new customers will be insured, which implies they will have the ability to pay for drugs.[2] Estimating that perhaps one sixth of the $635 million found its way into campaign donations to the House of Representatives, and that it was given over two legislative cycles, it still is such a vast amount of money that it dwarfs most other legislative considerations for any congressman wanting to raise money to be reelected, which is the primary reason the law passed. If it were only $50 million per cycle that went into the House races, it would still be enough to average over $100,000 per congressman, a sizable chunk of the average amount spent to win reelection.

It is because of numbers like these that each congressman is acutely aware of his impact on the stock prices of the companies that are subject to government scrutiny. That is why there is such a competitive scrum for influential committee assignments. For example, the House Banking Committee, now under the name of the House Financial Services Committee, has 61 members. According to Opensecrets.org, in the 2010 election cycle, these members received over $34 million in donations from all political action committees (PACs), which included all manner of organizations on the left and right. In addition, these same members received over $37,900,000 in individual donations, many from the same people involved with the PACs. This represents an average of almost $1,200,000 per member, roughly the amount associated with running winning campaigns for reelection, as we saw earlier.

Following is a partial list of bills under active consideration in 2012, together with brief descriptions. Each proposed law represents an opportunity to raise funds and win over constituents. How many balls in play does Congress have at one time? This is a partial list from a recent summary by the Washington research firm Bradley-Woods of laws that came before

before Congress in March 2012, together with the industries affected and the stocks that were identified as being affected:

North American Energy Access Act (HR 3548)	To transfer permitting approval authority over the Keystone XL Pipeline to the Federal Energy Regulatory Commission (FERC).
Coal Residuals, Reuse and Management Act (HR 2273)	To amend subtitle D of the Solid Waste Disposal Act to facilitate recovery and beneficial use, and provide for the proper management and disposal, of materials generated by the combustion of coal and other fossil fuels.
EPA Regulatory Relief Act of 2011 (HR 2250)	To provide additional time for the administrator of the Environmental Protection Agency to issue achievable standards for industrial boilers, incinerators and for other purposes.
Currency Exchange Rate Oversight Reform Act of 2011 (S 1619)	A bill to provide for identification of misaligned currency, require action to correct the misalignment, and for other purposes.
Cement Sector Regulatory Relief Act of 2011 (HR 2681)	To provide additional time for the administrator of the Environmental Protection Agency (EPA) to issue achievable standards for cement manufacturing facilities, and for other purposes.
TRAIN Act of 2011 (HR 2401)	To require analyses of the cumulative and incremental impacts of certain rules and actions of the EPA, and for other purposes.

(*continued*)

Protecting Jobs From Government Interference Act (HR 2587)	To prohibit the National Labor Relations Board from ordering any employer to close, relocate, or transfer employment under any circumstance.
Budget Control Act of 2011 (PL 112-25)	A bill to reduce the deficit and raise the debt ceiling.
North American-Made Energy Security Act of 2011 (HR 1938)	A bill to expedite the Keystone XL pipeline application process.
Cut, Cap, and Balance Act of 2011 (HR 2560)	A measure to reduce the deficit, cap spending, and raise the debt ceiling.
Consumer Financial Protection Safety and Soundness Improvement Act of 2011 (HR 1315)	To amend the Dodd-Frank Wall Street Reform and Consumer Protection Act to strengthen the review authority of the Financial Stability Oversight Council of regulations issued by the Bureau of Consumer Financial Protection.
Department of the Interior, Environment, and Related Agencies Appropriations Act, FY2012 (HR 2584)	A measure to make appropriations for FY2012 for the Department of the Interior, EPA, and related agencies.
Jobs and Energy Permitting Act (House) (HR 2021)	A bill to expedite the EPA's permitting process to allow for increased oil and gas exploration in Alaska's Outer Continental Shelf (OCS).
A bill to repeal the Volumetric Ethanol Excise Tax Credit (S 1057)	A bill to repeal the ethanol blenders' tax credit and lift the ethanol import tariff.
Jobs and Energy Permitting Act (Senate) (S 1226)	A bill to expedite the EPA's permitting process to allow for increased oil and gas exploration in Alaska's Outer Continental Shelf (OCS).

Reversing President Obama's Offshore Moratorium Act (HR 1231)	To amend the Outer Continental Shelf Lands Act to require that each five-year offshore oil and gas leasing program offer leasing in the areas with the most prospective oil and gas resources, to establish a domestic oil and natural gas production goal, and for other purposes.
Putting the Gulf of Mexico Back to Work Act (HR 1229)	To amend the Outer Continental Shelf Lands Act to facilitate the safe and timely production of American energy resources from the Gulf of Mexico, to require the Secretary of the Interior to conduct certain offshore oil and gas lease sales, and for other purposes.
Restarting American Offshore Leasing Now Act (HR 1230)	To require the Secretary of the Interior to conduct certain offshore oil and gas lease sales, and for other purposes.

The sectors affected by these 22 proposed bills were Oil & Gas, Basic Materials, Industrial Goods, and Electric Utilities. Some of the companies included the majors in the energy sectors, such as Baker Hughes (NYSE: BHI); Chevron (NYSE: CVX); ExxonMobil (NYSE: XOM); Halliburton (NYSE: HAL); Schlumberger (NYSE: SLB); TransOcean (NYSE: RIG); BP (NYSE: BP); Chevron (NYSE: CVX); ConocoPhillips (NYSE: COP); ExxonMobil (NYSE: XOM); Shell Oil (NYSE: RDS.A); and Transocean (NYSE: RIG). Each one of these bills could change, sometimes dramatically, the profitability of each company mentioned.

So what is it that legislators do? They are always legislating. Sometimes they are planning legislation, sometimes they are passing legislation, sometimes they are amending legislation—but pretty much they are in a permanent state of agitation. So what does the average company see coming when it hears that there is going to be new legislation in its industry?

Well, health care reform is a good example. Why would the pharmaceutical industry have paid $635 million over several years to lobby Congress? First of all, most large companies are happy to have some of the regulatory burdens that they bear—it keeps smaller competitors from getting to be too pesky. So at best, perhaps, big business has an ambivalent relationship with big government. They are often allies, and when they are, it is usually bad for the consumer. Why would business submit to being functionally partners with government? Because resistance is often very painful, and functionally partnering with government can be very profitable in the short run. In the long run, businesses that depend on government protection and get too entangled with the government suffer by losing their flexibility and competitiveness. This was the case with the domestic automobile companies. The health care industry provides a good example of what happens when the government encroachment is repulsed and when it is accepted.

In 1992, President Clinton was elected, and his biggest initiative was to revamp health care. The large pharmaceutical companies fought that effort with all the public relations tools at their disposal. But it was a difficult battle. Figure 3.1 shows what happened to stocks like MRK and JNJ compared to the Standard & Poor's (S&P) 500 Index during the course of the 1993 attempt to change that industry.

At its worst moment, the health care industry lost 25% of its equity value during the course of Congress's discussions, which was over $100 billion in 1992 dollars. This likely represented something like the past several years' accrual of option value for the industry veterans. Once President Obama was elected with a filibuster-proof majority, the industry had to make a calculation—do we reject what the politicians want to do, and potentially

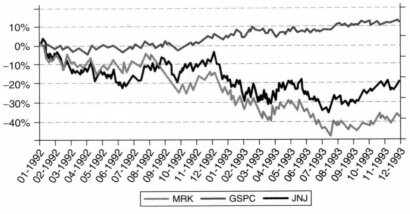

FIGURE 3.1   MRK, JNJ, and S&P 500 Index, 1992–1993. Source: Yahoo! Finance

lose a lot more than 25 percent again because government has more room to maneuver by virtue of a unified party control of government, or do we play ball and try to fashion laws that we think will help our companies over time? In this circumstance, there is enormous pressure on the companies to play ball because at any moment not only do they have a lot to lose (see the 1992 to 1993 industry chart), but if their competitors break ranks ahead of them, they can be frozen out of participating, while their competitors are made stronger. It is a Hobson's choice.

Once the Democratic presidential field was limited to Senators Obama and Clinton in 2008, Washington observers knew that there was at least a 50 percent chance that health care reform would get a major legislative effort in any new Democratic administration. According to Opensecrets.org, the pharmaceutical industry fractured its political giving and split its support evenly between the Democrats and Republicans in the 2008 election, having given Republicans the bulk of its support in 2006. But there is always an additional problem for each industry deciding to change the regulatory environment to better entrench their competitive position. The problem is that even if you make a pact with the devil, or perhaps because it is a pact with the devil, its final form may not be as advertised. Or stay done. Or guarantee that the government won't eventually turn on you and ask more, and then some, and so on. Certainly, the health care industry looked even worse in 2008 and 2009 as the health care bill came into focus, as seen in Figure 3.2.

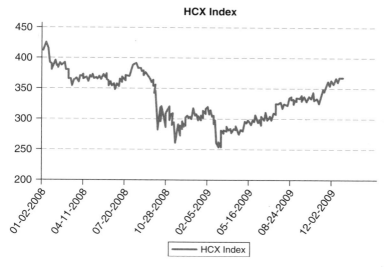

FIGURE 3.2 S&P Health Care Index, 2008–2009. Source: Yahoo! Finance

CONGRESSMEN AS TRADERS AND REAL ESTATE ENTREPRENEURS: MAKING MONEY OUTSIDE THEIR DAY GIG

There is one more aspect of what members of Congress do as issues entrepreneurs that is important to address. When you are an entrepreneur, you have to look at all opportunities to make money from your assets. For senators and representatives, their assets are largely the ability to influence the regulatory environment and to get early warnings on what it will be. Campaign donations are helpful for paying for the next election, but trading profits that go directly into your bank account are also one way to make money from your political assets.

That is why, as shown in a recent academic study,[3] the *average* senator had a portfolio earning *10 percent above the market for five years in a row* during the greatest bull market ever. Professor Alan Ziobrowski and his colleagues showed that from 1993 through 1998, a five-year period, the average senator made 85 basis points more than the market on their purchases, offset only slightly by losing 12 basis points more than the market on their sales. To put this in perspective, in 2000, Barber and Odean[4] found that the average household underperformed the market by 12 basis points per month during the period from 1991 through 1996. In 2001, Jeng, Meck, and Zeckhauser[5] found that from 1975 through 1996, the average corporate insider earned positive abnormal returns of 50 basis points per month. In effect, the *average* senator beat the market by 10 percent per year, year in and year out, over a five-year period. To put this in perspective, there are roughly 10,000 domestic mutual funds. From February 2007 through February 2012, less than 1 percent of them beat the stock market by 10 percent per year. The obvious conclusion of their senatorial study, which they analyze in the framework of modern portfolio theory (MPT), is that the only reasonable explanation for this result is that the senators were trading on inside information.

In fact, the study found that the average purchase was up 25 percent 12 months later. The researchers concluded that as to the Senate, in the time period analyzed, there was no statistical difference between Republican and Democratic senators. They did find, however, that junior senators had statistically significant higher returns than their less active senior colleagues. They probably needed the money more.

In Ziobrowksi et al.'s follow-up study of the House of Representatives in 2011, they looked at approximately 16,000 trades by 300 members of the House of Representatives from 1985 through 2006.[6] The average member of the House beat the stock market by an average of 6 percent per year. In that study, Democrats were found to have statistically significant higher trading returns than Republicans. The charitable view is that the Democrats were better traders. The same statistical analyses as above suggest this outsized success was in fact due to insider trading.

The real issue here is that public servants enter Congress from all walks of life, but they almost all emerge rich, and the implication is that they all used their influence to feather their nests. In fact, both Democrats and Republicans routinely traded stocks on inside information, or to get access to initial public offerings (IPOs) or otherwise use their positions of influence to make profits from federally funded programs to gather real wealth.[7] For example, Speaker of the House Dennis Hastert saw his net worth increase from the time he entered the House of Representatives as a former high school wrestling coach from $100,000 to over $10 million upon his retirement from Washington. Wealth like that is usually built from many transactions over time, where each one has a very favorable risk-reward profile. In one such transaction, Speaker Hastert purchased real property, and the subsequent federal funding of a major road near to the property caused it to quickly soar in value.[8] Similarly, Speaker Pelosi was instrumental in arranging over $600 million in funding for a light rail project that had the incidental impact of making an office building she owned several blocks from the route much more valuable. In 2010, Speaker Pelosi's minimum net worth increased 62 percent to $35.2 million. She was also one of the members of the House most active in trading IPOs.[9]

Equally important from a conflict-of-interest point of view, Speaker Pelosi had privileged access stocks that were front and center before Congress with key regulatory issues at stake. Speaker Pelosi purchased Visa stock on its IPO in March 2008.[10] To be fair, purchasing an IPO is not insider trading and Speaker Pelosi is from California, a hotbed of tech investing—but most ordinary people do not get access to hot IPOs. Peter Schweizer concluded she intervened to prevent the consideration of any bill to help retailers force lower debit card interchange fees for two years with Visa and MasterCard and their bank partners.[11] The Visa IPO that Speaker Pelosi purchased more than doubled, while the overall market declined over the next two years.

It is worth recalling that in the 1990s, denunciation of access to hot IPOs was one of the favorite issues of critics of underwriters, and cited by many as an important cause of the collapse of the Nasdaq market in 1999. "Spinning" or allocating IPO shares to individuals who were in a position to influence the company's subsequent selection of investment banking services was found to be a prominent conflict of interest. By 2011, the Financial Industry Regulatory Authority (FINRA) had adopted rules outlawing spinning by underwriters. In that context, the main difference between Speaker Pelosi's receiving IPO shares and preventing harmful legislation so that her shares do better, and a corporate insider's receiving

IPO shares for spinning is mostly just the time frame. The spinner's profits are immediate only if they choose to sell immediately, and Speaker Pelosi's developed over two years. Neither one is guaranteed, although Speaker Pelosi is taking more risk. However, the beneficiaries of spinning were usually people who had a lot at stake in the success of the IPOs they were in a position to influence as to the selection of underwriters. Speaker Pelosi occupies a position of public trust and should avoid even the appearance of putting her interests ahead of the public interest, however that is defined. If Speaker Pelosi, or all of Congress for that matter, were compensated based on the performance of a basket of the entire U.S. stock market, there would be less appearance of impropriety because there would be less personal interest in favoring or protecting one industry over another.

Finally, in 2010, Dodd-Frank was passed. Under the Durbin Amendment to the bill, the Federal Reserve was given the power to set lower interchange fees on behalf of the retailers. When the Fed finally announced in December 2010 on a preliminary basis that it planned to lower the average debit card interchange fee from $0.44 per transaction to $0.12, MasterCard fell more than 14 percent over six trading days, and Visa fell more than 17 percent over three trading days.

Recently, there has been much publicity regarding Congress's stock trading and the investment of government money to enhance the members' private property. In response to compelling documentation of congressional self-dealing[12] in both stock picking and property-enhancing earmarks, even *60 Minutes* disapproved of Congress in an episode featuring Peter Schweizer. Congress had been caught with its hand in the cookie jar. After much wrangling, on March 22, 2012, the Senate passed the House's version of the Stop Trading on Congressional Knowledge Act. This law, known as the STOCK Act, generally heightens the disclosure of the personal finances of congressmen, requires reporting of stock transactions within 45 days (as opposed to 18 months), and specifically prevents congressmen from trading on inside information. It also improves the availability of personal financial information on the Web. One item that was specifically deleted from the bill was the tightening of disclosure regarding the financial industry that studies Washington looking for clues about how Congress and the regulators will affect stocks.

Watching *60 Minutes* made it clear that any actual trading on inside information by Congress had to be stopped. But insider trading itself is difficult to spot. What was really offensive about the actions of Congress was that they had an informational advantage over the average trader and exploited it. Whether it took the form of insider trading, which has always been illegal for the average citizen and recently has been made explicitly illegal for Congress, or getting access to IPOs which most of the public could not; or access to direct benefits from earmarks, which are still not illegal; or helping companies they own stock in legislatively, they are still getting richer from a perk of their public office, and that is offensive. The work of Ziobrowksi proves statistically that Congress has an informational edge when it trades. Congressional insider trading was probably slowed down but not eliminated by the STOCK Act because the reputational harm the publicity caused or the potential for publicity will stop many Congressmen from even attempting it. That is the way a good preventative law is supposed to work. But the profit that Speaker Pelosi made on Visa IPO will still be there for the taking in the future. More important, although both sides of the aisle say they want to end the practice of earmarks, neither side actually appears to want to do that. It is the earmarks more than anything else that contributed to locked-in property gains. Astonishingly, in spite of all the adverse publicity associated with earmarks, both parties want to use them more again and are searching for fig leaves for cover. This is a classic instance of the incumbents agreeing they should be able to do what helps them keep their jobs.

From a Congressional Effect point of view, what emerges is that the business plans of all our major industries have become and are still playthings in the sandbox of Congress. How did this happen? Let's consider an industry that is 80 percent government controlled, like the banking industry, as characterized by John Allison, former CEO of BB&T, the nation's 10th-largest bank. When 80 percent of an industry's business plan is controlled by the government, it is easy for Congress to play it like a violin. Why was there any need for congressional interference on either side of the interchange fee issue? Is Wal-Mart so inept and defenseless as a company that it cannot effectively negotiate with MasterCard? Or vice versa? Moreover, once you have the power to locate a road, or a railroad, or an Army base in your district, or any federal trifle, you as a congressman have the ability to make money, either directly or indirectly from the exercise of that power.

SUMMARY

The fact remains that 535 congressmen (or issues entrepreneurs, as some consider themselves) can routinely outperform Fidelity, Vanguard, Merrill Lynch, Goldman Sachs, Morgan Stanley, and most other financial professionals. The precise formulas under which they monetize their knowledge advantages and their influence—whether it be through extracting campaign donations, favors for friends, insider trading, or using them to drive issues that increase their popularity—will always be subject to change and avoiding bad appearances. One thing has been true for over 100 years, and it is going to be true for the foreseeable future: with 535 issues entrepreneurs fighting for the limelight, there will be a constant eruption of news and proposals that relentlessly try to alter the existing business plans of each sector of American industry. The trick is to understand that congressional dysfunction is the norm and that it is likely to be permanent and that very little can be done about it except to minimize its negative impact on your life and your investments, and to occasionally see if you can genuinely profit from congressional pathologies.

NOTES

1. Timothy P. Carney, *The Washington Examiner*, August 3, 2011, http://washingtonexaminer.com/politics/2011/08/birth-control-plan-conscience-vs-special-interests/116930

2. http://health.usnews.com/health-news/news/articles/2012/03/22/analysts-debate-importance-of-the-individual-mandate-to-health-reform-law

3. Alan J. Ziobrowski, Ping Cheng, James W. Boyd, and Brigitte J. Ziobrowski, "Abnormal Returns from the Common Stock Investments of the U.S. Senate," *Journal of Financial and Quantitative Analysis* 39(4), December 2004.

4. Brad M. Barber and Terrence Odean, "Trading Is Hazardous to Your Wealth: The Common Stock Investment Performance of Individual Investors," *Journal of Finance* 55(2), April 2000.

5. Leslie A. Jeng, Richard J. Zeckhauser, and Andrew Metrick, "Estimating the Returns to Insider Trading: A Performance-Evaluation Perspective," *Review of Economics and Statistics*, May 2003, 453–471.

6. Ziobrowski et al.

7. Peter Schweizer, *Throw Them All Out: How Politicians and Their Friends Get Rich Off Insider Stock Tips, Land Deals, and Cronyism that Would Send the Rest of Us to Prison* (New York: Houghton Mifflin Harcourt, 2011).

8. Ibid., p. 54.

9. Ibid., pp. 38–50.

10. Aliyah Shahid, "House Minority Leader Nancy Pelosi's Wealth Grows 62% to $35.2M, Boehner, Reid's Worth Increases Too," *New York Daily News*, June 16, 2011, http://articles.nydailynews.com/2011-06-16/news/29687626_1_stock-gains-house-speaker-charles-rangel

11. Schweizer, pp. 42–46.

12. Ibid.

CHAPTER 4

Behavioral Finance, the Stock Market, and Congressional Dysfunction

W hen I first took geometry I had a terrific teacher named Mr. Kerbin, who wanted us to really imagine a universe of parallel straight lines and flat planes. To help us visualize that clear, unconflicted universe of the rational Greek mathematicians, we had a classroom in which we constructed parallel lines using tau strings that looked like they were the exact same distance apart across the whole room. For planes we had cardboard panels intersecting globes and slicing out circles. And, of course, there were triangles with right angles. It was inspirational teaching, and it fostered a love of math. Academic finance has for many years inhabited the same universe of parallel lines that never touch or bend apart. But as we learned from Einstein, in the real universe, straight lines of light eventually can become curved by gravity, and things are not always rational. A close measurement of those parallel strings would have shown them different distances apart at different points in the classroom.

Over the past 30 or so years, there has been a growing branch of finance theory generally known as *behavioral finance*. Traditional finance is expressed in a series of rational, Newtonian equations. I use the term *Newtonian* as shorthand for "unbiased," without being impacted by the act of measurement itself, and for constant equations. As Meir Statman pointed out, the vast bulk of traditional finance theory is the interplay among the four pillars of investing theory: the capital asset pricing model, modern portfolio theory (MPT), the Black-Scholes option pricing model, and (I believe to a lesser extent) Modigliani and Miller's work on corporate capital structures.

In Chapter 2 we saw how MPT and the capital asset pricing model posit that stocks in a portfolio generally have a level of reward commensurate with the risk incurred. The Black-Scholes model uses volatility and probability discounting to discover the right price for an option with a given level of volatility for an underlying stock and a given level of interest rates. Finally, in Modigliani and Miller's work on corporate capital structures, enterprise values of companies with differing levels of debt were said to have comparable overall valuations regardless of the debt-to-equity ratios. (I believe the extreme markets of 2008 went a long way toward proving that capital structures really do make a difference in the valuation of different companies.)

All of these theories are rational in the sense that they solve for investment prices that assume a constant level playing field. For example, in discounting, interest rates used to make an analysis are constant over the period studied, and a dollar of loss and a dollar of gain have equal weight—both are worth a dollar. But what if you could empirically prove that a dollar of loss is not equal to a dollar of gain as measured by a human? Behavioral finance is different from MPT and other traditional finance theories in that it tries to scientifically understand the biases that we bring to investing and account for that in what kind of results we get. It turns out that when thinking about how we are as investors, it's important to not only think of us as human beings but as, perhaps, higher primates. One branch of behavioral finance looks at our different decision-making systems, which range from our cerebral cortex to our amygdala. When we are in our higher-primate mode, we don't always do the rational thing. In our minds, and therefore in real life, a dollar of loss is completely different in its distance from zero than a dollar of gain.

OVERVIEW OF BEHAVIORAL FINANCE CONCEPTS

Concepts of behavioral finance are important in understanding how the stock market actually works, how investors actually view their returns, and how to calibrate our reasoning so our biases do not undermine our investing success. I think it also particularly useful for understanding how Congress organizes its activities. This chapter has a brief overview of behavioral finance concepts, followed by how Congress uses these concepts to consolidate its power. We calculate rationally with our rational brain, but we also calculate with an emotional brain. While theories like MPT assume that we are always rational, we clearly are not. Behavioral finance makes explicit the flaws in our reasoning, which typically divide into two kinds of flaws—faulty logic or calculation and the emotional override of logic. Like traditional finance academics, as a nation, or certainly in the dominant media, we embrace a myth of a rational Congress stately sorting out the rational answers for guiding our country. The Senate, for example, likes to think of itself as the world's greatest deliberative body. In reality, neither investors, voters, nor Congress are rational in their approach to our problems. This chapter explores how Congress exploits voter irrationality to stay in power.

SURVEY OF BEHAVIORAL FINANCE CONCEPTS

Behavioral finance tries to describe how we process information and how we uncover data that we use to make decisions. We tend to start with the information that is most readily available, such as recent stock prices or headline news. If we get too much information, we often shut down or slow down our decision-making process. To manage the burden of getting too much information, we prejudge data that comes to us in order to process it more quickly. This was an enormous advantage in our hunter-gatherer days when we were hanging out by the watering hole and trying to decide *quickly* if some new piece of data (for example, another creature) required a fight-or-flight response. Because we are humans or, better still, higher primates, we have emotions, and emotions allow us to process some information very quickly but also with bias. Also, as primates, albeit higher primates, our logic isn't always all that it's cracked up to be. But we have in many ways progressed from those days, and the most successful investors have the luxury of "cognitive reflection" or taking their time and fully gathering relevant information to analyze an investing opportunity.

Satisficing

Sometimes that prejudgment includes taking information that is more recent and giving it greater weight. One term of art coined by Herbert Simon that appears in the literature about behavioral finance is the concept of *satisficing*, a combination of satisfying and sufficing, or, as I would put it in this context, "close enough for government work."[1] This is the way we characterize decisions that may not be optimal but appear adequate because we are not presented with all of the rational solutions. For example, in your 401(k) you may have a limited choice of investment options and have to choose one even though it may not be optimal out of all possible solutions but it is the one that is available and fits the regulatory framework.

Hyperbolic Discounting

Another key concept of behavioral finance is the concept of *hyperbolic discounting*.[2] If we were able to be just human calculators always assessing

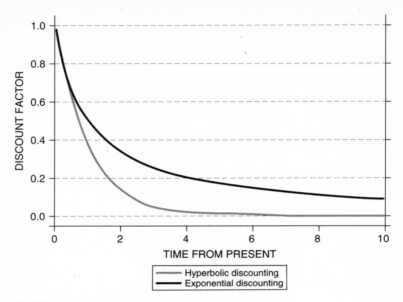

FIGURE 4.1   Hyperbolic Discounting

accurately and with a constant level playing field, the possibility of future profit, particularly over a long period of time from a particular investment, we would think of ourselves as rational, but in fact we have a bias toward short-term gain, as compared to long-term gain, and an even greater bias against short-term loss. Behavioral finance scientists have done experiments where they have scientifically determined our prejudices by empirically measuring them. The simplest example of this is our tests where subjects are asked whether they would accept $1 tomorrow or $2 in two days, and they typically answer that they would like $1 tomorrow. When asked to discount the same amounts over a long period of time, for example, would you like $1 in five years or $2 in six years, they answer they would definitely like $2 in six years. So they're applying different discount rates to different time periods. Short-term rates are sky high, and long-term rates are significantly lower. Hyperbolic discounting has more variance in the discount rate, and even exponential discounting changes the rate over time, but at a slower rate (see Figure 4.1). The key is that hyperbolic discounting is almost discontinuous depending on whether the time period is short or long.

Endowment Effect

In hyperbolic discounting, short-term returns are given much greater weight. Similarly, the pain of loss has been shown by behavioral finance theorists to be greater in the mind of investors than the hope of gain. Another key concept of behavioral finance is the *endowment effect*. The endowment effect stands for the idea that for anything that we own, we've already invested time and resources and identity in proving to ourselves that the idea is worthwhile, and that's why we discount any information that now contradicts what our earlier research confirmed. For example, using coffee mugs, one investigator of the endowment effect found that investors would be willing on average to buy sample mugs for $1, but, when asked to sell them, would not sell them for less than $2. The experiment's subjects experienced $2 worth of pain when the coffee mugs were taken away. The endowment effect particularly applies to any thesis we have staked our reputation on by telling our friends or clients or the public about our views or our performance.

The endowment effect is an outgrowth of our proprietary instincts toward something we own already. In a rational world, the right price for a stock is one at which I should be indifferent to buying and selling it at the same time. That is its fair price. With the endowment effect, once I own a stock I want more than $6, maybe $8 or $9. If I don't own it, it can't possibly be worth $6 per share; otherwise, I would have owned it already. The most I would pay is $3 or $4. This sort of internal narrative of pride illustrates our emotional bias toward discovering the right price for any asset we are already endowed with.

The endowment effect and hyperbolic discounting together largely explain why many people often procrastinate. Why should I feel the pain today when my measurement of how painful the loss will be in the future is much less because I'm discounting it in a hyperbolic way?

Anchoring

Anchoring occurs whenever we become locked in on certain data and use that as shorthand for making decisions about a stock. The easiest version to understand is "I am not selling Citibank until it hits $50 per share" or whatever round number suits your fancy. A variation of that is the concept that I paid $6 per share for this stock, it has to be at least $6 for me to sell it. The truth is the stock may or may not be worth $6 per share anymore, but whether you should buy it or hold it at this price has nothing to do with the price at which you bought it. It has to do with whether it's worth $6 today. Anchoring occurs any time nonlogical reasons are used to set typically numerical goals with respect to an investment. Anchoring can take the form of the price last paid, or the average price, or the first price paid for a stock. It can also simply be a round number, or an investors' lucky number, or a number that was chatted about the night before. We are constantly linking data points in our environment, when often there is no compelling reason to do so. We are suggestible, and we like to fill in voids in explanation. Some experiments in anchoring have found that if a number is mentioned in casual conversation, and serious financial goals are mentioned in the next conversation, people will have the casual numbers on their mind and use them to set value.

The most sensational example of anchoring I can think of is the one depicted in Amity Shlaes' book, *The Forgotten Man*. In the 1930s, the Secretary of the Treasury, Henry Morgenthau, is talking about nation's finances one morning with President Roosevelt still in his bed:

> *Then, still from his bed, FDR would set the target price of gold for the United States—or even for the world. . . . It did not matter what the Federal Reserve said. Over the course of the autumn, at the breakfast meetings, Roosevelt and his new advisers experimented alone. One day he would move the price up several cents; another, a few more.*
>
> *One morning, FDR told his group he was thinking of raising the price of gold by twenty-one cents. Why that figure? his entourage asked. "It's a lucky number," Roosevelt said, "Because it's three times seven." As Morgenthau later wrote, "If anybody knew how we really set the gold price through a combination of lucky numbers, etc., I think they would be frightened."[3]*

Morgenthau was frightened by that conversation because it was an extreme example of a price being set by anchored expectations that had little do with fundamental value. In this case, what was frightening was that casual anchoring was being used to set the core value of the gold exchange standard used to run our financial economy.

Separate Mental Accounts

Another form of shortcutting is setting up separate mental accounts. We all tend to have mental accounts in our head when we say to ourselves, "Oh, I'm using this account to save for college and this account to save for my retirement, and this account to pay for my beer and poker." In reality, we have only one account or, better, one overall portfolio. Optimizing for one account is not necessarily optimizing for your overall portfolio.

Herd Behavior and Groupthink

Herd behavior or groupthink is another phenomenon categorized by behavioral finance. Perhaps the best way to describe it is we don't mind being wrong, but we really don't like looking stupid. When we find something that everybody else is doing, there is a perception that, "Hey, everybody's doing it, so we should just go with the crowd." There is some safety in numbers or the crowd, especially in the very short term. The problem with groupthink is that the group as a whole may be wrong and sooner or later will definitely be wrong. In effect, everyone in the group is thinking "everyone is doing it" as a substitute for a considered opinion and due diligence. Everybody was buying houses in 2007, but it was a bad time to buy houses. Everybody was in the market in 2007, but it was a bad time to be in the market.

Sunk Costs

Sunk costs are another version of "I paid $6 for this stock. I'll be damned if I'm going to sell it below six, even though it is two right now." If you could sell it for twice what it is worth today, you should. Behavioral finance warns us that the fact you paid $6 is mostly irrelevant. At the margin, behavioral finance teaches us to ignore not only the price we paid for the stock but whatever sunk costs we have paid in terms of time, dollars, or reputational damage.

Confirmation Biases

One of the other ways we irrationally form narratives that affect our investing is that we develop "confirmation biases." We give greater weight to data that supports our view and too little to contradictory data. Once you invest time, effort, and emotions in a narrative, it is very difficult to change your mind. This is why investors fall in love with stocks, and why advisers constantly tell their clients that they're not married to stocks, that they can change their mind if they want to. Most of all, this is why investors come to believe in certain stories and are very unwilling to change their mind, sometimes even when there's a lot of data telling them that they should be changing their mind.

Overconfidence

Another concern of behavioral finance is what happens to our investments when we become overconfident. There is not one seasoned human investor on this planet that has not been at one time or another overconfident of their judgment based on objective measures of their successes and failures. A different way of describing this phenomenon is that when we've had success we get overconfident about our ability to predict the future and to recreate that success. Certainly, most investors in 2008 understood that they had been too confident. Nothing is more dangerous to an investor than to be too confident. It is important to approach the stock market with the sense that you're going to be wrong many, many times, during the course of investing in it, and to accept that error is inevitable.

One of the other concepts of behavioral finance is that investors form an illusion having built a story around a particular stock or a particular investment that because they have the "illusion of knowledge" that they really know more than they do about a particular investment. The shorthand way of saying this is that even though with Excel I can make projections for a company that detail to the tenth of a penny what it should make next year, in fact just because the model appears to have greater accuracy and more data doesn't mean that my decision is actually going to be a more accurate model than the next guy's. The question is do you have the important information and have you weighed it correctly.

Cognitive Reflection

To have rationally and thoroughly weighed the right data requires a great deal of what behavioral finance specialists call cognitive reflection. Cognitive reflection is the ability to not make any hasty decisions about what you're doing, and it requires the opposite of a flight-or-fight response.

Choice Bracketing

Another aspect of behavioral finance is making it clear to investors that they should not engage in choice bracketing. This involves making choices independent of the portfolio when in fact it is the job of investors to put together an overall portfolio that will do its job as well as possible. There may be components of the portfolio that are underperforming at any given moment in time. In fact, by definition, there will be, but the point of a good investment program is to construct a portfolio that over time provides broad diversification and assembles enough assets to uncorrelated returns so that the portfolio as a whole performs well and not necessarily at any one particular asset class.

Taking all of these concepts and summarizing them and trying to boil down behavioral finance to several concepts, I would make the following observations: Investors have to do their best to avoid hyperbolic discounting. Short-term results and short-term focus is almost always worse than long-term focus. It is a constant battle to understand what your true biases and idiosyncrasies are and then calibrate for your own weaknesses, but it must be done, and it can only be done by regularly reviewing your performance against the market and against your goals. One of the keys to successful investing as demonstrated by behavioral finance is taking advantage of short-term irrational valuations that allow investors with long-term horizons to succeed.

CONGRESS'S APPROACH TO BEHAVIORAL FINANCE

What does behavioral finance tell us about the behavior of Congress? To answer that, it is probably best to start by looking at the time horizon of Somali pirates. Every now and then we will see a headline that tells us that Somali pirates have just taken over another freighter or another ship or another oil tanker. But if you step back and think about it, the Somali pirates are in a regular business just like a hamburger stand or a department store. In fact, in Eyl, the pirate capital of Somalia, Toyota Land Cruisers are quite common. Life goes on after a raid. So what is the time horizon for the typical Somali pirate on a project that they might do? It turns out that the average pirate time horizon for a new project is several months. If you're a Somali pirate planning on hijacking an oil tanker, the first thing you have to do is identify an oil tanker, then ride out to it on the high seas, which may take anywhere from three to six weeks. If you're lucky enough to get a freighter hijacked on the high seas, you then have to contact the German or Austrian or Swiss insurance company, as the case may be, and negotiate a ransom. It's happened often enough in recent years so that there's precedent for it—there's kind of a market. The Somalis know that if they have a ship that's worth, say, $150 million, they can pretty much always charge something like $3 to $5 million and get away with it, but if they try to make it $10 or $20 or $30 million they won't get away with it. So now that precedent's been built up, with a set of historical ransom prices, it's a repeatable successful formula for the Somali pirates. All it takes is one or two months to get to the ship, some time to capture it, and several months to negotiate a ransom. This represents a business planning horizon of several months.

The average time horizon for entrepreneurial congressmen to bring issues on, as we saw earlier, is for all practical purposes of the same order of magnitude as that of a Somali pirate. If you are a congressman running for reelection, from the day you are reelected you are focused on your next election, and in order to have power and influence and raise money for that next election, you have to assemble your legislative initiatives that will allow you to get the donations you need to be reelected. As an issues entrepreneur, if your legislation is going to be introduced in March, it may take you several months as a congressman to see if you can get other congressmen to support your cause. By the time the issue comes to a head in the public arena, it may be only six months ahead of an election. Your goal is to find a breakout issue that you can "nationalize" so that your brand in Congress has added distinction and can command more attention from the voters, the political action committees (PACs), and the lobbyists. So while the average congressman may have an extra few months over the average Somali pirate in terms of the time frame for realizing a project, that project being a new piece of legislation, for all practical purposes both have the same short-term horizon. One advantage the congressmen have is that they only have to threaten some legislative effort in order to collect a ransom; they don't necessarily have to succeed at it. The poor Somali pirates actually have to seize the hostages, with all the downside risk that entails. Moreover, congressmen can perennially threaten the same industries over and over again, each time extracting new rents.

There are three important distinctions to be made between congress-men and Somali pirates in addition to the fact that they operate on different continents. The Somali pirates run a cash-on-cash business: if one of their projects fails, they can lose money, or even their lives. Congressmen, however, are first and foremost issues entrepreneurs. If one of their ideas succeeds and they impose a new layer of regulation on the American people, it can be years, or decades, before the full impact of the legislation can even be conceived. In many cases, the unintended consequences of their legislation far outweigh the impact of the intended results. Also, since they are not spending their own money, their programs always cost more than promised, and occasionally cost 10 times or 100 times more than advertised. The only penalty to a retired congressman of having his pet projects cost more than promised or achieve the opposite of the pol-icy results he wanted is the indignity his place in posterity suffers. To give this penalty its proper weight, can you imagine any self-respecting Somali pirate with his booty in hand caring much about posterity? Neither can I.

Causes of Dysfunction

All the dysfunctionality and pathology of Congress flows from these three issues: (1) their true time frames for reelection and issue mongering are perennially short; (2) they are only spending vast sums of other people's money (the technical term for this is *OPM*); and (3) onerous laws often do not apply to or affect them. All of which brings us to the nature of Congress's instincts. While Congress nominally spends other people's money for legislative results, for the most part each congressman's real business objective is to be reelected. It is as if a trustee evaluated a financial adviser solely on the basis of how nice the restaurants were at which the trustee was entertained.

There is a famous Seinfeld episode called "The Opposite" in which the perennial loser, George Costanza, owns up to the fact that "every decision" he has ever made has been wrong. Using a form of behavioral finance, he decides to calibrate for his instincts on every course of action, and resolves to do the exact opposite of what his instincts tell him to do. In that episode, the Anti–George Costanza meets a beautiful girlfriend by introducing himself forthrightly and immediately as unemployed and living with his parents. She falls for him, gets him an interview with George Steinbrenner, and in the interview he is brutally, outrageously honest with Steinbrenner. As a result of doing the opposite of his instincts, and directly addressing his flaws and being straight in his communication, he gets the beautiful girl, a job with the Yankees, and moves out of his parents' house.

Looking at "The Opposite" episode in reruns recently, it struck me that one only has to pause for a moment, looking on the brief behavioral finance survey, to realize that almost every action taken by Congress represents precisely the opposite of what behavioral finance tells us is the right way to think about things. Taking each one of the behavioral finance analytical tools mentioned earlier and looking at it, we can see that whenever there is an opportunity to uncover a bias to prevent bad investment, in the world of policy that faulty bias is used to drive the legislative process. For Costanza, doing the opposite leads to success, but in real life, our Congress is doing us no favors by doing the opposite of what behavioral finance calls for.

Let's review of some our major legislative issues over the past 10 years or so and how their outcomes would be characterized by basic behavioral finance. It has been several years since the Senate has passed a budget as required by the Congressional Budget and Impoundment Control Act of 1974 and, therefore, by each senator's oath of office. The main reason for this is that the majority does not want to be on record as formally proposing any cuts for government spending, which would entail withdrawing benefits from constituents. In politics, there is a concept of "third rails"—these are usually entitlement programs where *any* suggestion of cutbacks is generally thought to be politically fatal. Social Security, Medicare, Medicaid, Food Stamps, and No Child Left Behind are examples that come immediately to mind. In the political calculation of Congress, using "endowment effect" analysis, taking away any amount of benefits is like confiscating voters' coffee mugs for $1 when the voters believe they are worth $2. Rather than experience the backlash of threatening the withdrawal of a benefit, the Senate figures that delaying the pain into future, past the next election cycle, is vastly preferable to experiencing it now. In this regard, the Senate is engaged in hyperbolic discounting: the short-term pain is to be avoided at all costs, while the long-term costs are tolerable because many of them may not even be in office when the required cuts have to be made, and the *then* members of the Senate have to experience the *then* wrath of the voters.

Anchoring

Anchoring clearly applies to the budgeting process. Because last year's allocations, plus a generalized growth factor, have been Washington's starting point for budgeting, the Senate has had more latitude to avoid making any serious decisions or even thinking. Continuing budget resolutions that roll last year's allocations forward without any meaningful change except for inflation are clearly relying on anchoring for an emotional pass from the voters. In fact, Washington has so enshrined anchoring as its approach for deeming a budget appropriate that if the consensus is that there ought to be 5 percent growth in the budget every year, a reduction in the planned increase to only 3 percent is said to be a cut, and by definition, all cuts are Draconian. Only in Washington do normal English words lose their meaning or take on the opposite meaning. In the rest of the country, an increase of 3 percent over last year is an increase. In Washington, if they had been notionally thinking about raising the budget at issue 5 percent, a 3 percent increase is a Draconian cut. There has been bipartisan agreement on this usage for many years.

Anchoring, the endowment effect, and hyperbolic discounting were at the heart of our recent budget and debt ceiling processes. All three biases as applied to Congress's political calculations result in a Congress that is incented to enormously procrastinate on every budget and financial issue.

In the actual event, in the run-up to August 2011, a politically split Congress had almost a year in which to reach a compromise about whether to raise the debt ceiling of the United States. Unable to reach a compromise, they fashioned a super-commitee consisting of six senators and six congressmen, whose job was to identify the tough budget cuts that really had to be made. Faced with a budget where 43 cents out of every dollar was borrowed, but not wanting to make *any* short-term cuts, Congress settled on a budget with less than one half of 1 percent of the cuts occurring in the first two years.[4] Standard & Poor's Corporation, watching the United States completely unable to realistically manage its budget and debt ceiling process, gave a historical downgrade to U.S. debt—our first ever, but apparently not our last.

If the super-committee didn't come up with cuts, the defense budget and a key entitlement budget would be subject to automatic "Draconian" cuts. No one in the super-committee wanted to be associated with specific cuts, and the Gang of 12 failed to reach agreement. From an anchoring point of view, last year's budget was the most readily available anchor, so there was no need to make any tough choices, especially if they required sacrifice.

If the budget last year was $3.7 trillion because of anchoring, the correct starting point for opening the budget debate is always last year's number—$3.7 trillion—plus a growth factor, which may be 5 percent. The growth factor used, by the way, is almost as arbitrary as President Roosevelt's assertion that three and seven are lucky numbers. In fact, since World War II, there was at least one occasion when anchoring was challenged. In 1977, President Jimmy Carter introduced "zero-based" budgeting to Congress, which reduced the size of several bureaucracies, and then went back to its old ways.

Status Quo Bias

We saw earlier that one of the biases that behavioral finance warns us against is "status quo" bias: why should I sell any of the stocks that Daddy left to me? In government, and particularly in our budget process, status quo bias is the ruling zeitgeist.

The tax code, with its million lines of code, has grown so cumbersome that no one person can understand it all. Whenever tax reform is proposed, the political class groans that it is too complicated to truly reform the tax code. It is also to the benefit of the permanent political class to not reform the tax except in incremental bits and pieces because each reform is a source of campaign favors that can be converted into money, which can then be converted into votes. In terms of "sunk costs," our investment, as a country, in the tax code represents an enormous sunk cost that resists assault because everyone's eyes glaze over at the thought of such massive change. In fact, in actual policy, we would all be much better off from eliminating the regulatory and tax drag on the economy. There would be minor increases in risk offset by massive reductions in prices, generating massive increases in standard of living.

Current Lack of Cognitive Reflection

The idea of the Senate is that it would provide the major source of cognitive reflection required to govern wisely. When Benjamin Franklin was asked in 1787 by a Mrs. Powell during the Constitutional Convention, "Well, Doctor, what have we got, a republic or a monarchy?" Without the slightest hesitation, Franklin answered, "A republic, if you can keep it." Once upon a time, the Senate referred to itself as the world's greatest deliberative body. It was designed to be that way by virtue of the six-year senatorial term, which must have seemed like a very long commitment in the late 1700s, and by the fact that each state chose its senators to negotiate with a then much weaker federal government. For our first 100 years, senators were not selected by popular vote, but rather by the governments of each state, and were more viewed as agents of the individual states, rather than the

United States. Now that they are elected by popular vote, we have less of a republic and more of a democracy and less cognitive reflection.

The following story about a meeting between Thomas Jefferson and George Washington has been repeated many times: There existed a variety of opinions as to a legislature of one or two houses. It is said that when Jefferson returned from France he was breakfasting with Washington, and asked him why he agreed to a senate.

"Why," said Washington, "did you just now pour that coffee into your saucer before drinking it?"

"To cool it," said Jefferson, "my throat is not made of brass."

"Even so," said Washington, "we pour our legislation into the senatorial saucer to cool it."

In the current state of paralysis, the Senate has abandoned that role. In the current state of affairs, as the Senate lapses into default budgets consisting of continuing resolutions and no meaningful new initiatives, the United States has become more and more of a mere democracy. This is not attributable to one election or one party, but rather represents the drift of the past 100 years, as the voting franchise has expanded, and the power of the federal government relative to the states and the people. But mere democracies have shorter-term outlooks than republics. One of the key biases identified by behavioral finance is "self-control" bias—the inability to take care of long-term goals because of surrendering to short-term goals. It is this single bias or weakness that is responsible for most Americans retiring with too little money to properly support themselves in old age. This is exactly what has happened at an accelerating rate in the past few years, as we have seen in the breakdown of budget discipline.

Confirmation Bias

One of the other hazards discussed earlier was confirmation bias, giving too much weight to confirming data and too little to contradictory data. The remedy for this is to try and freshly look at your portfolio and regularly ask, "Would I own this stock if I didn't own it already?" In Congress, there really is no such remedy routinely applied to legislation. For example, Head Start has been funded year after year even though there is no measurable data showing it provides sustained improvement in reading scores for its kids. In fact, because Congress measures the success of its legislative programs with whether they were reelected as opposed to whether they achieved their intended results, it is safe to say that by the standards of a company, Congress for the most part never evaluates whether its programs have performed as promised, or within budget projections, and very rarely cancels any program. It is as if they are married to every stock in their portfolio. As President Ronald Reagan put it, "Actually, a government bureau is the nearest thing to eternal life we'll ever see on this earth!"

Our Innumerate Congress

One of behavioral finance's identified pitfalls is that as investors we some-times simply miscalculate or apply faulty logic. These mistakes are not necessarily bias mistakes but, rather, more like mathematical errors. As the sums have become bigger and bigger, Congress is more and more incompetent with respect to basic calculation, or more accurately, innu-merate. This is true for small programs and for ones affecting the entire government. In the summer of 2009, to help "jump start" the economy, Congress passed a "Cash for Clunkers" law, thinking it would boost overall demand for cars by offering bounties for people surrendering less fuel-efficient cars. In reality, it brought demand forward by several months, so that people planning on buying a car in September decided instead to buy in July. But annual demand was not materially lifted, and the unintended consequence of the act was that used cars became more expensive. But the extent of government miscalculation in this act was a laboratory example of how ineffective government calculation can be. "Cash for Clunkers" allowed people to turn in their old cars and get a bounty on the purchase of a new car. The government thought that plan, which officially started on July 24, 2009, would last until November 1, 2009, with a budget of $1 billion. In the actual event, the government ran through its appropriation in less than one week, and the plan had to be suspended on July 30, 2009.[5]

Perhaps the biggest example of faulty logic in the past two decades of domestic policy has been Congress's approach to the housing market. At its core, the mostly bipartisan logic was "it's always good if we help more people buy more homes." As the unrelenting collapse in the housing market has shown, sometimes you can have too many people buying houses, and when this illiquid market became overheated, it nearly brought down the entire world economy. There is a difference between promoting government-sponsored mortgage credit, where the processing bank is relieved of all risk, but the borrower has taken on more than they can handle, on the one hand, and a sustainable market that will not suffer a major crash, on the other. There was no meaningful logical review or oversight of Fannie Mae or Freddie Mac in the 10 years leading up to the housing crash. Despite warnings and major fraud issues uncovered at Fannie Mae and Freddie Mac in 2004, Congress continued with its unstinting support and protection of these institutions. In fact, Congressman Barney Frank literally said, "I'd like to roll the dice" one more time as the justification for leaving the housing lending in its status quo state. Rolling the dice is likely to lead to faulty calculation. This insouciance about managing one of the most important asset classes in the United States, one that is the foundation of the solvency of the United States itself, continued through the passage of Dodd-Frank, which disrupted the business plan of every single major financial institution in the country but left Fannie and Freddie largely untouched.

A cognitive bias that is a favorite of mine is the concept of "the illusion of control" that occurs when investors believe they can more accurately forecast the future than they really can, or when they think they can affect the outcomes of investing, for example, by trading actively, more than they really can. You may think you know everything there is to know about one stock. Perhaps you have invested a lot of time as well, and even know some aspects of their business issues that very few other investors know. But the market *always* knows better than you. After all, it represents the collective, organic, networked information of millions of participants: even if you have a Phi Beta Kappa key from Harvard, you do not know as much as the market. Congress's experience with the housing market is a good example that even though government may have the "illusion of control," even the government, or perhaps especially the government, can never know as much as the market. For example, in 2009, the administration authoritatively predicted that without that year's $800 billion stimulus package being passed, the U-3 unemployment rate would go above 8 percent. But in the actual event, from the time the stimulus package was passed in early 2009, through May, 2012, the unemployment rate has never been below 8 percent. Similarly, Congress persistently miscalculates the future expense of its programs. As pointed out by Senator Rudy Boschwitz, when Medicare was being passed in 1965, Congress projected its cost at $10 billion per year in 1990. "Instead . . . 25 years later, the outlays were $107 billion. Government estimates were off by a factor of more than 10!"[6] When you miss your numbers by a factor of 10, your numbers start to lose their meaning, and you genuinely have no control.

Another bias to be on guard for in investing is "self-attribution bias"—the self-aggrandizing measurement that attributes all your port-folio successes to your brilliance, while the stocks that had problems had them because of some exogenous event outside your control. It is not very difficult to imagine every mainstream politician taking credit for the good things in the economy, and blaming the opposition, or foreign countries, or the weather, or sunspots for the bad things that happened.

When weighing decisions as investors, we often engage in "choice bracketing." Narrow choice bracketing is the limiting of the choice at hand to its immediate impact. In the seminal paper on this subject, Read, Lowenstein, and Rabin[7] framed the notion by the example that narrowly choosing to smoke one cigarette in isolation might not harm you very much, but the broad choice to smoke 7,300 over a year might. The goal of behavioral finance is to make you understand you are really choosing to smoke 7,300 cigarettes per year and consciously address the health implication of that choice. Each government program is reviewed in a narrow bracketing framework. That is why we have 1,339 different separate Agriculture Department programs. In fact, even when programs are duplicative, each one is left to stand in isolation. For example, Senator Coburn recently failed in an attempt to withdraw $10 billion in funding for duplicative programs.

"Mental accounting" is another bias we have to understand as investors. While it can be helpful, it can also be harmful. If we run up our debt in our 16 percent credit card account because we are buying groceries, but save for our vacation in a bank account yielding 0.1 percent, we are ignoring the opportunity to improve our overall performance. Obviously, the federal budget is a festival of "mental accounting" because the major entitlement programs have been authorized in perpetuity and as a result are massively slipping out of fiscal control. This is so much the case that we describe the vast majority of the budget now as nondiscretionary: between Medicaid, Medicare, and Social Security, over half the 2008 budget was mandated, and interest on the national debt and defense spending accounted for another 16 percent of that budget. As the Baby Boomers age, retire, and get sick, the 2011 budget has an even smaller percentage allocated to discretionary items.

The congressional budget process makes it exceedingly difficult to counteract false mental accounting and in fact institutionally requires it. For example, the Congressional Budget Office (CBO) scored health care reform as *reducing* the next 10-year budget deficit by $119 billion in a March 18, 2010, letter to Speaker Pelosi. In fact, most of the benefits and associated costs of the law start in 2014, while the revenues associated started in 2010, and the CBO followed a convention of only looking at the cash flows over an exact 10-year horizon from the year following the date of its CBO scoring. Two years have passed, and now the CBO scores that legislation as costing $1.76 trillion, almost double the $940 billion used when it was first announced.

Another bias that behavioral finance warns us against is emphasizing information with ready "availability" over more accurate, more difficult to get at information. In the world of stocks and bonds, you may readily know from looking at Yahoo! or TV that a stock has a price-to-earnings ratio (PE) of 12. That doesn't mean you know enough to make a high-quality decision about purchasing that stock as an investment decision. Similarly, CBO budgeting, which is cash-based accounting, is the information that has the highest "availability" to members of Congress, and is statutorily required for the decision-making process. However, it is extremely low-quality information judged by the standards of the private sector. The budget is not broken into an operating and a capital budget like those of major corporations, and there is no net present value representation of liabilities and assets. Some have estimated the unfunded liabilities of the United States to be in excess of $50 trillion. That is materially different than the $15 trillion of debt that was the focus of the rating agencies, and all citizens deserve an accurate and fair disclosure of our obligations in order to make intelligent decisions about which policy to support. In fact, it seems likely that if the United States were a bank and presented its financials exactly as it does now to the public market in a prospectus, it would be guilty of gross misrepresentation under the Securities Exchange Act of 1934.

There is rarely meaningful analysis of whether last year's budget was spent wisely, whether funds achieved what they were supposed to achieve or promised to achieve—none of that. In behavioral finance terms, that would be deemed "status quo bias." In the policy arena, that means knowing how the budget process worked last year and just baselining it up. This is what passes for governance in the Senate now. Once we have gotten a government program to answer a particular wish that we want, not necessarily even need, the thought of giving up that program becomes much more onerous than the thought of leaving it in place. Again, in the world of behavioral economics, you have to ask yourself if you would recommit to a stock. In the world of Washington policy, you never have to ask, "Would I recommit to this government program?" It's always assumed that the government program is going to be back. That's true of the $1.5 trillion spent on Social Security, Medicare, and Medicaid, and it's true of the $50,000-a-year Cowboy Poetry Festival in Nevada, and every program in between.

Groupthink

Groupthink and herd behavior are obvious pitfalls for professional politicians gathered into political parties. But what behavioral finance tries to help us avoid is doing things because everybody else is doing them. The popularity of an idea in the world of behavioral finance is something that makes a particular idea suspect. In policy, however, there's nothing that a politician likes better than to be early on the side of an issue that appears to have manifest, widespread, and deep public support, but just because something is widely popular doesn't mean it's good for the country, particularly if it's popular with politicians. Sarbanes-Oxley was a law that had widespread public support and was passed 99 to 0 in the Senate and 432 to 3 in the House of Representatives. It had massive public support, but it was a law that had a horrible impact on the banks. Sarbanes-Oxley led directly to a dramatic decrease in the number ofinitial public offerings in America. So while it's the nature of the beast that politicians do things precisely because they have popular support, that doesn't mean that the popular policy solution is a good one.

Investment Fees and Conflicts

I could not end a chapter on Congress and behavioral finance without mentioning something that has bothered me for a long time. Under Congress's direction, the Securities and Exchange Commission (SEC) has made scrutiny of financial adviser conflicts and fees and brokerage conflicts and fees some of its primary targets for regulation and disclosure. I have no issue with disclosure: it makes for a competitive, informed market. I often think that this emphasis on fees and the complete elimination of conflicts is excessive given the high value the securities industry adds when it helps the average Joe avoid the pitfalls of behavioral finance. For example, a few years ago, the SEC, a creature of Congress, instituted rules requiring all mutual funds to have at least 75 percent of their directors be independent. Fidelity Investments, in opposition to this rule, submitted a study showing that mutual funds with management-led boards outperformed mutual funds with independent boards.[8] Why not just have full disclosure of fees and conflicts and let the market decide? Yes, it's true that the majority of mutual funds do not match the Standard & Poor's (S&P) 500 over time net of fees, but they fully disclose that. Why can't informed investors buy funds with more governance conflicts and higher returns if they so choose? What is galling is that the rules come from Congress, which tolerates much greater conflicts of interest in its day-to-day conduct of its own business.

What the marketing and branding of the mutual fund and securities industry does is bind their clients to a plan of action that is likely to create much greater long-term success and overcome the short-term thinking associated with behavioral finance. Moreover, the average investor is frequently driven to sell at just the wrong point because of the scare tactics of Washington. For example, Morningstar has demonstrated that some funds have good returns but that individual investors often jump in and out of them and the overall market at the wrong time so their returns as fund shareholders are not as good as the those of the funds themselves. For those unfortunate investors, who cares if they saved a few basis points by buying a fund with cheaper overall fees? A lot of the value added that an adviser has is in simply getting his client to think hard about the future, defer gratification, and undo the psychological damage caused by Congress. It is a valuable service worth more than its fees in the harm it avoids. but one that is mostly belittled by Washington, which is itself mostly just a big cost center. The rules of the finance industry make increasing commoditization of financial advice more likely, which to my mind means fewer people will be persuaded to think about the long term. And that commoditization is being driven by Congress, which seems to do nothing but defer tough choices and hide the giant hidden costs of its programs with great alacrity. If Congress were run by financial advisers, who try to make their clients focus on the long term, I doubt we would have had our national debt downgraded in 2011.

SUMMARY

Concepts of behavioral finance are important in understanding that even though we aspire to be completely rational in our investment decision making, we actually make investment decisions that have a great deal of emotional bias that is reflected in how the stock market actually works and how investors actually view their returns. Behavioral finance teaches us to calibrate our reasoning so our biases do not undermine our investing success. For example, we tend to start with the information that is most readily available such as recent stock prices or headline news. When we get too much information, we shut down our decision-making process and prejudge data in a variety of ways. Behavioral finance is also particularly useful for understanding how Congress organizes its activities. Congress acts in an illogical and short-term-biased manner.

This brief overview of behavioral finance shows that in almost every major legislative decision, Congress explicitly or implicitly is driven by the self-interest of each congressman to do the *opposite* of what behavioral finance would suggest. It celebrates its biases by enacting laws that are premised on faulty logic and emotion, and has increasingly abandoned its foundational role of providing "cognitive reflection" in favor of procrastination, and favoring short-term fixes over long-term solutions. The Congressional Effect exists in no small part because every day millions of market participants and thousands of their fiduciaries watch Congress with sustained dread knowing that they will spend most of their energy promoting the wrong thing to do at exactly the wrong moment. As investors, we can only flinch, often on a daily basis, watching our congressmen play on our worst fears in order to make our most important policy decisions, which in turn are quickly reflected in stock market valuations.

NOTES

1. Herbert Simon, *Models of Man* (New York: John Wiley & Sons, 1957).
2. Joseph P. Redden, "Hyperbolic Discounting," *Encyclopedia of Social Psychology*, ed. Roy F. Baumeister and Kathleen D. Vohs (Thousand Oaks, CA: Sage, 2007).

3. Amity Shlaes, *The Forgotten Man* (New York: HarperCollins, 2007), 147–148.

4. http://wsws.org/articles/2011/aug2011/budg-a02.shtml

5. Matthew Dolan, Corey Boles, and Josh Mitchell, "'Cash for Clunkers' Runs Out of Gas," *Wall Street Journal*, July 31, 2009, http://online .wsj.com/article/SB124898886526095011.html

6. Rudy Boschwitz and Tim Penny, "History of Gov't-Run Health Care Is a Study in Skyrocketing Costs," *Investor's Business Daily*, July 31, 2009, www.theabsurdreport.com/2009/history-of-govt-run-health-care-is-a-study-in-skyrocketing-costs-by-rudy-boschwitz-and-tim-penny/

7. Daniel Read, George Loewenstein, and Mathew Rabin, "Choice Bracketing," *Journal of Risk and Uncertainty* 19(13), 1999, 171–197.

8. www.sec.gov/rules/proposed/s70304/fidelity031804.htm

CHAPTER 5

If Congress Is Malfunction Junction, What's Its Function?

I t is the central thesis of the Congressional Effect that Congress generally hurts stocks. The support for this is overwhelming on a daily basis and on a longer-term basis, with sectors affected. Without trying to put too fine a point on it, I view Congress's efforts as mostly ranging from dysfunctional to extremely dysfunctional because their primary goal is to extract rents. Parasites that kill off their hosts have the most regret, and I am sure that someday there will be a recorded instance of actual regret for what might have been.

This chapter looks at several key industries, outlining the impact of Congress on them and their stocks, and uses those histories to show how you can profit from Congress's relentless dysfunctionality.

ECONOMIC LIFEBLOOD: INVESTMENT CAPITAL FORMATION, THE STOCK MARKET, AND CONGRESS

In order to get a feel for the persistence of Congress's dysfunctionality, it is worth taking a longer and somewhat cumulative view of regulatory constraints imposed on various industries. I'll start with the securities industry, having grown up in it. This brief, noncomprehensive overview covers disclosure rules, trading rules, sell-side research, Sarbanes-Oxley, and Dodd-Frank. Although it is a little bit like saying I am concerned that motherhood and apple pie are not always good, I will start with a regulation that on its face was uncontroversial: Reg FD. This disclosure regulation, supported by Congress and mandated by the Securities and Exchange Commission (SEC), required all companies to speak to analysts at the same time and to disclose material information to the entire market all at the same time. While its goal was laudable, it still results in less information reaching the market and less committed holders. It also played a role in reducing the number of research analysts, which I think has permanently hurt the U.S. capital markets. It was symptomatic of an attitude toward the entire capital formation industry that has taken us on a strange course. It also exacerbated a two-tier market: large companies did have research and got more of the long-term commitment that comes from thinking you understand a company, while smaller companies lost research support and sponsorship.

The next shoe to fall was decimalization. In 2000, in response to relentless pressure from Congress (which in turn was likely responding to prodding by the larger securities firms), the SEC mandated decimalization of stock prices, making it unprofitable to make markets or provide research coverage for small companies. It was ostensibly consumer friendly—but just for large company stocks and large brokerage firms. Commenting on that change, Ted Weisberg, CEO of Seaport Securities LLC, said in the *Financial Times* in 2010 that high-frequency trading (HFT) was not the source of the market's problems, but rather just a symptom of something that had gone wrong much earlier. He thought that the elimination of the uptick rule and the move to required decimalization drove market makers out of the market, and made the markets much more vulnerable to the accidents that can happen when computer-driven algorithms dominate the daily price and volume action. Speaking about the flash crash of May 6, 2010, where the market lost for a moment $1 trillion, he said:

> ... *[I]t is not HFT that is the problem, but rather Congress and the SEC... the losers sadly are the integrity of what historically were the most transparent and liquid securities markets in the world and the general investing public and corporate America. The winners are the computer geeks. ... What is good for them is clearly not good for the markets and the public confidence in our markets.*
>
> *It is almost impossible for the government to admit when it has made a mistake and is therefore also wrong.*[1]

Ted proposes a solution of reinstating the plus tick rule and allowing human dealers to earn a profit from wider spreads for smaller stocks. He finds that the markets lose too much transparency when you have dark pools. In seeking to optimize just for the narrowness of the bid-ask spread, the SEC has made the markets more vulnerable to volatility. By trying to protect us in one area, they have made life more dangerous in another. The impact of decimalization on brokerage firms, specifically ones that had market making as their main activity, was harsh. Their margins shrank and continued to shrink. The benefit for institutional investors was nominal: their bid-ask spreads narrowed considerably, but so did liquidity and market depth. Large blocks were traded in dark pools by the large shops, and the market had less transparency. The result was that the smaller dealers started to go out of business, and the market for initial public offerings (IPOs) shrank. Today, we have a lot of high-frequency trading but shallower commitment to individual stocks and higher overall volatility, which I think is a bad trade-off. Jim McTague covers this subject in depth in his book *Crapshoot Investing*. Since the flash crash in 2010, the public has steadily withdrawn funds from the mutual fund industry as a whole while the market has been rising, a sure sign that volatility is taking its toll on their patience.

On September 11, 2001, the World Trade Center was bombed. The stock market had been lagging, off of its euphoric highs in 1999. In October 2001, the Enron accounting scandal broke, revealing that a company that had been worth more than $60 billion had rigged its books and was now broke. There was a lot of bipartisan popular will to *do something*, and in Congress, some of this will was channeled, as far as the economy was concerned, into new securities regulation. In February 2002, the Senate held its first hearings on changes in the financial accountability laws. Years later, when asked to comment on the rationale for the law, Senator Paul Sarbanes commented:

> *The Senate Banking Committee . . . undertook . . . hearings on the problems in the markets that had led to a loss of . . . trillions of dollars in market value. The hearings produced remarkable consensus on the nature of the problems: inadequate oversight of accountants, lack of auditor independence, weak corporate governance procedures, stock analysts' conflict of interests, inadequate disclosure provisions, and grossly inadequate funding of the SEC.*[2]

But it was starting to look like Congress might be upstaged by New York. Merrill Lynch had settled a case with a retail client for $400,000 for insufficient disclosure regarding conflict of interest on the part of Henry Blodget, its star Internet research analyst. In May 2002, then New York State Attorney General Spitzer made startling use of the 1921 Martin Act of New York to threaten brokerage firms that had banked and provided stock research on the same companies. This law is the jurisprudential equivalent of the Creature from the Black Lagoon. It judges offerings using an amorphous standard of substantive fairness, not whether there had been adequate disclosure and intent to defraud, and, astonishingly, it limits the right to counsel. Attorney General Spitzer charged Merrill Lynch and its former research analyst Henry Blodget with illegally rewarding and punishing companies with favorable or unfavorable research depending on whether they were cooperative Merrill Lynch corporate finance clients.

By the summer of 2002, *Forbes* magazine published a "Corporate Scandal Sheet" listing the following firms as participating in financial irregularities, together with the regulators investigating them: Adelphia Communications (ADELA); AOL Time Warner (AOL); Arthur Andersen; Bristol-Myers Squib (BMY); CMS Energy (CMS); Duke Energy (DUK); Dynegy (DYN); El Paso (EP); Enron (ENRNQ); Global Crossing (GBLXQ); Halliburton (HAL); Homestore (HOMS); Kmart (KM); Merck (MRK); Mirant (MIR); Nicor Energy LLC, a joint venture between NICOR (GAS) and DYN; Peregrine Systems (PRGNE); Qwest Communications (Q); Reliant Energy (REI); Tyco (TYC); WorldCom (WCEQC); and Xerox (XRX). Faced with the publicity of a seemingly endless array of bad financial reporting, and in danger of falling behind in the race with New York Attorney General Spitzer for headlines, Congress felt compelled to act quickly, and Sarbanes-Oxley received very little public debate or scrutiny as it was fast-tracked for passage.

Notwithstanding that all 22 companies cited above were *already* under investigation by either federal or state law enforcement agencies, Congress passed the Sarbanes-Oxley Act of 2002 (SarbOx) to give the government even more firepower. This legislation was primarily a reaction to the bankruptcies of WorldCom, Global Crossing, and Enron, and the apparent failure of their auditor, Arthur Andersen, to be more proactive in stopping accounting fraud.

This law was so popular in Congress that it passed 99 to 0 with one abstaining in the Democrat-controlled Senate, and 423 to 3 with 8 abstaining in the Republican-controlled House of Representatives. It was signed within a week by President Bush. The law codified extra accounting reviews, known as Section 404 reviews, and lent weight to identifying and nominally eliminating apparent conflicts of interest at the board of directors level as well as in the accounting profession and the securities industry. It created the Public Companies Accounting Oversight Board (PCAOB), which would "establish auditing and related attestation, quality control, ethics, and independence standards and rules to be used by registered public accounting firms in the preparation and issuance of audit reports."[3] The members of the PCAOB were appointed by the SEC without accountability to Congress. They were charged with auditing the auditors, who were now no longer subject to mere peer review, and limited in the services they could provide. Accounting firms had recently doubled and tripled their donations to Senator Sarbanes, and in the wake of SarbOx, the price of high-end public accounting doubled or tripled on an hourly basis within a year or two. The law included 16 regulations that dramatically increased the complexity of and manpower required to do public audits, including extensive documentation of internal controls. It also sharply curtailed permitted conflict-of-interest transactions between directors and officers on the one hand and their companies on the other. The crowning requirement of the law was that every CEO had to personally attest that the proper procedures had been followed to provide accurate financial reporting.

SarbOx was a damper for the entire market. In the immediate aftermath of SarbOx, stocks accelerated their fall. Figure 5.1 shows the market from the first hearing on it through year-end.

In conjunction with the law's passage, federal and state authorities dramatically increased their enforcement efforts. After SarbOx, New York Attorney General Spitzer and the SEC teamed up to enforce an effective ban on research related to investment-banking clients. The outcome was a $1.5 billion research settlement by the large securities firms where they all conveniently agreed with the government to simultaneously drop research coverage of one third of the companies they covered without any immediate short-term competitive disadvantage relative to their large peers. Roughly a third of the settlement was paid for by insurance, a third was paid for by the large companies directly, and another third was paid for by cost savings in firing research analysts who had been viewed by their large companies as necessary loss leaders who they were now free to jettison. Five hundred million dollars was earmarked for "independent" research firms, who now would pretty much receive payments whether or not their research was worthy in the arena of competition.

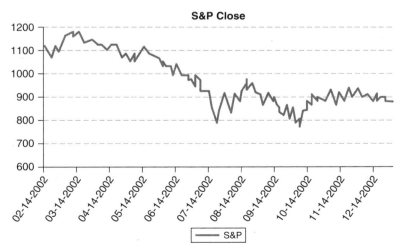

FIGURE 5.1 S&P 500 Index, February 14, 2002, through December 31, 2002. Source: Yahoo! Finance

The real effect was to prevent research analyst participation in banking revenues, even with disclosure of conflicts, so analysts stopped helping bankers figure out where best to spend their time, and the bankers focused only on the largest deals. Cutting investment bankers off from industry knowledge leads to very poor capital allocation. To be honest, investment bankers seldom know as much as they would like us to believe they do.

SarbOx did little to truly improve disclosure, but it did dramatically increase the compensation paid to accountants and lawyers. In the 1990s, I had worked at the institutional equity research firm, which acted as investment banker to many firms seeking to go public, and our research analysts would follow these companies. The analysts would participate in the investment banking fees from these small IPOs. Our clients knew that our research analysts received fees and were conflicted, but they valued the research because it gave them a feel for whether or not the companies were performing as planned. After the global research settlement, without the ability to benefit from investment banking, but with the threat of sanction from the SEC and the requirements of SarbOx, it was effectively impossible to find research analysts willing to cover small companies. The immediate impact of SarbOx in July 2002 was to reduce the prices for the banks stocks in general, which then led the S&P 500 Index down over the year following its passage (see Figure 5.2).

By 2004, small companies were budgeting $2 million for IPO expenses and an extra $1 million in annual oversight expenses, and often avoiding going public. I went from having 150 institutional clients willing to look at small-company IPOs to having perhaps seven. The traditional public market

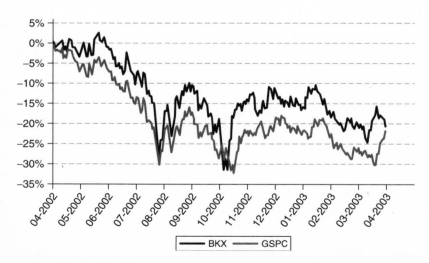

FIGURE 5.2   S&P 500 Index after SarbOx.   Source: Yahoo! Finance

for small-company IPOs effectively disappeared. Before decimalization, an institutional investor knew it could find enough liquidity to get out of a big position in a small company. After decimalization, it knew it could not. Before SarbOx, an institutional investor knew that there would be a nominal burden for a small company being public. After SarbOx, most institutional investors could not justify buying stocks where 10 percent or 20 percent or sometimes even *all* of their bottom line was consumed by regulatory overhead. Before the Global Research Settlement engineered by New York Attorney General Spitzer, many small public companies had or could hope to get independent sell-side research coverage. After that settlement, most of that research disappeared, and institutional investors cut back on their small-cap exposure because they didn't want to own stocks without available research. Taken together, these reforms crushed the IPO market. By 2005, 24 of the 25 largest IPOs were done overseas. In my opinion, as damaging as the loss of IPO business was in any year, the loss of the sell-side research infrastructure was equally damaging to the long-term interests of the U.S. economy.

Less understood is the impact of the systematic change to sell-side Wall Street research, whereby analysts cannot directly participate in deal revenues. We have removed the most well-informed observers from the capital-formation process. Now, research analysts are barred from identifying and courting and economically participating in IPOs. Our capital markets talent is going overseas. My college interns are visiting Singapore and noticing its nice weather. Why should capital markets talent return to the United States? What is to stop the kids from starting their careers in Singapore? The world of private equity is more elitist and less inclusive than the public markets, and allows less feedback from the markets as to whether a company is on track. Without realizing it, in the name of perfection regarding the forms of compliance, and the forms of price quotation, we have separated and atrophied portions of the feedback loops in our capital markets so that we are like those patients whose right brains cannot communicate with their left brains: we have the appearance of normalcy, but we do not have normalcy. Our left hand no longer knows what our right hand is doing. Our smartest, most thorough capital markets people—our research analysts—have been forbidden from participating in the capital-formation process at the most crucial stage: the IPO stage. It is bad policy. And it has enormous long-term stock market consequences.

In the United States, the perceived regulatory drag on valuation became so great that private equity investors found they could offer some companies higher valuations than they could achieve in the U.S. public markets. In addition, some U.S. companies found themselves raising money overseas because the capital environment was more hospitable. Historically, private equity had a lower valuation than public equity because the initial investment was discounted based on the belief that someday the company would go public and that first investors would be rewarded for their risk taking and patience. Investors want to invest at a discount to that event of liquidity. Put differently, there was a much larger pool of potential buyers of public equity than private equity, so as a traditional rule, public equity carried higher relative valuations. Things became so out of whack that by 2007, in many sectors, private equity was available at higher valuations than public equity. I referred to this at the time as an "inverted equity curve." The regulatory burden had become so great that the public markets were less desirable sources of capital than the private market. In July 2007, I published an op-ed in *Investor's Business Daily* that said:

> *In the bond market, an inverted yield curve is often a precursor of a recession. An inverted equity curve should be understood in the same light, with potentially greater severity, as its consequences are not fully understood either by regulators or Wall Street.*[4]

After the equity curve inverted, there was indeed a recession of unusual severity in 2008. In fact, it was the worst recession since the Great Depression, and official NBER scoring notwithstanding, it may not be over.

So up through 2008, what was the net result of Congress's efforts to improve oversight of capital formation in the United States? It was the near strangulation of capital for small business. The past three years' unemployment figures have been startling—worse than expected by almost every economist surveyed. Unemployment will likely stay surprisingly high because government is winning its long war of attrition against the primary driver of employment: small business. Small businesses are starved for capital and inundated with regulations. For small companies, there are four main sources of outside capital: public or IPO money, venture capital, bank loans, and family and friends. At the U.S. peak of the 1990s, we had several times as many IPOs as we have had in the past few years, and many of the recent ones have been mostly for larger companies, many of which were Chinese.[5] Today, small U.S. companies are effectively shut out. Billion-dollar U.S. valuations are required to go public, up from $50 or $100 million in the 1990's. Intel, it should be recalled, went public raising $6.8 million. Without a robust IPO market, the venture capital market suffers. Venture capitalists need IPOs to validate their judgments and gain their limited partners' confidence. Bank loans to small business were down an astounding 69 percent from 2007 through 2009 as banks struggled with bad mortgage paper primarily induced by government housing policies, higher capital requirements, and an avalanche of new regulations. And families and friends had their seed risk capital impaired by the epic housing collapse.

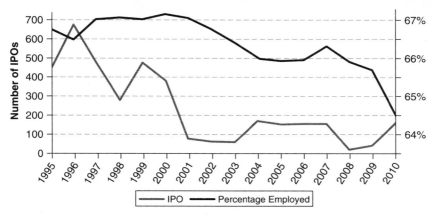

FIGURE 5.3 Percentage Employed vs. IPOs, 1995–2010. Source: Yahoo! Finance, Bureau of Labor Statistics

Figure 5.3 shows the percentage of the population employed as compared to the number of IPOs since 1995.

Figure 5.4 shows the U-3 unemployment rate against the number of IPOs since 2000.

This stewardship of the U.S. capital markets was largely bipartisan in its thrust during the period from 1995 through 2008, even though the Republicans were in control of the Senate through 2008 and the House through 2006 as well as the presidency from 2000 through 2008. I believe the causation stated above regarding the capital markets and job formation demonstrates that Congress is dysfunctional in its regulation

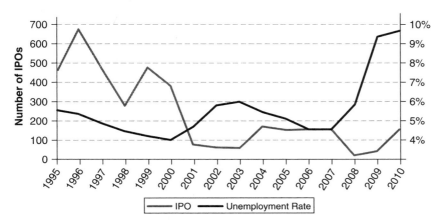

FIGURE 5.4 U-3 Unemployment vs. IPOs, 1995–2010. Source: Yahoo! Finance, Bureau of Labor Statistics

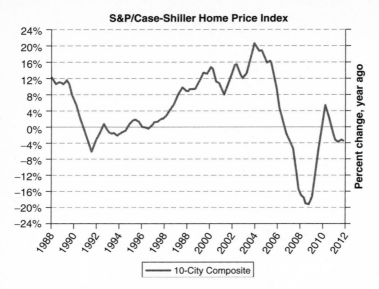

FIGURE 5.5   Case-Shiller Home Price Index. Source: Standard & Poor's

of the economy even in good times. In bad times, when it has crises to invoke, and is in more partisan hands, Congress is, if possible, even more dysfunctional.

Having strangled small business for capital, when the recession finally did hit, it was unusually severe, as predicted in the *Investor's Business Daily* op-ed. Housing plummeted, creating a panic in the housing market (see Figure 5.5), which spread to the banks, and then to the stock market.

DODD-FRANK OVERVIEW

While much of current political debate focuses on the potential impact of the new health care law (which will likely be still debated many years from now), I believe that Dodd-Frank represents a scale of government oversight and intervention that is in fact unprecedented and completely unmanageable. While it is possible to look at discrete sections of the law and imagine them somehow constitutional, I do not find it possible to comprehend how Dodd-Frank can contribute positively to grow the economy. The law is 2,319 pages, and I am sure that two years after its passage its full impact is still not understood by Wall Street, the managements of the banks, and most especially, by the regulators. One thing is certain: it has helped to depress bank stocks more than other sectors.

In law, if you have an agreement to agree, but do not actually agree, generally speaking you do not have a contract. SarbOx did the damage it did to the capital markets and our employment prospects with only 16 regulations. Dodd-Frank has 243 separate regulations. It is so vast in its rule-making authority that it is best thought of as the regulatory equivalent of an endless agreement to agree. Nothing is in stone yet, and the regulators can play gotcha with the banks all day long. In turn, the banks will have their profitable businesses mostly curtailed; they will suffer enormous new regulatory burdens and become much more like utilities over time. I am told in actual practice at the large banks, the compliance people are trying to draft operating procedures anticipating what the new rules *might* be. How can you lend without knowing the new rules? The highlights of Dodd-Frank, which are set out below, should be read with the understanding that each one is a hook for another several hundred pages of explanation, and potential liability:

1. Moving financial derivatives on to exchanges, highly regulating counter-parties, and perhaps even requiring industrial end users of commodities with natural supplies to still post collateral for hedging contracts. This will have the net effect of driving some of this business from New York to Chicago, and some overseas to places like Hong Kong, with a net loss to the United States. One consequence of this will be that a lot of assets will be frozen or liquidated or just idled to provide "safety" at a time when our biggest danger is that the velocity of money has slowed to a crawl, making business formation more difficult.

2. Implementation of the Volker Rule, sharply limiting banks' proprietary trading, and preventing banks from investing in hedge funds.

3. Requiring all hedge funds with over $100 million in assets to register with the SEC.

4. New wind-down procedures will be put in place that essentially codify the ad hoc seizure of banks like Washington Mutual that left sharehold-ers with nothing when under normal procedures they might have gotten something. This will apply to arguably solvent banks, too. Once-burned, twice-shy investors will not as easily invest in bank equity knowing that Fed seizure has become easier.

5. Raising capital requirements for banks in accordance with Basel 3 and disallowing most Trust Preferreds as capital.

6. A new "consumer watchdog" agency will limit the products consumers can buy, especially when they're in real trouble. (Suppose the only lender who will lend to you is a payday lender, but you need the money to keep your car insurance in force? Will the consumer really be better off with these loans having been regulated out of existence?)

7. The Fed has gotten to referee the fight between "defenseless" merchants like Wal-Mart and Target on one hand and Visa and MasterCard and their bank partners on the other hand on debit card interchange fees.

8. Given all the pressure on their profits from this and other provisions on their noncore products, banks may make it up by charging for bank accounts. So now the consumer will earn no interest on their checking accounts but get charged for keeping their cash with banks. Huh? It looks like savers will be penalized and spendthrifts rewarded. Many savers, angered by the fees, may simply pull their deposits out of banks and put their money under the mattress, sort of like the Great Depression.

9. Asset-backed securitization will be permitted, but the originator must retain 5 percent of the total risk of the asset. This actually follows a recommendation articulately stated by George Soros at the height of the crisis. It may provide better risk allocation in the housing market, but one unintended consequence is it will make the banks even less likely to lend because the 5 percent "holdback" will not be considered equity capital.

10. Additional proxy requirements regarding compensation. It is incomprehensible to me that a Senate that has not submitted a budget for over three years can hold executives' feet to the fire by requiring proxy approval of executive compensation.

11. Credit rating agencies would have two more years of monopoly power, finishing with an SEC study of their calls. Let the market make the calls and get the credit agencies out of public shelter for their oligopoly.

Sadly, this does not begin to be a comprehensive list. In theory, the bill is not all bad, just mostly bad, in a fragile economy that needs animal spirits more than anything else. In the short term, this law is terrible for banks because it requires so much time and effort to fill in the blanks on the regulations and because it restricts their businesses so much. It is difficult to overstate the paralysis this kind of a bill can generate. For example, in just the asset-backed area, after a year of frenzied effort, the SEC recently released a 667-page proposed rule amending disclosure requirements for asset-backed securities. The Congressional Effect applied to the bank stocks as they underperformed the S&P 500 Index from the day Dodd-Frank was passed in July 2010 (see Figure 5.6).

It had a similar impact on some individual stocks subject to new rules in Dodd-Frank. For example, Figure 5.7 shows a chart of MasterCard stock during December 2010 when the impact of the Durbin Amendment was crystallized for the market with the announcement that the Federal Reserve

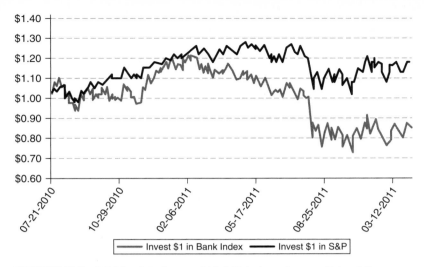

FIGURE 5.6   KBW Bank Index vs. S&P 500 Index. Source: Yahoo! Finance

had decided MasterCard and Visa and their partners could collect only 12 cents instead of 44 cents on every debit card interchange transaction fee.

This is a classic case of the Congressional Effect on a specific stock. What interest was it of Congress whether MasterCard or Wal-Mart has higher margins? In total, the estimated regulatory drag on the United States economy has been estimated at approximately two trillion dollars per year. Dodd-Frank probably makes that estimate low. And Dodd-Frank

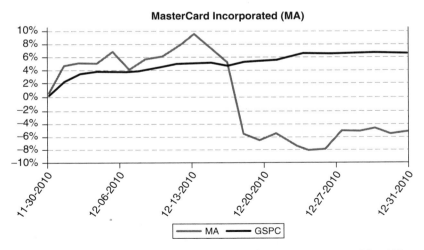

FIGURE 5.7   MasterCard vs. S&P 500, December 2010. Source: Yahoo! Finance

was not the end, just one more hit, although a massive one, in a parade of burdens placed on the banks. By the summer of 2011, the Fed had proposed another surcharge on the surplus of large banks. In response, at a public meeting the CEO of JP Morgan Chase asked the Fed chairman, Ben Bernanke: "Has anyone looked at the cumulative effect of all these regulations, and could they be the reason it's taking so long for credit and jobs to come back?" Chairman Bernanke was flustered in his response, and his body language made it clear that in fact, no regulator had thought about the cumulative effect of "all these" regulations. That is, no one except the market. From the day Dodd-Frank passed, on July 21, 2010, through December 31, 2011, the S&P 500 Index dramatically outperformed the KBW Bank Index (see Figure 5.11).

It should be added that even at the regulator level, there is a growing awareness that government intervention, particularly in the form of capital requirements, can be procyclical—that is, they can make the normal business or lending cycle have greater ups and downs. See, for example, the International Monetary Fund's paper on this subject. The Congressional Effect is an expression of the nearly relentless nature of Congress's procyclical impact.

From the middle of 2007 through January 2009, the market capitalization of the banking sector went from $2.95 trillion to $959 billion,[6] representing a loss of about $2 trillion. At the precise bottom, the KBX Bank Index was down almost 80 percent from its 2007 highs, representing a loss of about $2.4 trillion for the entire sector. Since then, the market value of the industry has recovered, although not as much as the broad market. Overall, the market capitalization losses for the industry from the peak are over $1 trillion, even with the recovery since the lows in 2009, while the broad S&P 500 Index has recovered most of its losses from that time. The government is clearly on a drive to make the banks much more like utilities, and the market is discounting their diminished business models in estimating their value.

All of this begs the question: how much wealth was destroyed by Congress and how much just by the natural forces of a slowing economy? It is a very difficult question to answer with any precision. We know from the MasterCard and Visa stocks that a one-week plummet based on new regulation was about 15 percent. Just working with a very rough estimate, as an educated guess, I would attribute roughly a quarter to half of the loss in market capitalization to the presence of new government regulations. This represents anywhere from $250 billion to $500 billion of lost market capitalization available to fund growth, or use for margin to buy other stocks, and so on.

There are many plausible counterarguments to this figure, and no doubt the most forceful ones start with, "If we didn't do the bank bailouts, the whole system would have blown up!" But my point is, the government relentlessly intervened in those markets to distort credit and capital allocation, whether it was with the securities market discussed earlier or in the mortgage markets, where the scope of damage caused by the government distortion was much greater. Picking the moment of greatest financial disaster caused in large part by the government and then asking if we needed the government to save us does not acknowledge government's dominant role in creating the crisis of wealth destruction in the first place.

I do not want you to come away from this book thinking I am a total pessimist. "Total" is such a strong word. Even I admit that there are times that Congress, as dysfunctional as it is, will try to make amends when it thinks it can help incumbents by doing so, particularly if no new cash outlay is required. So after witnessing a lost decade in which our IPOs collapsed in number, the overall stock market mostly lost money for investors, the economy went into a deep recession with the worst recovery ever (including the Great Depression), and the job market turned horrible without capital to help small businesses, Congress recently passed, and the President recently signed, the JOBS ("Jumpstart Our Business Startups") Act. This law seeks to undo some of the nonsense that SarbOx, Reg FD, and Dodd-Frank applied to small public companies. Whether it will be effective in an environment where the regulators have been overzealous for 15 years or more remains to be seen. In business, when a large company makes a mistake on its business plan, the managers know within a year or two that they will suffer. In the case of Congress, a decade can go by without the slightest acknowledgment of policy error, because each member is acting primarily in his "issues entrepreneur" mode.

The take-away for traders and investors trying to make money is that when a large industry is in Congress's gun sights, it will likely underperform the market for an extended period of time before Congress starts to realize the unintended consequences of its actions. Once these are known, the industry can stabilize relative to the rest of the market, and even occasionally get regulatory relief.

HEALTH CARE REFORM

Health care reform is particularly compelling to look at in the context of the Congressional Effect because it is such a regulated portion of our economy and because reform was tried and failed in 1993 and succeeded in 2010 with predictable capital market impacts each time.

At the end of 2007, if you had followed election politics, you would have seen that the Democrats were rising in the polls and, more specifically, that health care reform was an issue that both Senator Obama and Senator Clinton agreed on as a priority. Even if you estimated the Democrats' chance of winning the presidency and control of both chambers of Congress at only 50 percent, you could have reasonably viewed health care as a sector to underweight in your portfolio because it was more likely than others to wind up in Congress's crosshairs. Let's review briefly the health care industry, starting in modern times.

As we saw earlier, in late 1992, the new President-elect Clinton began pushing for comprehensive health care reform, and the health care companies plunged in value. The insurance companies, to create public pressure against the bill, planted seeds of doubt about the wisdom of the proposals with the "Harry & Louise" commercials. In these commercials, sponsored by the medium-sized health insurance companies, an everyday couple, played by some actors, wondered aloud what was going to happen to their health care protection with the new 1993 law. It went down to defeat. In the wake of the Republican victories in 1994 with the "Contract with America" and the sweep in both the House and the Senate, health care reform was left for dead.

But it lived as an idea. In May 2006, Governor Romney of Massachusetts signed a state bill requiring every citizen of Massachusetts to have health insurance, and portions of that law then went on to be the model for health care reform in 2008. Both Senators Clinton and Obama had competed for the Democratic nomination with a platform of health care reform, and as it became clear to the market that Senator Obama would become President Obama, and the overall stock market began to deteriorate, health care stocks, housing, and financials led the charge down the hill. Obviously, not all of the market's decline was attributable to the market's discounting of the impact of a Democratic sweep. But as to health care, the market knew there would be significant reform, but it did not know how big the reform would be. In fact, the HLV, the health care S&P Depositary Receipt (SPDR), hit its bottom within a few days of the overall market bottom in March 2009, although its biggest individual down days were in 2008, ahead of the election, as you can see from Table 5-1. These were extraordinary moves in such a compressed time for an entire nominally recession-proof industry.

Individual stocks, like UNH, hit bottom even before the election on October 10, 2008. On that day, the *CBS Evening News* show featured candidate Obama talking about the need for a national health exchange and a voice over suggesting this issue needed to be the highest priority of the incoming leaders, as compared, say, to the crashing financial system and the crashing housing market, and the dramatic plunge in employment, and the Troubled Asset Relief Program (TARP), and so on. One shibboleth of Wall Street is "buy the rumor, sell the fact." When the rumor is negative, and caused by what Congress might do, people easily imagine Congress

TABLE 5-1	S&P Health Care Index Top 10 Daily Losses in 2008
Date	**Daily Loss**
9-Oct-2008	−7.15%
15-Oct-2008	−6.70%
20-Nov-2008	−6.40%
1-Dec-2008	−6.15%
19-Nov-2008	−5.01%
22-Oct-2008	−4.76%
29-Sep-2008	−4.69%
6-Oct-2008	−4.64%
5-Nov-2008	−3.56%
14-Nov-2008	−3.45%

Source: Yahoo! Finance

might do anything. That is what comes with a 10 percent approval rating for Congress. As Will Rogers once said, "This country has come to feel the same when *Congress* is in session as when the *baby* gets hold of a hammer."

The world turned upside down. Large portions of the health care industry decided to play ball with the government. Harry and Louise went to work for the Man, saying it was time for health care reform in industry commercials praising the changes in the law.

In the actual event, the Democratic Senate waited on health care reform until Senator Franken was seated in July 2009 so that it had a filibuster-proof majority to consider the law. But that was put on hold with the illness and subsequent passing of Senator Kennedy. As a result, the effective time of a filibuster-proof majority could be said to have really begun from the time Senator Kirk replaced Senator Kennedy on an interim basis in late October 2009. The Patient Protection and Affordable Care Act completely revised 16 percent of the U.S. economy, and was moved along without any Republican support in the Senate. In November 2009, I said:

It is not a coincidence that the dollar's decline relative to other currencies and gold has accelerated over the last three months as the health care debate has culminated for the moment in the passage of the Affordable Health Care for America Act, H.R. 3962 by the House of Representatives. To get a true sense of the irresponsibility of Congress it is necessary to outline at least a portion of the breathtaking scope of what Congress is attempting. As listed before, the act is grossly inflationary because it mandates or results in (1) more coverage requirements per person; (2) more people covered; (3) fewer doctors per patient to provide care; (4) more adverse selection; (5) [lack of tort reform]; (6) sharply higher health care unionization; and (7) less private interstate competition.

By CBO estimates, the Act commits U.S. taxpayers to spending over one trillion dollars over the next ten years. Through the magic of a projection that would be fraudulent if done by a publicly traded company subject to Sarbanes-Oxley, the law was deemed to be a revenue enhancer because it collects taxes beginning in 2011, while only providing benefits beginning in stages in 2013, one year after the presidential elections. Deficits in the years beyond 2019 have been ignored. . . .

There is not the slightest chance that the assumptions underlying the bill will be reflected in reality once people have the chance to game the system [by skipping coverage until they are sick, and knowing they can't be denied when they finally decide to insure]. In the same way the government could not keep up with the acceleration of demand created by the cash-for-clunker law, healthcare insurers and providers will not be able to keep up with the distortion in demand created by not having use of the system tied to a cost . . . Congress acts as if we can borrow and borrow and never have to worry about repaying. We have issued $12 trillion in debt, and the new law would add another $1 trillion at a minimum. This is in an economy that only has $14 trillion of nominal GDP. As the total United States debt begins to climb over 100 percent of our GDP, other nations will increasingly move away from the dollar.[7]

It may sound partisan to say that Congress was irresponsible in passing the law, but it cannot be denied that Congress broke sharply with its normal procedures to rush the bill out at a breakneck pace once it appeared even possible that the Democrats might lose their filibuster-proof majority. Senator Reid broke precedent by not making the bill available three days before a vote and then by having the Senate work over the weekend several times in December 2009. In the end, the Patient Protection and Affordable Care Act was passed with exactly 60 votes, all Democrat, in the Senate, on December 24, 2009. Once the Senate passed the law, and its composition changed, making it susceptible to filibuster, only the House could bring it forward; there could not be a conference committee to reconcile House and Senate versions of a new law as is normally the case.

As the focus shifted to the House of Representatives, when asked about the health care bill and what was in it, on March 10, 2010, Speaker Pelosi replied " . . . we have to pass the bill so that you can find out what is in it, away from the fog of the controversy." On March 21, 2010, it passed the House with a narrow majority of 219 to 212 that allowed Blue Dog Democrats to say they were against it while simultaneously continuing to caucus with Speaker Pelosi. The unprecedented 2,730-page bill had many provisions that were read by perhaps a handful people. To make the bill more difficult to overturn, there was no "severability" clause. Some have argued this was an oversight in the rush to completion, perhaps having to do with severability clauses usually being added in House and Senate Conferences. In general, I would agree with Lily Tomlin, "No matter how *cynical* you get, it is impossible to keep up." In that spirit, I think the best explanation for the lack of severability is that leaving it out made it more difficult for any of it to be overturned. In that sense, that tactic is similar to a poker player with a weak hand in Texas Hold 'Em going "all in" bluffing his way to constitutionality.

In fact, it has only been two years since the law was passed—a two-year anniversary without any announced celebration by the White House. And in that time period alone, the average health insurance bill has increased by over 14 percent in 2009[8] and another 9 percent in 2010[9] and another 8 percent in 2011,[10] as compared with a cumulative CPI of 7.4 percent for those three years. At these rates of increase, many Democratic allies, primarily unions and state organizations, immediately began petitioning for, and receiving, waivers from the health care bill they had worked so hard to pass. In fact, once the law was signed, over 1,200 total waivers were allowed as of January 1, 2012.[11]

The Congressional Effect analysis suggests that once you know an industry or a company is going to be subject to intense new regulation, it is wise to underweight that industry or that company. In health care this was especially true, because the industry had always been presented to Wall Street as recession resistant, so now with a looming burden of excess regulation, this industry was poised not only to not keep pace with the market but to underperform the market. A good example is UnitedHealthcare, which from the end of 2007 through the election of 2008 sharply underperformed the S&P 500 Index, as can be seen in Figure 5.8.

Of course, if an industry has fallen because of excess regulation, to the extent it appears that regulation may be lifted, that may be the time to begin investing again. On December 13, 2010, a federal district court found the health care reform law unconstitutional: If you had invested in UNH, you would have outperformed the market by almost 50 percent in less than a year and a half (see Figure 5.9).

In March 2012, after being sued by 26 states, and with a split in the circuit courts, the Supreme Court took on the issue of the unconstitutionality of the health care reform law, and in a controversial 5-4 decision, with Chief Justice Roberts casting the deciding vote, upheld the constitutionality of

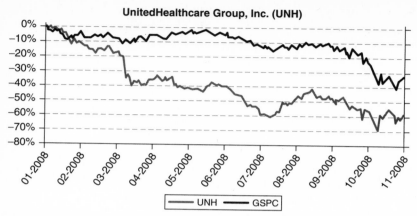

FIGURE 5.8 UNH vs. S&P 500 Index, January 2008 through November 2008. Source: Yahoo! Finance

the law. It is safe to say, however, that the intense debate at the Court showed that Congress had reached a moment of true dysfunction simply with respect to its process. At one point, one of the justices asked about the severability of the law: the idea that even if the individual mandate was unconstitutional, it was the justices' duty to parse through the law and find which sections could be kept and which could not. One frustrated justice asked, "Do you really expect us to read all 2,730 pages of this law, identifying which sections should stay and which should go?" What was "bad"

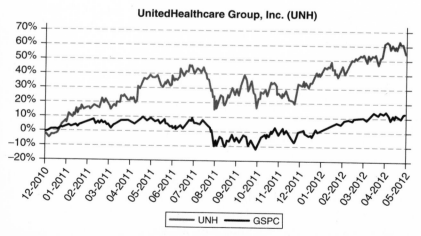

FIGURE 5.9 UNH vs. S&P 500 Index, 2010–2011. Source: Yahoo! Finance

for the administration was good for UNH, as the stock finally broke back above its close from the end of 2007. The point is that the Congressional Effect tends to damage stocks, and when it is removed, or when the market is discounting the removal of excess legislation, they tend to recover.

The overall value of the health care sector, as measured by Standard & Poor's, was about $2.3 trillion as of the end of 2011, very slightly above its price levels at the end of 2007. At the bottom of the 2008–2009 sell-off, the industry had lost roughly $700 billion in market capitalization during the course of the health care debate and the collapse in the stock market (see Figure 5.10). While it is clear that different constituencies within the health care industry were deeply involved in trying to get the health care reform law to be favorable to them, it is also clear that the market had to discount the potential damage from changing the existing business model of the industry.

In contrast, the long-term charts of companies like Merck, Johnson & Johnson, and UnitedHealthcare show companies that have sharply outperformed the broad market over long periods of time in prior markets and were historically considered to be largely recession-proof. Over the long term, and in spite of the recessions of the 1980s, 1990s and 2001, this sector and these stocks sharply outperformed and represented a defensive

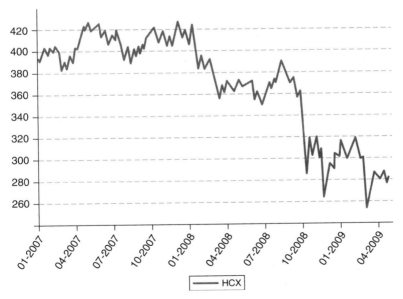

FIGURE 5.10 Health Care Index, January 2008 through April 2009.
Source: Yahoo! Finance

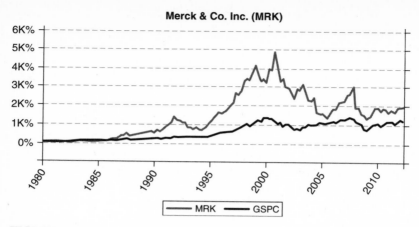

FIGURE 5.11   MRK vs. S&P 500 Index, 1980–2011. Source: Yahoo! Finance

store of equity value (see Figures 5.11, 5.12, and 5.13). While we now know they continued to somewhat outperform in the last recession as stocks, the threat of a change in business model has eroded the Wall Street perception that these stocks are safer than the broad market.

Asking the same question we asked about the financial services sector, I would attribute roughly half of the $700 billion in lost market capitalization to government intervention, or $350 billion. This is not a scientific guess: it is only a directional statement, but there is no question that health care reform and its impact was the single biggest concern of investors in this industry over the past four years.

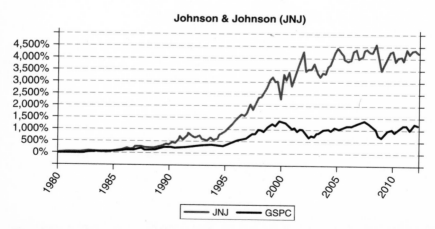

FIGURE 5.12   JNJ vs. S&P 500 Index, 1980–2011. Source: Yahoo! Finance

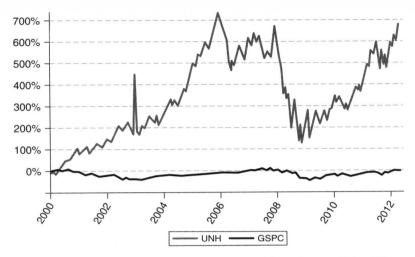

FIGURE 5.13   UNH vs. S&P 500 Index, 2000–2011. Source: Yahoo! Finance

BURNING COAL AND OTHER ENERGY INVESTORS

These two industries were not the only ones to be affected by the election. There are many others. To pick another one, for example, let's look at portions of the energy industry. From June 2008 through February 2009, as oil prices plunged, the price of all energy-related stocks fell. Compare the Oil & Gas Index (XLE) to the Coal Index (KOL) in Figure 5.14, and you will see a sharply higher fall-off in the value of the coal industry in the immediate aftermath of the 2008 election.

As you can see from the chart, the oil and gas industry has suffered a 24 percent drop since June 2008, while the coal industry has suffered a 50 percent drop. Because both produce energy, and because most energy products can be substituted over time to some degree for other forms of energy, the difference is largely explainable by government regulation developments. In the case of oil and gas, there was a moratorium in the Gulf of Mexico on drilling in conjunction with the BP oil spill, but it was lifted.

But the coal industry has been singled out as one that should be subject to particularly severe regulation. In fact, the Environmental Protection Agency (EPA), with the support of the administration and Congress, has subjected the coal industry to very costly new regulations, and as a result, the value of the entire industry plummeted on a relative basis, as shown in Figure 5.15.

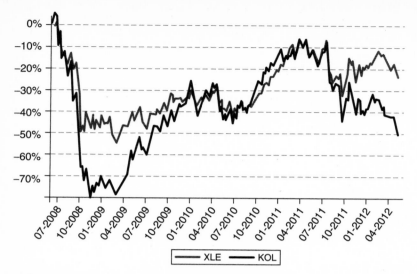

FIGURE 5.14   XLE vs. KOL, July 2008 through April 2012. Source: Yahoo! Finance

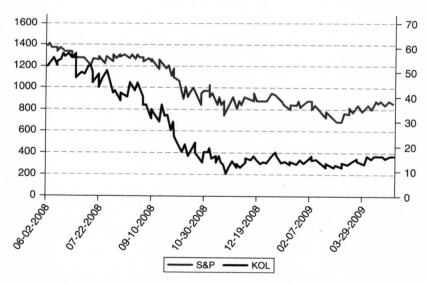

FIGURE 5.15   KOL vs. S&P 500 Index. Source: Yahoo! Finance

In the case of coal, the industry was hit with several potentially devastating regulations. One requires a buffer of up to 800 feet below any seasonal creeks or rivulets above a coal mine. The entire surface area of the land portion of earth is subject to seasonal rivulets. So, if a mine is underground, which by definition includes 100 percent of all underground mines, and an efficient layout requires access to coal that is less than 800 feet below the surface, that coal will now be off limits. This regulation alone, heavily enforced, likely makes the majority of the underground mines in the United States uneconomic.

As if that regulation were not enough, the EPA, again with Congress's blessing, is promulgating an anti-mercury regulation that seeks to cut coal plant emissions by 90 percent. These regulations are implementing the Clean Air Act of 1990, so it is difficult to understand the urgency of their implementation. The coal industry estimates that implementation will cost $170 billion, which will then be added back into electricity prices to be recovered by the utilities. The government claims thousands of lives will be saved.

For example, the state of New Jersey's Department of Energy believes that implementing these regulations for utilities would prevent 68 pounds of mercury from entering New Jersey's air from New Jersey itself every year. Sixty-eight pounds is the equivalent of 30,872 grams, spread over 22,588 square kilometers, or roughly 1.4 grams per square kilometer. Once the dispersion attributable to the first kilometer of atmosphere is incorporated in this calculation, the density of mercury from these emissions would be 1.4 grams per cubic kilometer. Since the average household is about 1,000 cubic meters, it would avoid exposure to 1.4/1,000,000s of a gram per year with this law.

The average compact fluorescent (CFL) bulb sold has 3 to 5 mg or 3/1,000s of a gram of mercury,[12] so if you break one new bulb in your house per year, you will have experienced 2,000 times the exposure that is currently projected to cost consumers $170 billion to prevent. So the average New Jersey household of four people will pay over $2,000 to prevent an annual exposure to mercury 1/2,000 of the exposure from one broken light bulb. And these bulbs are dangerous and ten times more expensive than the bulbs they replace. Special material handling procedures are advised for picking up that broken light bulb.[13] This is not a good trade.

In March 2012, the EPA published its CO_2 regulations. Having identified CO_2 as a cause of global warming because it is a "greenhouse gas," the EPA requires all new coal-fired utilities to adopt expensive carbon capture and storage equipment. In its announcement, the EPA states that under the rules it expects no new coal plants to be built before 2030 with the new regulations. In practice, whenever utilities upgrade old equipment, they are generally held to a standard of upgrading what would be required under the new regulations. As a result, if these regulations stand, the coal industry will gradually go out of business. The industry lobbying groups estimate the combined effect of all the anti-coal regulations will be to lose 250,000 coal-related jobs as a result the implementation of these rules.

For the sake of these kinds of regulations, the coal industry has truly suffered under the Congressional Effect. The overall industry has a market capitalization of roughly $70 billion. Had it been subject to new regulations only as stringent as those for the oil and gas industry, and participated in the improvement in energy prices, its market capitalization would arguably be an extra $10 to $40 billion higher today. In closing on the subject of coal, energy, and global warming, I would just add one caveat that relates back to Chapter 4, where we discussed the dangers identified by behavioral finance. To construct global warming models, scientists use as many as 2,000 variables to create models going out 50 or even 100 years. In reality, over the past 10 to 15 years, at least some empirically collected data shows no actual global warming.[14] So we have both a data issue and a causation issue: If there is global warming, is it primarily caused by mankind? Or is it caused primarily by other factors, such as the presence or absence of sunspots?[15] Taken together, these two facts suggest that much of the driving impetus behind the onerous environmental legislation we face is due to "the illusion of knowledge."[16] The "illusion of knowledge" particularly applies where the data has been challenged, as it was in the Climategate scandal regarding the East Anglia global warming data depository.[17] While there are scientists that have found evidence of global warming,[18] it strikes me as incongruous that the call to action is based on events modeled to occur decades from now while ignoring debt default by the United States, which can be modeled to occur in less than a decade and has, in my opinion, both a much higher probability than global warming and a much more severe potential impact on our pursuit of happiness. Just because we can take 2,000 variables and construct a temperature model to 17 decimal places does not mean it will be an accurate prediction. The model may well be precise but totally inaccurate. For example, the NASA/Hansen models predicted that higher levels of CO_2 would automatically result in higher temperatures but they have not.[19] In his book, *But Is It True?: A Citizen's Guide to Environmental Health and Safety Issues* (Harvard University Press, 1997), Aaron Wildavsky shows how most environmental risks we are asked to sacrifice for are in fact negligible.

All of this raises some very complicated questions. There is no doubt that one of the factors deeply affecting coal is the growing supply of natural gas. To the extent government has a legitimate interest in cleaner air and promotes regulations favoring natural gas, that is a good reason alone for investors to shy away from the coal industry. But there can come a moment when the government tilts the playing field so far and uses its police power to disfavor one industry so much that its regulations effectively wipe out that industry. This should not only be understood as regulation. This should be understood as a "taking" under the Fifth Amendment. Where regulation is so stringent that it eliminates an industry, there may be an enormous opportunity to invest because the market will eventually acknowledge the government has gone too far.

The oil and gas industry suffered as well from both lower world prices and the prospect of greater regulation. From the summer of 2008 through April 2012, it too underperformed to the broad S&P 500 Index even though oil and gasoline prices have been quite high recently (see Figure 5.16).

The defense stocks also suffered from the perception not so much that they would be more highly regulated and reduced in their budget (see Figure 5.17), but that the defense budget of the United States would be reduced. That, too, is a Congressional Effect. It should be added that these stocks have mostly recovered, and that they suffered very few meaningful budget cuts over the past four years.

The 2008 market debacle had many industries that got in trouble, and many were punished with more regulation for their being in trouble. Just looking at the industries profiled so far, the aggregate damage attributable to the Congressional Effect totaled at least $1 trillion though the bottom of the recent bear market.

But the Congressional Effect is not always and everywhere and in every single instance bad for stocks. When the political tide looks like

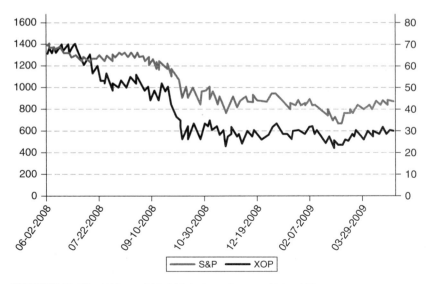

FIGURE 5.16 XOP vs. S&P 500 Index. Source: Yahoo! Finance

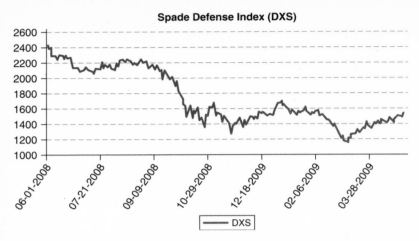

FIGURE 5.17 DXS vs. S&P 500 Index. Source: Yahoo! Finance

an industry is going to be sharply favored by Congress, it may be worth investing in that industry. In October 2004, the Republican-controlled House and Senate passed the Volumetric Ethanol Excise Tax Credit, which was promptly signed into law by President Bush. This law radically changed the economics of companies that benefited from the higher corn prices and higher ethanol prices. For example, Pacific Ethanol (PEIX) ran from a split-adjusted $67 per share in March 2005 to a peak of $294 per share in 2006, as shown in Figure 5.18.

Of course, when Congress has created an industry that is at its core uneconomic, like the ethanol industry, it is important to find "a greater fool" to whom you will sell, and do it before the collapse. In the case of PEIX, it went bankrupt, and its shares declined from that peak of $294 per share to less than a dollar per share in April 2012, which is a particularly bad return of −99.7 percent if you bought at the peak, as can be seen in Figure 5.19.

This is one of the hazards of Congress's fixing a price on an industry that is uneconomic. For a while, it can be heaven, and then if it is not truly economic, or there is not really a need for it, or it can be substituted, then it can be hell. The domestic ethanol industry had three legs of support: tariffs, crop subsidies, and mandated purchases. The subsidies were the first to go. My guess is that if there is a Republican sweep in the fall, the other legs of support for ethanol will be systematically reduced over time, but that is just a mere guess. In Spain, now that they have run out of money, they are also backing away from the idea of a "green" economy.

Other "green industries" were heavily supported by the incoming Democratic president and his supportive Democratic majority in the 110th

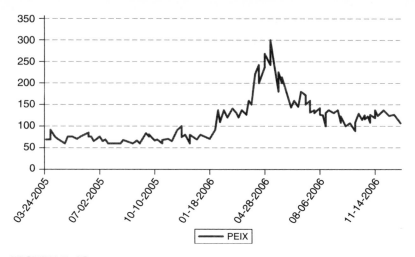

FIGURE 5.18   PEIX, 2005–2006. Source: Yahoo! Finance

Congress, including electric car companies, solar companies, wind energy companies, and algae companies, among other efforts. While some of these, like the VOLT division of GM, got billions of dollars of support, I tend to view most businesses that require cash outlays from the government as not easily sustainable. GM, which is surviving as an overall entity, still had to idle the VOLT line, at least temporarily, because demand for it was so soft.

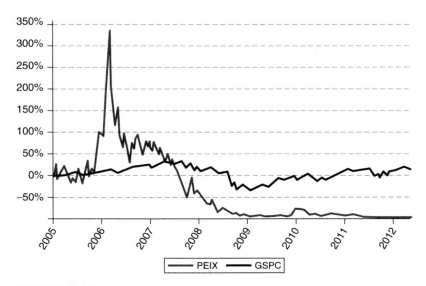

FIGURE 5.19   PEIX, 2005–2012. Source: Yahoo! Finance

As a general rule, when Congress picks a technology, it picks the wrong technology.

SUMMARY

Whenever Congress adds a new layer of in-depth regulation for an industry, the regulation usually has unintended consequences that adversely affect that industry and the sectors of the economy that industry serves. As evidence, this chapter took a closer look at the finance and health care and coal sectors. In finance, the wave of new regulation over the past 10 years has made our markets more volatile, less helpful to small companies, and arguably more dangerous for the small investor, and reduced the relative market capitalizations of the companies in that industry as part of the Congressional Effect. In health care, massive new regulation severely impacted the stock prices of the industry, both in 1993 when it was proposed and failed, and in 2008 through 2010, when it became law. Companies, knowing that their stock prices will suffer no matter what, have the bad choice of either embracing more regulation to shape it to their advantage, or resisting it. The coal industry has suffered greatly from both new sources of energy but in particular from massive new regulation. Either way, once Congress has an industry in its sights, that industry will suffer from both a regulatory point of view and, as a result, a market value point of view. President Reagan's famous saying was that the nine most dangerous words in the English language were: "I'm from the government and I'm here to help." It applies with even more force when Congress says it.

NOTES

1. Ted Weisberg, "Congress and SEC Should Admit They're Wrong," *Financial Times*, September 7, 2010.

2. Interview with Nance Lucas, *Journal of Leadership & Organizational Studies*, Summer 2004, http://findarticles.com/p/articles/mi_m0NXD/is_1_11/ai_n25101748/print?tag=artBody;col1

3. www.pcaobus.org

4. Eric Singer, "Thanks Sarbox for Inversion of Equity Curve," *Investor's Business Daily*, May 25, 2007.

5. www.thecourtneygroup.com/images/ipo-chart-a.png

6. http://bespokeinvest.typepad.com/bespoke/2009/01/sp-500-financial-sector-market-cap-continues-to-sink.html

7. Eric Singer, "Devaluing the Dollar by Trashing Private Healthcare," *Investor's Business Daily*, November 16, 2009.

8. Noam M. Levey, "U.S. Employers Push Increase in Cost of Health-care onto Workers," *LA Times*, September 2, 2010, http://articles.latimes.com/2010/sep/02/business/la-fi-healthcare-costs-20100903

9. Associated Press, "Report: Health Care Costs to Rise 9% in 2010," *USA Today*, June 19, 2009, www.usatoday.com/money/industries/health/2009-06-18-health-care-costs_N.htm.

10. Reed Abelson, "Health Insurance Costs Rising Sharply This Year, Study Shows," *New York Times*, September 27, 2011, www.nytimes.com/2011/09/28/business/health-insurance-costs-rise-sharply-this-year-study-shows.html?pagewanted=all.

11. Sam Baker, "HHS Finalizes Over 1,200 Waivers under Healthcare reform Law," *The Hill*, January 6, 2012, http://thehill.com/blogs/healthwatch/health-reform-implementation/202791-hhs-finalizes-more-than-1200-healthcare-waivers

12. www.sfswma.org/hazardous-waste/florescent-lights-mercury

13. www.scientificamerican.com/article.cfm?id=are-compact-fluorescent-lightbulbs-dangerous

14. www.dailymail.co.uk/sciencetech/article-2093264/Forget-global-warming--Cycle-25-need-worry-NASA-scientists-right-Thames-freezing-again.html

15. www.thelongview.com.au/documents/NASA-PREDICTION-SUPPORTS-GLOBAL-COOLING-by-Kevin-Long.pdf. See also www.cato.orgpubs/regulation/regv15n2/reg15n2g.html

16. http://wattsupwiththat.com/2012/04/23/why-there-cannot-be-a-global-warming-consensus/

17. www.foxnews.com/scitech/2010/01/28/scientists-climate-gate-scandal-hid-data/

18. www.nytimes.com/2010/11/14/science/earth/14ice.html?_r=1&ref=temperaturerising and www.nytimes.com/2010/11/14/science/earth/14ice.html?_r=1&ref=temperaturerising and http://www.nytimes.com/2011/10/01/science/earth/01forest.html

19. www.c3headlines.com/climate-models/

CHAPTER 6

Where Will Washington Strike Next?

W hen I was a young lawyer coming out of law school, I interviewed for a prestigious job with a very large law firm with one of the top regulatory litigators at the firm. At one point the discussion turned to having kids and the state of television. He casually mentioned that he was really bothered by how hackneyed and puerile TV had become, and in response he sharply limited what his children could watch.

I asked, "how limited are their choices?"

He replied, "I only let 'em watch *Mutual of Omaha's Wild Kingdom*, and that's it."

"Really?"

"Yes, really. Once they know about the jungle, they've learned everything they need to know from TV."

Impressed with the partner's success in litigation in Washington, D.C., it occurred to me I needed to know about the jungle. I found myself occasionally watching naturalist films, many of which were made by Sir Richard Attenborough. Describing the danger in which a wounded animal found itself in the savannah, increasingly surrounded by predators who were increasingly aware of the wounded animal's weakness, I remember vividly the voice of Sir Richard Attenborough intoning, "There are no secrets on the Serengeti," as the predators went in for the kill. I think having a heightened sense of the law of the jungle explained why that partner did so well in his D.C. practice. But the truth is that while Washington may appear to be open, it is not for the ordinary citizen on many issues. Understanding what will really happen with a law or an issue is very

113

complicated and uncertain work both because of the incentives for the Washington ecosystem to keep things complicated and because of the shifting political winds.

There may be no secrets on the Serengeti, but there are plenty in Washington, D.C. Nevertheless, the work of figuring out how Congress will affect your portfolio as to specific industries and companies is knowable, and can be entered into from the most casual levels all the way down to the most in-depth. If you're an investor, how do you figure out where Congress will strike next and how it will affect the companies that you own? The purpose of this chapter is to give you guidelines, sources, and road maps for thinking concretely about what could happen to your companies or your sector.

WHERE YOU CAN FIND INFORMATION

In general, there are three major areas of research or data available to the analyst researching what will happen next on Capitol Hill. Many of these sources are simply the ones you would turn to daily for general news about politics and can be loosely defined as what any political junkie would have either on the left or on the right as their daily diet of Washington drama. This chapter categorizes sources that are not traditional "investment" sources such as investment blogs, newsletter, and investment research. Rather, it is aimed at the political media, with some overlap for the larger Wall Street media.

Traditional Print and Mainstream Televison Sources

For someone with simply a passing interest in politics, the major news outlets at least cover some of the issues of the day, even if not in-depth. TV obviously tends to cover more issues with just sound bites and personality as compared to print, and there has been a lot of crossover between the media as more reporters have appeared on the major networks news shows. Even though the TV coverage is not in-depth, it is important for obvious reasons: more people get their news from TV than from other sources. In spite of the importance of politics in their lives, almost half of the public is completely unengaged in politics. It is likely that in the 2012 election less than 60 percent of the eligible voters will actually vote, and of those voting, at least 20 percent will decide in the last two weeks of the election.[1]

The major mainstream TV and newspaper sources are:

- *New York Times*
- *Washington Post*
- *Los Angeles Times*
- *Time* magazine
- CNN
- NPR
- *CBS Evening News*
- *NBC Nightly News*
- *ABC World News*
- *USA Today*
- MSNBC
- *Newsweek*
- *The Atlantic*
- *The New Republic*
- CNBC
- McLaughlin Group
- C-SPAN (all channels)
- *The Nation*
- *Financial Times*
- *Christian Science Monitor*

On the right, there are fewer traditional TV and print sources:

- Fox News
- *Wall Street Journal*
- *Investor's Business Daily*
- *National Review*
- *Reason*
- Newsmax
- *New York Post*
- *Human Events*
- *Weekly Standard*

- *Washington Examiner*
- *American Spectator*
- WorldNetDaily.com

Radio

The Center for American Progress released a study in 2007 asserting that 90 percent of programming for talk radio was conservative and 10 percent was progressive. Most of the radio personalities listed below would argue that the mainstream sources listed above are progressive and that a similar imbalance—only favoring the left—exists in television journalism. Conservative radio shows include:

- Rush Limbaugh
- Sean Hannity
- Mark Levin
- Glenn Beck
- Michael Reagan
- Laura Ingraham
- Michael Medved
- Hugh Hewitt
- Larry Elder
- Jesse Lee Paterson
- Dennis Prager
- Mike Gallagher
- Thomas Sowell
- Cal Thomas
- Walter E. Williams
- G. Gordon Liddy

There are a handful of progressive radio commentators, including Bill Press, Ed Schultz, Stephanie Miller, Mike Malloy, Democracy Now!, Thom Hartman, and Mark Thompson.

In addition, there are numerous programs produced by government-supported entities like National Public Radio, which try to provide in-depth coverage of major legislative issues.

These lists are not intended to be comprehensive. They are simply a reflection of the public's enormous appetite for information on our political discourse.

Online

The largest web sites now increasingly control much of the political dialog.
On the left, there is:

- HuffingtonPost.com
- Politico.com
- dailykos.com
- tnr.com
- dailybeast.com
- salon.com
- OPEdNews.com
- Politicalwire.com
- thinkprogress.com
- wonkette.com
- MyDD.com
- talkingpointsmemo.com
- firedoglake.com

On the right there is:

- Breitbart.com
- Drudgereport.com
- Newsmax.com
- theblaze.com
- freedomworks.com
- DickMorris.com
- Cato.org
- Americansforprosperity.com
- Freerepublic.com
- AmericanThinker.com
- Lewrockwell.com
- Hotair.com
- Pajamasmedia.com
- Americanthinker.com
- Townhall.com
- Washington Times

- Washington Examiner
- Citizensunited.com
- NYSun.com
- Futureofcapitalism.com
- Ibtimes.com
- Crookandliars.com

The aggregators, beginning with the DrudgeReport.com, play a very significant role in channeling the political discourse of the day. The Associated Press, which is very progressive, provides many media outlets with their base news stories. When they ignore a story, it tends to die, even if it is sensational. Yahoo!, Google, Bing, and Comcast all play a much more dominant role in news dissemination than ever before. More and more people are curating news to serve to their friends than ever before.

Also, Facebook, Twitter, LinkedIn, and other social media outlets now dominate the political debate. Curating news for friends is one of the major activities of the several hundred million people now on Facebook. America is getting more balkanized, with more people gathering their news on the Web and gathering self-sorted news. Fifty years ago, most news was received from one of the three then major network anchors. Walter Cronkite almost alone could bring the Vietnam War effort to an end. Not anymore.

The search engines also offer major opportunities to see which stories are developing. If you go to Google.com/trends and type in "health care legislation," you will see the historical rise and fall of searches on this issue. Some searches, like that for Dodd-Frank, reveal not enough traffic to be tracked even though that law profoundly affects the banking industry. Twitter.com has a very up-to-the-minute trending analytical capability, as does Yahoo.com, but most of the results involve pop culture.

Think Tanks and Blogs

Then there are think tanks on both the left and the right. Policy papers that appear on these sites eventually become the intellectual basis for much of the thrust of the major political parties. The most significant think tanks include:

- American Enterprise Institute
- Heritage Foundation
- Cato
- Reason

- Pacific Research Institute
- Americans for Tax Reform
- Competitive Enterprise Institute
- Independent Women's Forum
- Brookings Foundation
- Center for American Progress

D.C.-Specific Media

Having kept abreast of general politics through one, some, or all of the preceding sources, to track what will happen in Washington, D.C., itself, there is a more limited group of D.C.-specific media to which one can turn to narrow the scope of inquiry. These include:

- *The Hill*
- C-Span
- Politico
- *Congressional Quarterly*
- *Federal Register*
- House.gov
- Senate.gov
- The blogs of each of the federal agencies
- *National Journal*
- Fivethirtyeight.com
- Redstate.com

Following are the web sites of the major examples of legislative impact during election years and guidelines on sources on where to look for and how to handicap what will be the dominating legislative agendas and which politicians are likely to have the most input:

- realclearpolitics.com
- Rasmussen.com
- Foxbusiness.com
- Bloomberg.com
- Strategas.com
- Potomacresearch.com
- Bradleywoods.com
- Intrade.com

How Congress Passes a Law

Against this background of a tsunami of media, it is worth stepping back for a moment and looking at how Congress makes a law. See Figure 6.1 for the process.

The first source of information about Congress's impact on different industries is the publicly available information outlined earlier, some of which is free online, and some of which is available to anyone by subscriptions that are worth the money. The next level of information is what to do once you have found a bill is starting to work its way through Congress? Well, if you are part of the Washington establishment, you would try to determine which exact congressman or congressmen are going to be responsible for the bill's becoming a law, which means tracing the decision-making flowchart in Figure 6.1 at every step to figure out if a bill is going to become a law. For example, is the proposed bill going to be voted on by the appropriate committee in the House? If so, which member of the House will shepherd it through? How many cosponsors are there for this legislation? Was it introduced before? Last year? What happened then? Did it get to a committee vote? Will an identical bill be introduced in the Senate? Will it be passed by the House and then sent to the Senate? These are all things that can be determined with research, and you can familiarize yourself with the process of how laws are created. Thomas.gov is an excellent source for expanding your parliamentarian understanding of how things work in Congress. The key idea is to determine who will be responsible.

Once you know who will be responsible, you can start to make an educated guess on where they stand on a particular law. In a prior Congress, Senator Coburn and then Senator Obama teamed up to cosponsor a law on increased government transparency. Had you visited senate.gov, you could have seen official web site announcements leading you to realize where they stood on this issue, and you could have easily predicted its passage.

The third leg of understanding the inner workings of Washington is not as accessible to the general public, but it can be approximated to an extent by the diligent newcomer. There exists a multibillion-dollar industry that lobbies the interests of every conceivable interest group, and in particular those of big companies and big labor. The members of Congress have a duty to relate to the public. That doesn't mean you can count on getting face time with a senator, but it does mean with persistence you can reach someone who is on their staff, or in the staff of the regulatory agency of the law you are interested in. Let's say you are an owner of UnitedHealthcare, and you are trying to figure out if Congress's real agenda is to have only one single payer of health insurance claims, in which case your company will at some point be forced out of business. You are unlikely to get a

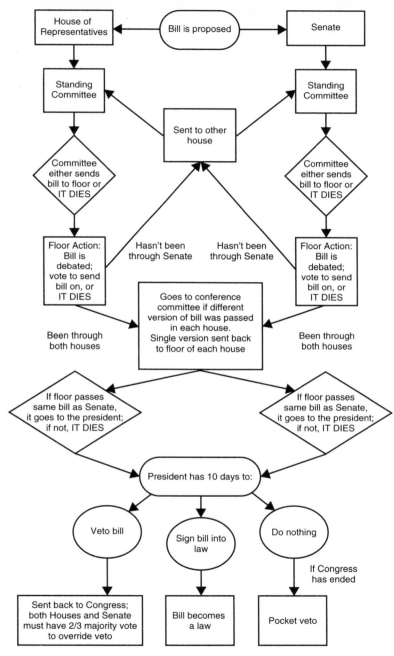

FIGURE 6.1 How Congress Passes a Law

completely straight answer (ever), but you can get some additional sense of the likelihood of that happening even just doing your own investigating. Also, if you use sources like the excellent site opensecrets.org, you can follow the major donations to each congressman and get a better sense of to whom they are beholden. One wag once suggested that congressmen should be wearing outfits like the NASCAR drivers so that we can know who is sponsoring what for whom more quickly.

I think it is worth spending a little more time on this issue. I am relentlessly struck by the discrepancy between mandated speech in the private sector, and the treatment of conflicts of interest in that sector, and those of required speech in the public sector. For example, in an earlier chapter it was observed that research analysts are now prohibited from participating in the banking fees for an initial public offering (IPO). This is an outgrowth of the research settlement imposed on the industry in 2002, and now codified in the Financial Industry Regulatory Authority (FINRA) rules. The recently passed JOBS Act may eventually modify this rule but the damage to the sell-side research industry will take years and years to undo. To the extent that a research analyst works at a firm that collects investment-banking fees from a company he researches, that conflict must be highlighted in every written communication he has about the stock. Shouldn't the same idea apply to Congress? Shouldn't every law have required disclosures of the funds received by each congressman to ensure its passage?

All of this raises another interesting conflict-of-interest question. Access to Washington staff raises an interesting question. As we saw earlier, the Securities and Exchange Commission (SEC) adopted Reg FD in 2000, which materially contributed to a decline in research coverage, particularly for small companies. This rule makes it so that everyone gets to hear at the same time any new material about a company, which in real life translates into a very staccato flow of information. Those research people are mostly gone now and cannot be compensated for IPOs under current rules. This is why I think the JOBS Act just signed, which is designed to promote capital formation for small companies, will not succeed as well as the infrastructure we had in the 1990s in spite of the change in some of the laws. Congress is now subject to the STOCK Act, and no longer able to freely trade on inside information without any potential liability other than reputational damage. Shouldn't they, under the same philosophy, only have contact with the public at the same time on the pressing lobbying issue of the day? Of course, if they do that, they will be regulating much of the lobbying business out of business, which would be adverse for getting funding for reelection.

HOW TO LEVERAGE THIS GLUT OF INFORMATION

This chapter has tried to suggest a lengthy list of Washington, D.C.–related resources. I use them mostly by scanning them just to see if there is any new trending information of political gossip. The mathematically oriented ones will give you clues as to which people will prevail. For example, although the presidential race may turn out to be quite close and not usefully predictable, it may well be that several weeks ahead of the election in November 2012 you can get a feel for whether there will be a split Congress or a unified Congress. You can estimate this based on polling. You can further handicap the political horse races of the elections by tracking the audience figures for different web sites and media outlets. In the fall of 2004, Fox News beat out its news rivals including ABC, NBC, and CBS by two million viewers for coverage of the Republican convention, and that represented a new level of hard-core support for the president in hindsight. At the time, I thought that it boded well for President Bush's reelection chances.

Between trends in polling, audience ratings, sites like intrade.com, and donation tracking, it may be possible to handicap the political outcome in Washington, D.C., better than the average market participant. Site traffic is also something to watch, as are digital indicia of loyalty. For example, Quantcast.com tracks traffic to the sites mentioned earlier, and trends in that traffic are similar in informational value to trends in TV and radio audience. Google and Bing and Facebook search counts can also suggest real-time trends in support. I remember a point in the 2008 election race when Senator Obama had 1.4 million Facebook friends as compared to 200,000 for Senator McCain, indicating extremely high youth support for Senator Obama. The performance of certain sectors will also likely give a little bit of advance notice of the election outcome. In 1980, the defense sector went straight up in anticipation of a Reagan victory.

One other way to use the news from political sources listed in this chapter is for contrary indications. As discussed in Chapter 11, another way to reduce Congress's impact on your portfolio is to invest using a value or contrarian orientation. When you see what looks like fresh political news regarding an industry, and there is no follow-on reaction by the sector or stock that should be affected, that is a signal that the political story may have run its course and that you can now do the opposite of what the political media coverage suggests.

Scanning these sites in the aggregate is time consuming and obviously a burden when you are already trying to keep up on more pure financial news. Some of the aggregators, like realclearpolitics.com and drudgereport.com, can give you a very quick feel for the day's news. It is also useful to see if an issue seems to be getting rising attention. It is harder to notice when it is getting less attention. If you couple the media attention with tracking the corporate donations, which you can do to some extent with opensecrets.org, and the campaign war chests, you can start to make better-educated guesses as to the new power alignments in Congress, and from there make choices about which sectors to overweight and underweight. One final caveat is in order, particularly for financial advisers and portfolio managers genuinely trying to invest for the long term. One of the smartest people I know, Dr. Joe Plummer (see Chapter 1) once told me he never reads *any* newspaper. When I asked him why not, he replied, "It interferes with pattern recognition." As a political junkie, I cannot eliminate my urge to find out the latest tidbit of political news. But if you review many of the sources listed earlier, out of respect for Dr. Plummer, I think it is a good idea to relentlessly ask, "Is there a larger picture here than just this particular political race that I am missing?" For example, at a time when partisan political forces on both sides describe the 2012 election as the most important of our lifetime, it is likely that an ongoing trend of declining voter participation since 1960 will continue, and that 40 percent or more of the voting-age population will not vote. I don't have an answer for the significance of that fact; I just know that it means I am missing something in my understanding of the body politic in the United States.

SUMMARY

If you're an investor, how do you figure out where Congress will strike next and how it will affect the companies that you own? Use television, newspapers, radio, and online political resources: they will be the first to inform you when there is legislation affecting a specific sector or company. Think tanks and political blogs will also provide secondary insight into the goings-on in Washington, as do search engines and other Internet resources.

Try to determine exactly which congressmen are going to be responsible for a particular bill's becoming a law, which means actually understanding which committee will wind up with responsibility for drafting the proposed law in question. The members of Congress still have a duty to relate to the public, and while you may not be able to get face time, you currently can usually reach someone who is on their staff or in the staff of the regulatory agency of the law you are interested in to get deeper insight as to what may happen.

In the long term, unfortunately, this is likely to change. The more Washington talks about transparency, the less transparency we actually get. Reg FD in the securities sector requires companies to disclose material information at the same time to all analysts and investors. In Washington, such a rule applied to political communication by incumbents may come to pass because it could perversely give congressmen even more leverage on shaping legislation in proverbial smoke-filled rooms. In addition, the lobbying and research ecosystem that has grown up around Washington has a vested interest in charging rents to sort through the clutter of the thousands of proposed pieces of legislation every year and, in turn, to affect key legislation. To the extent you can follow which issues have attracted the most lobbying money or have changed traditional donation patterns, you may get early clues about new legislative risks. Finally, all the media cited in this chapter can also be tracked for their ratings to give coincident indications of how elections may turn out, which can be helpful in sector allocation.

NOTE

1. Brian Brox and Joseph Giammo, "Late Deciders and the US Presidential Elections," Tulane. The American Review of Politics, Vol. 30, Winter, 2009–2010: 333–355.

CHAPTER 7

Sidestepping Congress's Wealth Destruction with a Macro Approach

W hat if you could have a portfolio that filtered out much of the bad news and its impact on your portfolio, and pretty much reacted only to the good news your companies generated? It would probably feel like waking up and finding yourself in a beer commercial having a blast with your ideal buddies, or living in a MasterCard commercial doing something "priceless" with your family like diving into tropical waters from your own yacht.

The Congressional Effect approach can't guarantee the lack of bad news or even the yacht (especially the yacht), but it does allow you to tactically allocate a portion of your assets so that they are usually less proportionately affected than most domestic portfolios by news from the government. In effect, by screening a disproportionate amount of news that is political, your portfolio will tend to trade more based on the commercial news cycle, which is a more predictable cycle. CEOs are paid to guide shareholder expectations accurately and suffer when (for example) there are negative earnings surprises. By contrast, they have little influence over what Washington might do, so bad news from Washington can make their stock more volatile. The Congressional Effect approach emphasizes the pure commercial news flow and stays neutral for the time legislators are in session. So it is a less volatile way of investing.

This chapter shows you how to systematically apply the Congressional Effect on a daily tactical basis. The key is that even though it is applied on a daily basis, historically it has been most effective when applied consistently over very long periods of time. In the short term, no one can predict daily price moves, and there may be quarters or even longer periods where it is not an advantageous trade. But the historical data, which is never a guarantee of future results, does suggest that over one or more full investment cycles it has been a good risk-adjusted way to seek returns.

11,832 DATA POINTS SUPPORT THE CONGRESSIONAL EFFECT THEORY

We saw in Chapter 1 the massive data support for the proposition that Congress affects the market on a daily basis. From 1965 through 2011, there were 11,832 trading days. By comparison, the Super Bowl indicator discussed in a jocular way in Chapter 1 had just 46 data points. On the 7,767 days they were in session, excluding dividends and transaction costs, the annualized price increase in the Standard & Poor's (S&P) 500 Index was 0.72 percent on the days Congress was in session. This works out to an arithmetic average of 0.00286 percent per day during the average of 165 per year that they were in session. The vast bulk of the price return in the S&P 500 Index over this long period of time occurred on days Congress was out of session. During the 4,065 days they were out of session, the annualized return was 16.60 percent or 0.19 percent per average trading day on the average annual 86 days they were out of session. Just for reference during these 47 years, the annualized total return in the S&P 500 Index was 9.27 percent per year.

On a daily basis, from 1965 through 2011, a dollar invested only on in-session days would have compounded just through price action into $1.25 and on out-of-session days would have compounded into $11.91 (see Figure 7.1).

I first published on this topic in 1992 in *Barron's*. Since then, there have been a number of academic studies finding the statistically same results over even longer periods of time. Reinhold P. Lamb and colleagues released a study in 1997 taking the data all the way back to 1897 using the Dow Jones Industrial Average. They concluded:

> *This study reports on the existence of a curious calendar effect—a relationship between stock market performance and the schedule of the United States Congress. Almost the entire advance in the market since 1897 corresponds to the periods when Congress is in recess. This is an impressive result, given that Congress is in recess about half as long as in session. Furthermore, average daily returns when Congress is not meeting are almost eight times greater than when Congress is in session. Throughout the year, cumulative returns during recess are thirteen times that experienced while Congress is in session.*[1]

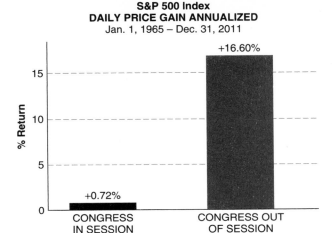

FIGURE 7.1 Price Gain in S&P 500 Index In-Session Days vs. Out-of-Session Days, 1965–2011. Source: Congressional Effect Management, LLC

This study was completed before the bull market of the 1990s ended. In the hundred years of the past century, the United States had only once, during World War II, experienced massive deficits. In the 1990s the Congressional Budget Office (CBO) version of the budget was balanced and the federal government expanded, but not at a rate that seemed to accelerate. During this period, the federal budget as a percentage of gross domestic product (GDP) was relatively constant. Although the CBO budget was balanced on a "cash basis," from the beginning of President Clinton's first term through the end of his second term, the outstanding U.S. Treasury debt increased from $4.177 trillion to $5.662 trillion. I believe that as the 1990s yielded to the 2000s, the real economy became weaker, primarily because of the continued expansion of the major entitlement programs, the launch of a new entitlement program, Medicare Part D, and the cost of the wars in Iraq and Afghanistan.

Another comprehensive study was completed in 2005, which included years up to and including 2004. In that study, entitled "Congress and the Stock Market" by Michael F. Ferguson and Hugh Douglas Witte, published in 2006, they also studied the Dow Jones Industrial Average from 1897 through 2004. They concluded:

We find a strong link between Congressional activity and stock market returns that persists even after controlling for known daily return anomalies. Stock returns are lower and volatility is higher when Congress is in session. . . . [2]

Using the Dow Jones Industrial Average, Professors Ferguson and Witte found that over 90 percent of the gains in the market historically occurred when Congress was out of session.[3] One of the important innovations of this extensive research was to relate the Congressional Effect to the popularity of Congress. The less popular Congress, the greater the Congressional Effect. They found that when Congress was extremely unpopular, the Congressional Effect tended to be greater than when Congress was relatively more popular. They also thought that rent-seeking behavior by Congress could explain their findings. The period they surveyed was exhaustive, going back day by day to 1897. There were approximately 32,000 trading days in the period they reviewed.

Most stunning, though, was the cumulative effect. They found that a theoretical dollar invested in 1897 only on days Congress was in session (again ignoring dividends and transaction costs) would have compounded from $1 into $2 in the course of 108 years. The same dollar invested only during the out-of-session days would have compounded into $216 through the end of 2004. Updating their work through the end of 2011, the in-session dollar would have fallen from $2 to slightly below $2, and the $216 would have further compounded into over $300. The statistics using the Dow Jones Industrial Average (DJIA) and the S&P 500 Index are consistent from a statistical point of view. Because Congress is in session on average about a third of the year, the 16.60 percent annualized price gain attributable to the days Congress was out of session in the S&P 500 Index over a 47-year period translates into a compounding rate of 5.4 percent. By comparison, the 5.1 percent annual compounding rate for the longer 108-year period from 1897 through 2004 reflects the DJIA and is remarkably similar for such a long period of observation. It is this price action, coupled with dividends, that accounts for most of the total return of these two indices.[4]

CONGRESS AND THE TRAGEDY OF THE COMMONS

"No man's life, liberty, or property is safe while the legislature is in session." This quote, usually attributed to Mark Twain, apparently first appeared in print in a case decided by Judge Gideon Tucker. When you think of Congress and realize that there are 535 issues entrepreneurs, it is easy to imagine that almost every day the legislature is in session is a day where there may well be legislative risk. For example, in the 109th Congress (2005–2006), there were 9,141 laws introduced with no major action, 930 with some major action, 22 that failed, and 465 that were passed.[5] While "only" 465 became law, each one required investors to notice it, understand it, and, if necessary, change their investment strategy. If you were short Archer-Daniels Midlands (ADM) in 2004, you should have been doing your best to see if Congress was going to tilt the playing field. From January 2004 through the passage of the ethanol law, and into the summer of 2006, ADM stock roughly tripled.

One way to systematically reduce legislative risk is to have little or no equity exposure just on the days Congress is in session. With 535 issues entrepreneurs introducing literally thousands of bills, of which several hundred will routinely be passed, you can think of each day as a relentless fight for who gets to be on camera with yet another new idea. But for congressmen, the fact that that visit in front of the camera is something that may depress the stock market is not something that bothers them. In fact, if it leads to more lobbying dollars, it is likely to be considered internally a good thing.

In his essay "The Tragedy of the Commons" (*Science*, 1968), Garrett Hardin brought focus to the idea that common areas can suffer if everyone gets to exploit them bit by bit, but no one individually suffers immediately if they are overused. Think of cows grazing in a town commons. Adding one more cow to the herd doesn't seem to do anyone harm, so individuals will do that. But eventually, with enough cattle, the town commons is denuded, and the whole herd dramatically starves. Aristotle was the first to notice this, and pointed out "what is common to the greatest number has the least care bestowed upon it."

The Tragedy of the Commons applies to Congress,[6] and for that matter, to most government activity. For example, no individual congressman ever feels responsibility for the market's going down, or for its roughly staying neutral over their *entire careers* on pretty much only the days they are visibly at work, but in fact that is what happens. Unlike physicians, congressmen do not think, "First, do no harm." In fact, they seem to think a little harm never hurt anybody. Every day they are in session is like a day in the hospital. You never know what could go wrong having nothing to do with your original illness. The most successful states, like Texas, limit the time their legislatures can be in session, and I believe this plays a significant role in the relative outperformance these states have had in growing their economies.

ADAM SMITH, CALL YOUR OFFICE!

In *The Wealth of Nations*, Adam Smith described the beauty of a mostly laissez-faire capitalist society where each party, possessing their own property, bargained for their own self-interest and freely transacted because they were better off from advantageous trading. The result was a widespread market for every good, and an understanding that self-interest properly channeled could truly benefit society as a whole. It is one thing for a merchant to bargain for his self-interest. He is committing his own property, so he will do his best to get value for it. It is quite another for a congressman to spend trillions of dollars of other people's money to perpetuate his role in an office with nominal public pay. The temptations and opportunities for corruption and just plain poor policy are legion when you are not spending your own money and when there is, as a practical matter, no accountability because you are from a gerrymandered district.

In this context, it is worth taking just a moment here to make an aside regarding the budget, the budget deficit, the fate of the dollar, and the Tragedy of the Commons. When each congressman is an issues entrepreneur, think of each issue as one more cow being introduced to the town commons. No one issue feels like it is too much, but here we are strangling in a tax code with a million words and thousands upon thousands of special favors. Similarly, the United States budget has relentless bloat, and there are now thousands of government agencies, each with a budget that requires a major fight just to slow down its nominal growth. Each congressman with a funded pet issue looks at his cause and says, "My project is not causing the dollar's decline or impacting the United States' credit rating." But in the aggregate, they are creating world war–style deficits, without a world war, and without the economic benefits that come with winning a world war. The purchasing power of the dollar has materially eroded. As a result, the common man in the United States has been brought ever closer to the brink of disaster by the slow but relentless devastation of the dollar and the increasing debt burden created by Congress.

In his masterful overview of the forces shaping our market and our economy entitled "Why Countries Succeed and Fail Economically," Ray Dalio of Bridgewater Associates, L.P. identified five stages in the life of a nation[7]:

Stage 1: Countries are poor and think they are poor.

Stage 2: Countries are getting rich quickly but still think they are poor.

Stage 3: Countries are rich and think of themselves as rich.

Stage 4: Countries become poor but still think of themselves as rich.

Stage 5: Countries deleverage and go through relative decline, which they are slow to accept.

Dalio views these cycles as evolving over generations within each country, in cycles of greater than 100 years, but impossible to meaningfully manage because the politicians typically have the short year or two time horizons we have documented so much in this book. Arguably, the United States has left Stage 3. Our first debt downgrade in August 2011 was perhaps the most objective milestone in this process. In between Stage 3 and Stage 5 are all bad choices from a congressman's point of view. Once debt is in excess of 100 percent of GDP, as it is now, as Dalio points out in "A Template for Understanding . . . How the Economic Machine Works and How It Is Reflected Now,"[8] when a nation has to undergo deleveraging, it can achieve it only by a mix of (1) debt reduction, (2) austerity, (3) redistribution of wealth, and (4) debt monetization (or printing money). None of these are attractive in a democracy, let alone a republic, and to the extent the market knows Congress is failing to do its real long-term job, the market has historically underperformed on the days Congress is in session.

In the context of Congress's large and persistent derogation of duty, such as the Senate's not passing a formal budget in three years, by avoiding equity exposure when they are in session, you are less likely to suffer short-term "legislative risk" in the mix of news affecting stocks that particular day. If that is the case, the macroeconomic news and the industry-specific business news is more likely to move the market. Both of these forms of news are more predictable than legislative surprises, and I think that is one big reason stocks perform better when Congress is out of session. Think of it as a way to manage the news cycle so that you try to get the same overall performance with fewer surprises.

One way to take advantage of this anomaly is to seek equity exposure only on the days Congress is in session. This can be achieved by buying S&P 500 Index analogs such as the S&P Depositary Receipt (SPDR; "spyders") ETF or S&P 500 Index futures only on the days Congress is out of session. Alternatively, you can have a portfolio that is both long and short these S&P analogs, where the short position is eliminated on days Congress is out of session. For information on Congress's schedules, you can look at the web sites of the House of Representatives at House.gov and the Senate at Senate.gov. I consider any day that is a legislative day for either chamber to be an "in-session" day. You can also follow Congress's activities on C-SPAN. I should add that Congress often changes its schedule at the last minute as part of the legislative jostling it does every day, and that you have to check frequently on Congress to be up to date. A representative account by an investor generally using the Congressional Effect approach had the following publicly audited* returns over the past five calendar years compared to the S&P 500 Index:

	Congressional Effect Approach	**S&P 500 Index**
2007*	9.58%	5.50%
2008*	−7.42%	−36.99%
2009	−4.35%	+26.45%
2010	15.31%	+15.06%
2011	−4.87%	+2.11%

*The representative account was directly managed applying the Congressional Effect approach from January 2007 through May 2008, and was invested in a mutual fund managed in accordance with the Congressional Effect from May 2008 to December 2011. The results shown are calculated net of fees and trading costs (e.g., brokerage costs, management fee, and internal mutual fund expenses), and reflect reinvestment of dividends and interest.

Cumulative annualized compounded returns from January 1, 2007, through December 31, 2011, were 1.26 percent using this approach as compared to −0.25 percent for the S&P 500 Index (see Figure 7.2). It is visually presented as a graph plotted against standard deviation in Figure 7.3 and beta in Figure 7.4. This period was one of the most difficult

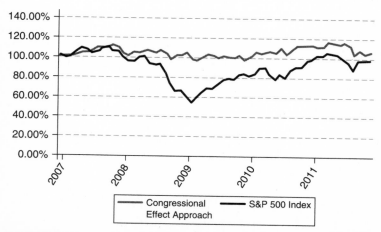

FIGURE 7.2 Congressional Effect Approach vs. S&P 500 Index, 2007–2011.
Source: Congressional Effect Management, LLC

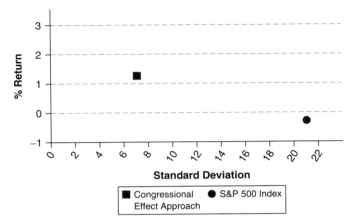

FIGURE 7.3 Congressional Effect Approach vs. S&P 500 Index, 2007–2011.
Source: Congressional Effect Management, LLC

for investors in the past 50 years, and these returns were favorable on a risk-adjusted basis compared to the S&P 500 Index during that period. To get updated, SEC-compliant information on the Congressional Effect Fund, please visit www.congressionaleffect.com.

Most important, in my estimation, these results show that the investor slightly beat the S&P 500 Index while being exposed to much less risk as measured by his standard deviation and the beta of his portfolio. For the five-year period from 2007 through 2011, this investment had a standard deviation of 7.71 percent, while the S&P 500 Index had a standard deviation

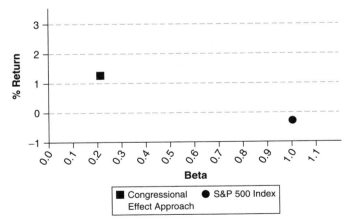

FIGURE 7.4 Congressional Effect Approach vs. S&P 500 Index, 2007–2011.
Source: Congressional Effect Management, LLC

of 21.14 percent. During the same period, this investment had a five-year beta of 0.23 and a five-year alpha of 0.84.

SUMMARY

"No man's life, liberty, or property is safe while the legislature is in session," said Mark Twain.

The Congressional Effect approach should allow you to shield a portion of your assets from government news, and trade more based on the predictable commercial news cycle. When you think of Congress and realize that there are 535 issues entrepreneurs, it is easy to imagine that almost every day the legislature is in session is a day where there may well be legislative risk. No individual congressman ever feels responsibility for the market's going down, but the cumulative impact of their aggregate actions results in vast unpredictability and volatility.

One way to systematically reduce legislative risk is to have little or no equity exposure just on the days Congress in session. This can be achieved by buying S&P 500 Index analogs such as the SPDR ETF or S&P 500 Index futures only on the days Congress is out of session. Alternatively, you can have a portfolio that is both long and short these S&P analogs, where the short position is eliminated on days Congress is out of session. By avoiding equity exposure when they are in session, you are less likely to suffer short-term "legislative risk" in the mix of news affecting stocks that particular day. The more predictable and stable macroeconomic news and the industry-specific business news is more likely to move the market positively because that news is either largely created and communicated by CEOs who have a vested interest in being accurate or is part of the economic cycle, which has less potential to surprise the market as a whole compared to legislative news. With your portfolio having less headline risk, it should be positioned over time to have better risk-adjusted returns The better your risk adjusted returns, the more likely you are to have the discipline to save for successful long term results.

NOTES

1. Reinhold P. Lamb, K. Ma, R. Daniel Pace, and William F. Kennedy, "The Congressional Calendar and Stock Market Performance," *Financial Services Review* 6(1), 1997. Available at http://ssrn.com/abstract=8314

2. Michael F. Ferguson and H. Douglas Witte, "Congress and the Stock Market," March 13, 2006, 1.

3. Ibid, p. 8.

4. *Source:* Congressional Effect Management, LLC.

5. www.govtrack.us/blog/2011/08/04/kill-bill-how-many-bills-are-there-how-many-are-enacted/

6. After this book was submitted for publication, but before it was published, Walter Williams wrote a column expressing a similar view about the "Tragedy of the Commons" and Congress: www.creators.com/conservative/walter-williams/our-nation-s-future.html

7. www.bwater.com/Uploads/FileManager/research/deleveraging/why-countries-succeed-and-fail-economically--ray-dalio-bridgewater.pdf, June 2011.

8. Created October 31, 2008, updated March 2012.

CHAPTER 8

Are Democrats or Republicans Better for Your Portfolio?

I am asked all the time, "Which political party is better for the stocks?" This leads to a host of follow-up questions:

- Does this refer to the president or Congress?
- Just the presidency or a unified government where one party controls the presidency and both chambers?
- Nominal rates of return or real rates of return?
- Bonds as well?
- All asset classes?
- Commodities?
- Or only large company stocks?
- Or only small company stocks?
- What is the relevant time frame?
- Who actually controls the government?
- Is it the president?
- Congress?
- The Supreme Court?
- Some of the above?
- All of the above?
- Does it depend on the issue?

- Can the president genuinely claim responsibility for stock market success?
- Or is it Congress that has a bigger claim to causing stock market success?
- Or are they both more like the Supreme Court, which rarely directly affects the economy?

These questions are meant to make the reader question the media characterization of who exactly controls the economy, or the stock market for that matter. For dramatic effect, our media, especially our television media, typically ascribe the power to influence the economy to the president. While this makes life easier for getting good photo ops, things are much more complicated that. The government has little power to really improve the economy. In fact, it has more power to make the economy worse. The real economy is what the stock market reflects, and the president has less influence over it than Congress does. In turn, a unified government is generally worse for the economy than a divided government. This chapter looks at different configurations of government along the lines of whether it is split or united, Democrat or Republican, and whether the investor is focused on nominal or real returns.

Before we dive into the numbers, note that the sample sizes are small, particularly compared to the 11,832 daily observations used for the daily measure of the Congressional Effect since 1965. We've had only 44 presidents, and for a long time the stock market was entirely under the Buttonwood Tree on Wall Street. That is to say, for example, there is not much good daily data concerning the stock market and Tippecanoe and Tyler too, the popular Whig candidates, as you may recall, from the 1840 election. So with mostly just the 1900s and thereafter to work with, are the election cycle sample sizes big enough to be really meaningful? And most important, what is the causation within the cycles? We are in Super Bowl indicator territory, but one with intuitive explanations that make sense. It's hard to say why the Giants winning the Super Bowl will make the market go up. It's not as hard to see why, say, less restrained one-party government is good for inflation. Rigorous statisticians may not feel comfortable with this limited data set, nor with parsing it, but I think taken as a whole it adds to what we know about the market. With that caveat, let's start with the gross nominal numbers just for presidents.

WHO GETS THE CREDIT FOR THE BULL MARKET IN 1980?

The stock market rallied 32 percent in 1980 when Ronald Reagan was running for office. Was the gain in that period attributable to him or to Jimmy Carter? Did the market know Reagan would help engineer a big economic recovery? Or was it just happy Jimmy Carter would be in the rearview mirror? Or was the presidency largely irrelevant because interest rates were bound to go down anyway? Over some, or even most, periods, if the criteria are only nominal returns and who was president, the answer is likely to be the Democrats. In "The Presidential Puzzle: Political Cycles and the Stock Market,"[1] Pedro Santa Clara and Rossen Valkanov found that, from 1927 to 2003, the excess nominal stock market returns have been about 11 percent for Democratic presidents, but only 2 percent for Republican presidents. They also found that the smallest 10 percent of stocks did particularly well with Democratic presidents, earning a whopping 22 percent more in excess returns with Democratic presidents than with Republican presidents.

Based on my own work, looking first at just nominal returns, since 1926, and using the Standard & Poor's (S&P) 500 Index, Republican presidents have an arithmetic average return of 8.62 percent, while Democratic presidents have an average return of 14.92 percent. This assumes that that the returns attributable to, say, 1980 are properly attributable to the Democratic president in office. I think it is valid to challenge that assumption. Few market participants who were around in 1980 think that the rally that year was attributable to the market liking President Carter. Rather, they mostly think it was the market liking the idea of getting rid of the President Carter.

Let's take the years of presidential change—1932, 1952, 1960, 1968, 1976, 1992, 2000, and 2008—and assume that they apply to the winner and not the loser of presidential election. When the returns reflect the upcoming president as opposed to the existing president, there is a 2 percent swing in the total return figures given above. In fact, going back to 1960, if we use the earlier year convention there is less difference between the Republican presidents and Democratic presidents; the gap narrows from 6 percent to 4 percent. The more intriguing question, though, is what happens when government is unified and what happens when government is split, and is the president really in charge or is Congress in charge? One of the ironies of public polling is that the president consistently polls much better than Congress does. As of the Spring of 2012, the president has an approval rating ranging between 40 and 50 percent, while the nation as a whole only gives 10 percent approval to Congress.

Nevertheless, as pointed out by many observers, a unified Congress plays a bigger role in governing the United States. Looking at the unadjusted returns for the Dow and the S&P 500 Index from 1960 through 2011, Republican presidents resulted in average total returns of 8.6 percent while Democratic presidents resulted in average total returns of 14.55 percent. During the same period, Republican presidents resulted in average price returns of 5.41 percent with the Dow Jones Industrial Average (DJIA) and 9.48 percent for Democratic presidents. Again, just looking at the unadjusted returns, when we had a Republican Senate the S&P average total return was 18.16 percent, and the Democratic Senate total return was 8.12 percent. During this period, when we had a Republican House, on average we had a 14.56 percent total return for the S&P and for the Democratic House we had a 10.26 percent total return on average. What's remarkable about these returns is that with a Republican president the S&P 500 Index had a standard deviation of 18.18 percent, but with a Republican Senate the S&P 500 Index had a standard deviation of 13.05 percent. With a Democratic Senate, the S&P 500 Index had a standard deviation of 17.3 percent. With a Democratic president, the S&P 500 Index had a standard deviation of 14.14 percent. If we were to take the Sharpe ratios associated with these using a simple chart where we had just gross returns divided by the standard deviation, we find that the Republican Senate, Democratic president had the most compelling risk-adjusted nominal return. The Sharpe ratio, originally used by Professor William Sharpe, determines whether the performance returns of a portfolio are attributable to good stock choices or to taking too much risk. The equation is most commonly expressed as the return of the portfolio less the risk-free rate divided by the portfolio's standard deviation:

$$R_p - R_{rf}/SD$$

Using the market data for a Republican Senate, the market had a Sharpe ratio of about 1.00. By contrast, a Democratic Senate had a Sharpe ratio of less than 0.20—a big difference. It also turns out that a Republican House is very good on a nominal basis. The market with a Republican House previously had an average return of 14.56 percent in nominal terms, while the market with a Democratic House had a nominal return of 10.26 percent. In fact, on the unadjusted price action, a Republican Senate just using the Dow had a return of 14.91 percent, while a Democratic Senate had a return of 3.74 percent. A Republican House had a return of 12.51 percent in price using the DJIA, while a Democratic House had a return of 5.62 percent.

UNIFIED GOVERNMENT FAVORS NOMINAL RETURNS

What happens if we look instead of at the political parties whether or not government was free to function and free to do its will? We also looked at this period of time into whether government was unified or had gridlock, and we defined total gridlock as a split Congress and partial gridlock as one party controlling both houses of Congress and the other party controlling the White House. With total unity, the S&P average total return was 12.92 percent from 1960 to 2011 and the average price return in the DJIA was 6.97 percent. With a total gridlock, meaning a split Congress, the S&P total average return was 9.48 percent. The DJIA price return was 8.63 percent. With partial gridlock, meaning one party controlling both houses of Congress, the S&P total average return was 10.46 percent and the Dow had 7.13 percent price return.

What emerges from the nominal numbers is a reflection of the bull market of the 1990s, which was far and away the biggest bull market we've had in nominal terms and reflected a market where we had President Bill Clinton, the Democratic president, and for most of the 1990s a Republican Congress from 1994 to the end of 2000. What happens if we step back and try to look at these markets adjusting for inflation? Republican presidents have much lower total returns, 3.97 percent, while Democratic presidents have an average total return of 10.91 percent. Again, this is simply taking the consumer price index (CPI) price inflator at its face and accepting it, which is something most people who are really familiar with the CPI do not like to do. Again, using the CPI when you have total unity, the S&P average total return is 8.98 percent. When you have total gridlock, the inflation-adjusted S&P average total return is 5.48 percent. When you have partial gridlock, it's 6.03 percent. There have been several important papers, including those by people associated with the CFA Institute, that look at these statistics and assert that unified governments are better for the stock market.

One very important paper about gridlock was done by Scott B. Beyer, CFA, Gerald R. Jensen, CFA, and Robert R. Johnson, CFA, entitled "Gridlock's Gone, Now What?" In this influential study of the stock market from 1949 through 2004, the stock market was divided into 10 deciles and looked at for whether it was in harmony, meaning the same party controlled the House, the Senate, and the presidency, or whether it was in gridlock, meaning one of those branches of government was controlled by a different party than the other. They looked at 13 periods of alternating harmony and gridlock and found that the smallest companies, those in the tenth decile, significantly outperformed during the periods of harmony, which is contrary to popular discussions of how gridlock is better for the stock market. Specifically during gridlock periods, they found that real returns ranged from 8.27 percent for the stocks of the very largest decile companies, which today represent about 75 percent of the weighted average of public companies. The largest six deciles, representing almost about 95 percent of the weighted average market value of all stocks, average about 8 percent total returns during gridlock periods. For each decile smaller in size, past the median decile, there was a fall-off in returns, culminating with a puny return of 4.65 percent for the smallest decile. In contrast, the largest decile companies averaged 8.78 percent real returns during the same period and each decile thereafter during periods of harmony had higher returns consistently ramping from 12.65 percent for the next decile to up over 27 percent for the very smallest companies. Their conclusion from this study is that with relatively constant inflation it is wrong to assert that gridlock is better for stocks.

However, in their own research, they also find that long-term government bonds do better during periods of gridlock than they do in periods of harmony by a wide factor, that the real returns for long-term government bonds are 5.5 percent during periods of gridlock and −1.67 percent during periods of harmony, a difference of 7.17 percent. Astonishingly, the study found that during periods of gridlock the real return on T-bills was 1.74 percent, and during periods of harmony the real returns on T-bills were 0.04 percent or four basis points per year. The official inflation rates for the two periods were approximately the same: 3.89 percent for the gridlock period and 3.70 percent for the harmony period.

This study offers a significant amount of data from a highly professional group of individuals, but I disagree with some (not all) of its conclusions, and would suggest that there's internal data within the study to give an alternative explanation for their findings. In the first place, once you've addressed the top six deciles, you've accounted for well over 90 percent of the market value of the overall stock market, and in fact on average the top decile alone equals 75 percent of the market value at issue. So minor differences in the true inflation rate or significant differences in the true inflation rate give a completely distorted view of what the real return is. In the article, the authors acknowledge that while the inflation levels appear to be similar, the expectation of inflation is much higher during the periods of harmony. I would embellish this by pointing out that to have a difference of 170 basis points on the real returns on T-bills over a 55-year period is a staggering difference, and I'd rather use the return on T-bills as the true measure of inflation discounting or even better the return on government bonds. If you discount the differences in returns between the two, the gridlock and the harmony equity returns, if they're discounted by the typical change in value in the bond market during the same periods, it's clear that at the end of a harmony period investors have higher nominal returns and lower real returns. This is consistent with our study using gold instead of the CPI. For reasons I don't want to get into here, I'm very suspicious of government versions of the CPI, which are changed often and always for less accuracy over the past 50 years.

The other explanation for why small companies do better in periods of harmony may be that the government is in fact printing more money, that the banks are given more money. They have more money they can lend, and small companies, which had less equal access to capital during periods of low inflation, find themselves in periods of higher inflation expectation with better access to capital, and that's why they outperformed.

SPLIT GOVERNMENT FAVORS REAL RETURNS

My concern in the Beyer study is primarily about using the S&P and accepting the CPI as an honest measure of inflation is that it just doesn't make sense in my own personal life. A trip to the gas station costs twice what it did three years ago. I know that last year my careful wife purchased weekly groceries that cost about $180 per week. I have been trying to lose weight for a while, and as a result I know that I'm eating exactly the same thing I ate a year ago. I am proud to say I have lost 15 pounds over that time with the kind of exercise you get from writing a book for the first time. Call me for my recipes. Today, the exact same amount of food costs $260. It is nearly a 44 percent year-over-year increase, but we're told by the government that there's been a negligible increase in inflation. It's simply not credible, and the average person knows it's not credible. The fate of the dollar and the emotion of purchasing power is not the main focus of this book, but it is safe to say that Congress thrives on the continued debasement of the dollar. Therefore, I think the best way to look at who's better for the stock market, whether it be the president, the Democratic Senate, Republican House, a gridlocked government, and so on, is to look at it on a real return basis using gold and the change in price in gold as a deflator. For most investors, the job of a long-term investment in the stock market is to preserve purchasing. If the S&P goes up 50 percent but inflation goes up 100 percent, you have lost purchasing power. The acid test of preserving purchasing power is looking at your investments in terms of the nominal market returns adjusted for the increase in inflation. Those are your real returns. If you use the S&P 500 Index return divided by the change in the price of gold, you will have an arguably honest description of the increase or decrease in wealth that occurred during a particular period. There are other inflation measures, such as those put out by John Williams at shadowstats.com. However, as to the CPI, it is difficult to do a CPI adjusted analysis and take the government CPI numbers seriously.

By the same token, any gold analysis is limited by the fact that dollars were not free to float relative to the price of gold in any substantial way really before 1973. They did move a little bit in the few prior years, but U.S. citizens were not permitted to own gold until 1974. What does this exercise of using gold as a deflator tell us about how we can earn the most wealth as a nation? First of all, from 1973 through 2011 it tells us that there's relatively little difference between which party controls the presidency. When there is a Republican president, the average gold-adjusted total return is 7.71 percent a year, and when there is a Democratic president, the average gold-adjusted total return is 6.02 percent a year. Most important, when there is a totally unified government, we know that the dollar is going to be more debased. So from 1973 through 2011 when there was a total unified government, meaning one party controlled the House, the Senate, and the presidency, real returns during that period were −6.32 percent. When there was total gridlock, meaning a split Congress, real returns from that period totaled +11.27 percent, and when there was partial gridlock, meaning one party controlled both houses of Congress and another controlled the White House, the returns were +12.94 percent. Since 1974, in round numbers, real returns were 18 percent to 19 percent when some form of gridlocked government existed. Having said that, I am reminded how Jim Grant refers to the fiat dollar, in existence since the Nixon shock of 1971 when we went off the gold standard, as the briefest of experiments by the standards of currency longevity. And I would add that the Great Depression had a gridlocked Congress from 1930 through 1932, during which time the DJIA fell from 164.58 to 60.26 on a dividend adjusted basis, or −63.38%.

REPUBLICAN CONGRESS VS. DEMOCRATIC CONGRESS

It gets even more interesting when you look at the House and the Senate party affiliations and stock market appreciation adjusted for the price of gold. A Republican House during the same period had real returns of 9.6 percent compared to a Democratic House, which had real returns of 5.08 percent, but a Democratic Senate had real returns over this entire period of minus 3.45 percent, and a Republican Senate on a real wealth basis had average total real returns of 20.20 percent. That's an astonishing 28 percent difference in real returns between a Republican Senate and a Democratic Senate. Now, the markets that made up the bulk of these returns are obviously the markets of the mid- to late 1990s when gold was either falling or stable in value and the market was roaring and the country as a whole had a sense that it was getting very wealthy very rapidly. The opposite occurred during periods of heavy inflation such as the late 1970s where the stock market meandered but the price of gold shot up. Similar phenomena happened over the past 10 years, beginning in the year 2000, where the stock market was relatively flat or down and the price of gold shot up. At the end of that period of time, what really happened is that the great majority of Americans found that they had much less real wealth. During the buoyant 1990s, the arithmetic average for real wealth gain was almost 19 percent a year. As we entered the 1990s, gold was almost $400 per ounce, and as we exited, it was down to $290 per ounce, a decrease of almost a third (roughly 27 percent). So between the nominal increase in the stock market and the drop in the price of gold and dollars, an astonishing sense of well-being was created.

FILIBUSTER-PROOF MAJORITIES HURT RETURNS

What can we learn from what happens when the government is really big and there's no power to even launch a filibuster? Highly unified government is usually horrible for the stock market. There have been four times since the Great Depression when the president has had a completely filibuster-proof majority in Congress:

1935 through 1942

1963 through 1966

1977 through 1978

2009 through 2010 (portions)

In gross price returns, excluding dividends, the stock market compounded at an average rate of 1.9 percent during these nearly 15 unfilibusterable years, as compared to an overall average of 6.2 percent since 1933. Without a filibuster threat, Congress is more likely to get drunk on power and redistribute the hangover to us.

Since the period where U.S. citizens were allowed to own gold again, there have been two periods where the president had a nearly filibuster-proof majority to work with, as well as controlled both houses: 1977 through 1978 and 2009 through 2010. In 1977, the S&P 500 Index total return was −7.18 percent, and in 1978 it was −6.56 percent. However, gold jumped 22.6 percent in 1977, and it jumped another 37.0 percent in 1978. Taking just these two years of filibuster-proof majority and looking at their impact on the real wealth of the country, the stock market was essentially neutral and our international purchasing power was cut in half in those two years because of the nearly 60 percent increase in the price of gold over those two years. That represents a drop in real net worth of over 40 percent in just a two-year period.

In 2008, the market fell by 37 percent and the price of gold went up, so that in one year alone there was a 52.2 percent loss in purchasing power. In 2009, the stock market went up 26.45 percent, but so did the price of gold, mitigating the increase. In 2010, the stock market went up another 15 percent, but the price of gold went up even more. So even with a more than 40 percent rebound in the price of the stock market from the time that Senator Al Franken was sworn in on July 8, 2009, through the time when Senator Scott Brown was sworn in on January 8, 2010, the S&P 500

Index was up 27 percent, while the price of gold was up 24 percent for a net gain in purchasing power of 3 percent over that half-year period where the Democrats had a genuine, usable, filibuster-proof majority. It was in the waning days of that majority, during December 2009, that the health care bill was passed against much hue and cry. Taken together, although these periods represent an extremely small sample, they indicate that while the stock market may go up—and go up sharply—in nominal terms when there is an extremely unified government, the increase in the stock market valuations does not necessarily reflect an increase in the sense of well-being for the average citizen.

The obvious lesson for investors is that when you see an extremely unified, filibuster-proof government, it is best to buy inflation hedges because that government is going to spend money like there's no tomorrow. In arithmetic average terms, the stock market went up at a rate of about 3 percent per year from 2000 through 2011. Gold, however, went up an arithmetic average rate of about 17 percent per year so that the average American in arithmetic terms lost 14 percent per year in purchasing power during the whole of the past decade. The bulk of the decade had unified government, whether it was on the Republican side or on the Democrat side. On a gold-adjusted basis, during the Reagan years from 1981 through 1988, with the exception of one year, the average increase between the stock market and the reduction in the price of gold was roughly 30 percent a year, and the years during the presidency of George H. W. Bush the same robust increase in real net worth occurred, and it occurred for President Clinton as well. So we had three administrations in a row mostly identified with partial or total gridlock, with the exception of two years.

It's worth pointing out that the two years where President Clinton had an unrestrained unified government with both a Democratic Congress and a Democratic presidency were the two outlier bad years of the 1990s on a real return basis. In those two years, the price of gold went up more than the stock market, the net result being a 3 percent net decline in real net worth.

The most important conclusion is that whenever you have a super majority of one party or the other, it's likely to be time to buy gold. Similarly, whenever you have split government, it's time to be cautious about gold, particularly when you have either total split or partial split.

SUMMARY

There are multiple ways to analyze which configuration of party affiliation and government coordination is best for total returns. In the popular press, most of the time the president is linked to nominal success or failure in the stock market. However, the limited data available suggest that it is Congress that really controls the purse strings of the government (or not, as the case may be) and that party configuration in the Senate and the House may have more implications for returns. Just by using the small sample size of data since 1926, statistics show that a Republican Senate combined with Democratic presidency had the most compelling risk-adjusted nominal return, although these data are probably dominated by the bull market of the 1990s. More significant than party affiliation is whether government is unified politically.

It is a Wall Street shibboleth that split government is good for the market. This is countered by some academic literature suggesting that nominal returns and real returns adjusted for the CPI are better when there is unified government. However, when real returns are assessed using the S&P 500 Index and adjusted for the change in the price of gold, there is a compelling validation of split government as being better for real wealth creation. I believe this is attributable to the fact that split government usually but not always reduces legislative risk because divided government is less likely to pass new legislation. The big exception to this rule is when government has gone too far and divided government is unable to undo what was handed to it. This was true in 1930 when the Smoot-Hawley Tariff Act was passed, and the market fell −63.38 percent in two years.

From 1973 through 2011, when there was a total unified government, meaning one party controlled the House, the Senate, and the presidency, real returns were −6.32 percent. When there was total gridlock, meaning a split Congress, real returns from that period totaled 11.27 percent, and when there was partial gridlock, meaning one party controlled both houses of Congress and another controlled the White House, the market's real returns were 12.94 percent.

NOTE

1. Pedro Santa Clara and Rossen Valkanov, "The Presidential Puzzle: Political Cycles and the Stock Market," *Journal of Finance* 58, October 2003, 1841–1872.

CHAPTER 9

Leverging the Election Cycle

There is a lot of belief in the investment world that the third year of every presidential cycle is good for the stock market. But given that we just finished a pretty mediocre third year of a presidential cycle, and are now in a fourth year, perhaps a better starting point for thinking about the presidential cycle in general is to think about the fourth year of the presidential cycle, and how to make money from understanding the little greater context for the upcoming election. The price returns of the Dow Jones Industrial Average (DJIA) from 1928 through 2007 are shown in Table 9-1 and exclude the impact of dividends.

This is the sort of data that has sparked interest of both academics and market participants. Once again, we are at least in Super Bowl indicator territory in the sense that 20 "cycles" is not a lot of data from which to draw statistically sound conclusions. Nevertheless, there is some statistical evidence that the third year of a presidential cycle is good for investors. In their paper "Financial Astrology: Mapping the Presidential Election Cycle in the U.S. Stock Market," Wing-Keung Wong and Michael McAleer found that "there were statistically significant presidential election cycles in the U.S. stock market during the greater part of the last four decades . . . stock prices decreased by a significant amount in the second year and then increased by a statistically significant amount in the third year of the presidential election cycle."[1] Since 1960, such years have resulted in gains of 10 percent more than the average year, or about double normal returns.

The usual explanation for this pattern is that presidents push to expand the money supply in the year preceding a presidential election.

151

TABLE 9-1	Presidential Cycle—Average Nominal Price Returns
Year 1 of presidency	3.82%
Year 2 of presidency	4.71%
Year 3 of presidency	13.24%
Year 4 of presidency	7.61%

Source: Congressional Effect Management, LLC

A study published by the CFA Institute found that monetary policy was expansionary 65 percent of the time during a president's third year in office versus 48 percent for the other three years. However, as the size of government has gotten bigger while the impact of ever-larger stimulus packages has gotten relatively smaller, this "third year" effect is more recently questionable. This chapter will deal with the impact of stimuli and their political timing. Here, a very comprehensive paper in the field was also done by Beyer, Jensen, and Johnson in 2008 entitled "The Presidential Term: Is the Third Year the Charm?"[2]

In that paper they cite numerous Wall Street sources claiming that the Fed is more expansionary in the third year of the presidential cycle, with the implication that the Fed is trying to help the incumbent have a more robust economy. They found "after controlling for monetary policy, [the] party of the president is not significant in explaining equity returns."[3] They find that Year 3 of the presidential election cycle is noticeably higher in equity returns than Year 1 and Year 2. Their work completed was in 2008, and covered the period from 1957 through 2004. It shows average Year 3 returns of 23.8 percent for large caps, and 38.0 percent for small caps. They also find "fixed income returns are below average in the third year of a presidential term." They accept inflation data as reported by the CPI and find nominal and real returns following similar patterns. Similar to what we saw in an earlier chapter, it's perhaps best to think of the members of the Fed, particularly in the last 20 years, seeking to assure their reappointment by helping the incumbent present better nominal results for the economy.

THE PRESIDENTIAL CYCLE AND REAL RETURNS

Instead of using the consumer price index (CPI) as a deflator, if we use the change in price of gold in dollars as a deflator, a different picture emerges. Table 9-2 shows the gold-adjusted returns of the Standard & Poor's (S&P) 500 Index with third years beginning in 1975 and the subsequent presidential election result in the following year.

Year	Third-Year Wealth Effect	Election Result
	TABLE 9-2 Real Investment Returns and Election Results	
1975	82.44%	Incumbent lost
1979	−47.72%	Incumbent lost
1983	46.44%	Incumbent won
1987	−15.48%	Incumbent successor won
1991	42.68%	Incumbent lost
1995	36.25%	Incumbent won
1999	20.02%	Incumbent successor lost
2003	7.33%	Incumbent won
2007	−20.03%	Incumbent successor lost
2011	−6.53%	?

During the period of their study, the third year still has stunning average real returns of 24.76 percent including 2003 in the calculation. But if we include 2007 and 2011, the overall average falls to 16.27 percent. Still, this is more than the 10 percent above the average arithmetic real return of 6.08 percent in that time frame for all years. Much more concerning is the third year average of −10.96% over the last three presidential terms, and the trend: 2.48 percent in 2003, −14.37% in 2007, and −20.99 percent in 2011. This is consistent with the observation of Robert Albertson of Sandler O'Neill & Partners regarding the stimulus packages that we as a nation are now spending five times as much on stimulus to get the same dollar of growth in the economy. Put differently, as we saw earlier, the Congressional Effect has accelerated as the size of government has gotten bigger, and the ability of the government to spend us into short-term apparent prosperity is decreasing.

I think the more valuable way to investigate is simply to go with the essential question for every presidential candidate. It was best framed by President Reagan: "Are you better off now than you were four years ago?" Look at Table 9-3. Looking at the first three years of the presidential cycle, and at both nominal returns and gold-adjusted returns, it is possible to discern a pattern for presidential elections.

Some observations jump off the page here. First, after Nixon abandoned the gold standard, gold, which had been suppressed, popped like a cork in water. The result was a real decrease in gold-adjusted wealth of −60.76 percent in the first three years of that presidential cycle!

Incredibly, President Carter had greater wealth destruction credentials. In his first three years in office, real wealth as measured by S&P 500 Index total returns adjusted by the change in the price of gold fell by −69.33 percent. It must have been astonishing to investors at the time to think that

TABLE 9-3	Investment Returns Adjusted for Change in Price of Gold		
Year	**S&P TR**	**Gold Price Change**	**Gold-Adjusted Total Return**
1973	−14.66%	75.64%	−51.41%
1974	−26.47%	66.15%	−55.74%
1975	37.20%	−24.80%	82.44%
1976	23.84%	−4.10%	29.13%
1977	−7.18%	22.64%	−24.31%
1978	6.56%	37.01%	−22.23%
1979	18.44%	126.55%	−47.72%
1980	32.50%	15.19%	15.03%
1981	−4.92%	32.60%	41.07%
1982	21.55%	14.94%	5.75%
1983	22.56%	16.31%	46.44%
1984	6.27%	−19.19%	31.51%
1985	31.73%	5.76%	24.55%
1986	18.67%	18.96%	−0.24%
1987	5.25%	24.53%	−15.48%
1988	16.61%	−15.26%	37.60%
1989	31.69%	−2.84%	35.54%
1990	−3.11%	3.11%	0.00%
1991	30.47%	−8.56%	42.68%
1992	7.62%	−5.73%	14.17%
1993	10.08%	17.68%	−6.46%
1994	1.32%	−2.17%	3.57%
1995	37.58%	0.98%	36.25%
1996	22.96%	−4.59%	28.87%
1997	33.36%	−21.41%	69.69%
1998	28.58%	−0.83%	29.65%
1999	21.04%	0.85%	20.02%
2000	−9.11%	−5.44%	−3.88%
2001	−11.89%	0.75%	−12.55%
2002	−22.10%	25.57%	−37.96%
2003	28.68%	19.89%	7.33%
2004	10.88%	4.65%	5.95%
2005	4.91%	17.77%	−10.92%
2006	15.79%	23.20%	−6.01%
2007	5.49%	31.92%	−20.03%
2008	−37.00%	6.06%	−40.6%
2009	26.45%	22.98%	2.82%
2010	15.06%	29.24%	−10.93%
2011	2.11%	9.25%	−6.53%

Carter was actually worse than the combination of Ford and Nixon in the deep recession of 1974.

With President Reagan, that all changed. Like night and day. In his first three years, real wealth increased 118.46 percent. In his second term, the first three years (which included the crash of 1987 cause in large part by Congress) only showed an increase of real wealth of 5.02 percent. Still it was an increase, and it came on the heels of a spectacular first term. President George H. W. Bush presided over an economy that saw real wealth grow by 93.38 percent in his first three years, but he broke his tax pledge, Ross Perot entered the race, and he ended his fourth year with a recession that the media loudly proclaimed.

President Clinton had a very respectable 41.11 percent increase in his first three years, although all of it occurred after he was forced to work with Republican Congress. In his second term, partially for reasons discussed in the chapter on impeachment, the market returned a stunning, and in hindsight, unsustainable return of 164.04 percent. The stock market climaxed in an incredible once-in-a-lifetime bull market at a time when gold was bottoming in a 20-year sell-off. And to top it off, he poured accelerant on the fire that was brewing in the housing market. We were all rich, or at least we thought we were. There is no question a major part of his enduring popularity is the wealth effect many Americans attributed to him because he was in the "chair" in our most prosperous period.

President Bush's first term saw the 9/11 attack, and in spite of a −48.52 percent loss in real wealth, he was reelected in an election where national security issues played a significant role. In his second term, real market wealth declined by −33.04 percent and his party lost the presidency. For many people, losses in the market were offset by a run up in housing prices. From the beginning of his term at the end of 2000 housing prices almost doubled through 2007 but had an incredibly sharp sell-off in 2008. For the 50 years prior to President Bush's term, housing was always either a benign or a very benign factor creating wealth in America. The S&P/Case-Shiller Home Price Composite Index of 20 Cities, which ended 2000 at 113.05, ended 2008 at 150.51, an increase of 33.14 percent. This housing wealth effect somewhat offset the real wealth destruction of the stock market during his terms.

In President Obama's first three years, the stock market has roared on a nominal basis, up 48.56 percent in his first three full years. Adjusted for the price of gold, though, between the market and the loss of purchasing power for the dollar, real wealth as measured by and stored in the stock market has declined by 14.40 percent from the beginning of 2009 through the end of 2011. (Of course, for the vast majority of Americans whose primary asset is their house, there has been an even greater erosion of wealth.) From the

TABLE 9-4   Real Investment Returns and Election Results

Year	Third-Year Wealth Effect	Three-Year Wealth Effect	Result
1975	82.44%	−60.76%	Incumbent lost
1979	−47.72%	−69.33%	Incumbent lost
1983	46.44%	118.46%	Incumbent won
1987	15.48%	5.02%	Incumbent successor won
1991	42.68%	93.38%	Incumbent lost
1995	36.25%	41.11%	Incumbent won
1999	20.02%	164.04%	Incumbent successor lost
2003	2.48%	−48.52%	Incumbent won
2007	−14.37%	−33.04%	Incumbent successor lost
2011	−6.53%	−14.40%	?

end of 2008 through the end of 2011, the S&P Case-Shiller Composite Index declined from 150.51 to 136.60, a decline of 9.24 percent.

Table 9-4 takes another look at the third year, adding the first three years' wealth effects just from the stock market.

I think that the real wealth effects of the market help at the margin to explain some but not all of the presidential election results. To the extent the last year is very different in tenor than the first three years, it may undermine the economics associated with the president in those years. In 2000, the market rally was decidedly over, and the incumbent successor lost. In 1992, there was a recession that was vigorously reported by the mainstream media, and the incumbent lost. As noted earlier, there is not much real wealth difference in the aggregate between Republican and Democratic presidents, although there is a sharp difference between Republican and Democratic Congresses and particularly Senates.

THE 2012 ELECTION AND BEYOND

There is some statistical evidence that the third year of a presidential cycle is good for investors. The usual explanation for this pattern is that presidents push to expand the money supply in the year preceding a presidential election. A study published by the CFA Institute found that monetary policy was expansionary 65 percent of the time during a president's third year in office versus 48 percent for the other three years. They also find that fixed-income returns are below average in the third year of a presidential term. However, this indicator has not been as good over the last three presidential terms as it formerly had been.

As this book is going to press, it is unclear how the election will turn out, at least to me. It is, after all, months before the election. There seems to be a good chance that the Republicans will win the Senate. Looking at the albeit brief and therefore statistically suspect history from 1973 through 2011, it turns out that Republican Senates are much worse for gold returns, with the average arithmetic return being 0.77 percent annually, as compared to 16.94 percent for Democratic Senates. In a historically rising stock market this has compelling implications for Democrat Senate historical real returns compared to Republican Senate real returns. In fact, the Republican Senate real returns average over 18 percent annually, while Democratic Senate real returns result in a loss of over −3 percent annually. A united Congress can effectively set policy for the nation as it did with respect to welfare reform when Bill Clinton was president.

Looking at these albeit brief historical returns, the logical macro trade is to reduce your exposure to gold if the Republicans win the Senate, and increase your exposure to stocks. Conversely, if the Democrats retain control of the Senate, it would be wise to have relatively more gold in your portfolio. Of course, these are relative statements. As mentioned earlier, you can also track on intrade.com the likelihood of the Republicans or Democrats winning the Senate. Given the inability of the United States to fund its budget without deficits, I believe it is always essential to have some gold in your portfolio. Hopefully, this review will help you in asset allocation.

NOTES

1. Wing-Keung Wong and Michael McAleer, "Financial Astrology: Mapping the Presidential Election Cycle in US Stock Markets," October 2008. Available at http://ssrn.com/abstract=1307643

2. Scott B. Beyer, Gerald R. Jensen, and Robert R. Johnson, "The Presidential Term: Is the Third Year the Charm?," *Journal of Portfolio Management* 34(2), Winter 2008, 135–142, DOI: 10.3905/jpm.2008.701624.

3. Ibid.

CHAPTER 10

Are Lame Ducks, Impeachments, Resignations, Vetoes, and Litigated Elections Good for the Market?

I once had the chance to meet Congressman Bob Barr in 2008 when he was running as a Libertarian candidate for president. The occasion was Freedom Fest in Las Vegas. It was a historic first meeting between Congressman Barr and his vice presidential running mate, Wayne Allen Root. Congressman Barr had made a short speech to the crowd about how we should do everything we could for liberty. Wayne Allen Root, who has a lively, talk radio personality, stressed that there was no better place in the world for the Libertarian Party to wave its flag and to start its campaign than Las Vegas, where people were free to gamble and use legal prostitutes.

Wayne said it with a twinkle in his eye, but it was clear that Congressman Barr, a Baptist from Georgia, was a little bit ill at ease with Wayne's celebration of Las Vegas's gestalt. After all, he had been unwittingly featured in the movie *Borat* with a prank by Sacha Baron Cohen where he thought that Baron Cohen was actually from a trade delegation from a country in central Asia. Baron Cohen gave him some cheese to eat and asked if he liked it. Congressman Barr replied, "It's very tasty," with a full mouth, at which point Baron Cohen revealed the human source of the milk used to make the cheese, causing Congressman Barr to almost lose his mouthful of cheese.

Sensing the congressman was not naturally at ease in Las Vegas, I sought to engage him in conversation. After we had a chance to talk a little bit, I mentioned my work and how the stock market did better when Congress was on vacation, and that when they were impeaching President Clinton they were effectively on legislative vacation during the entire impeachment process. In fact, the stock market did well when

President Clinton was in office, and it occurred to me that he had in fact benefited from the Congressional Effect. This chapter covers the research that Congressman Barr inspired with respect to extreme moments for our body politic, which I loosely refer to as disasters, frolics, and detours, but are commonly thought of as impeachments, resignations, lame duck sessions, and vetoes. It also covers the one big litigated election we have had—and may have again.

Figure 10.1 shows a chart of how the stock market did during President Clinton's second term. I suggested to Congressman Barr that President Clinton had probably gotten an extra year to 18 months of more positive stock market action caused in significant part by the absence of a Congressional Effect, which was the primary source of the good will surrounding his legacy. I pressed on, "It is ironic that in all likelihood you probably did more than almost anyone else to help President Clinton have such a positive image today for his legacy." At that point, Congressman Barr looked at me and gave me the same look that he had in the movie *Borat* when he had been informed about the cheese. Fortunately, Congressman Barr had nothing in his mouth.

I recognized from our conversation that it was worth going back and having a closer look at the timeline for the impeachment process and seeing if there was a link with the other work I had done on the Congressional Effect. There was. This chapter reviews the unusual moments of politics where the leadership is in flux because of either elections or out-of-the-ordinary transitions.

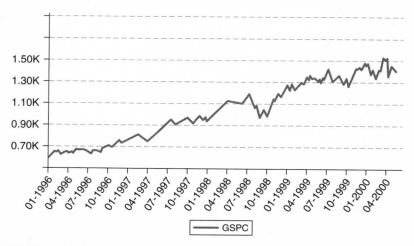

FIGURE 10.1 S&P 500 Index, 1996–2000. Source: Yahoo! Finance

PRESIDENT BILL CLINTON

At first glance, it would seem that the impeachment of a sitting president would always be bad for our country and therefore bad for the stock market. I am sure that was the political calculation that Congressman Barr and the Republicans in general made when they started the process. However, in the case of President Clinton, a close look at the actual performance of the stock market shows that, if anything, the market benefited from, shall we say, benign neglect.

The late 1990s were the most vibrant stock market we have ever had. As we saw in Chapter 9, not only did the market go up in great back-to-back-to-back annual rallies, but the price of gold fell by almost 30 percent, making travel and foreign goods tremendously affordable. We were rich, and we thought we knew it and we loved it. The tech boom was at its peak, and a new age was upon us. From a policy point of view, a Republican Congress had in 1996 forced the president to reluctantly adopt welfare reform, and the budget was, as scored by the Congressional Budget Office (CBO), mostly in balance. It is worth noting that we were still expanding our internal borrowings—during the course of the Clinton presidency, an additional $1.6 trillion in debt was added to the outstanding $4.0 trillion at the end of the presidency of George H. W. Bush, but the total debt of the United States was relatively constant as a percentage of the gross domestic product (GDP).

In 1997, the Taxpayer Relief Act of 1997 was passed. This act lowered the top capital gains tax rate from 28 percent to 20 percent, and the 20 percent bracket for certain capital gains was lowered from 20 percent to 15 percent. Most important, the first $500,000 of gains on the sale of a house owned by a couple was excluded from capital gains. Many people began to think of buying and fixing a house for resale as their main job. The housing market started to be much more vigorous, mortgage rates were declining, and the stock market was booming.

It was in this general environment that the impeachment news hit and probably had the opposite effect of that intended by the Republicans. While the conservative pundits were outraged, each new revelation regarding President Clinton paralleled stock market rallies for the most part. While there had been rumors of sexual peccadilloes concerning President Clinton for years, the first time that there was hard news that really seemed to break unprecedented ground was the Drudge Report on January 19, 1998, citing Monica Lewinsky as having an affair with the president. The market rallied 1.8 percent on that news.

During the remainder of January and into February there was a lot of back and forth regarding the sexual relationships that President Clinton may or may not have had, whether he would be called to testify in the Paula Jones lawsuit, and whether the independent counsel, Kenneth Starr, would be expanding his investigation of Whitewater into the allegations of sexual misconduct. By February 6, 1998, President Clinton had a news conference at which he said, "I would never walk away from the people of this country and the trust they've placed in me." The market rallied 0.9 percent that day. By the middle of March, the regular TV news outlets were beginning to focus on the story and there was a *60 Minutes* episode in which Kathleen Willey accused the president of sexual misconduct. On the day after the *60 Minutes* episode, President Clinton said nothing improper happened, and the stock market rallied 1 percent.

On April 30, 1998, in the first news conference after the Lewinsky story had broken, the president answered many questions and accused independent counsel Kenneth Starr of working hard to undermine the presidency. On that day, the stock market rallied another 1.6 percent. On July 25, 1998, Starr served the president with a subpoena, asking the president to appear in front of a grand jury regarding Monica Lewinsky. The stock market rallied a half percent. On July 30, 1998, the blue dress, the physical evidence, emerged into public awareness, and the stock market fell 1.5 percent. On August 17, 1998, the president, having once said that he "did not have sexual relations with that woman," admitted that he had had an inappropriate relationship with Monica Lewinsky. The stock market rallied almost 2 percent.

Finally, on September 24, 1998, the House Judiciary Committee began consideration of impeachment against President Bill Clinton in an open session. On October 8, when a formal vote was cast to authorize an impeachment inquiry of the president, the stock market fell 1.1 percent. On November 19, in a very long session, independent counsel Ken Starr brought his case against Bill Clinton to the House Judiciary Committee. The stock market rallied a half percent. Finally, on February 12, 1999, after a long impeachment process, the Senate failed to convict the president. The stock market fell that day by 2 percent. All in all, from the beginning of the news story's breaking in January 1998 to the president's acquittal in February 1999, the S&P 500 Index rallied over 28 percent, a stunning performance in a 13-month period. There were virtually no new legislative initiatives in 1998, and the 1998 congressional elections had national voter turnout that was the lowest since World War II. Voters just did not care.

I believe in response to the impeachment process, President Clinton came up with a plan to work hard to make the economy improve even further. The plan was brilliant in its simplicity. At that time, the number of U.S. Treasury bonds held by foreigners was declining, and a decision was made to stop using the 30-year Treasury bond as the anchor bond of the U.S. bond portfolio offering. This in turn made it so that there was a buying panic among institutions who needed nominally 30-year paper, which was filled largely with the 30-year mortgages issued by Fannie Mae and Freddie Mac. Excess institutional demand for these mortgages drove mortgage rates down. Lower long-term mortgage rates coupled with the 1997 change in tax treatment for residences created a combination of more favorable tax treatment and more favorable financing that in turn set off a secondary buying panic in real estate.

This buying panic got more seriously under way as the 30-year bond disappeared, and was in full force by the beginning of 2001 when President Clinton left office. With these two changes, housing prices, which had been rising 2 percent per year at the beginning of 1997, were rising 4 to 5 percent at the end of President Clinton's second term, and from 2000 to 2004 accelerated in their increase so that by the end of 2004 housing prices were rising at over 12 percent per year, creating a buying panic from the low-priced mortgages and the more favorable tax treatment. Figure 10.2 shows mortgage rates from 1995 through 2001.

By the time President Clinton left office, the average American felt materially wealthier. Their stock market holdings had gained in value even if there was a sell-off beginning in 1999 (Figure 10.3). The price of gold was down (Figure 10.4), the dollar was strong, and their homes were worth more (Figure 10.5).

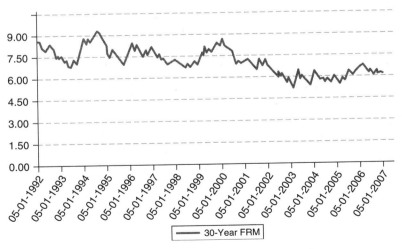

FIGURE 10.2 Mortgage Rates, 1996–2007. Source: Yahoo! Finance

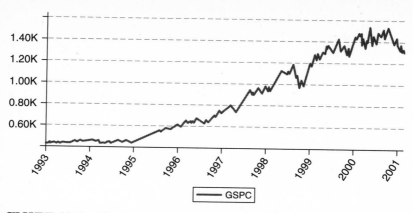

FIGURE 10.3   S&P 500 Index, 1992–2000. Source: Yahoo! Finance

In hindsight, a less overheated stock market and housing market would have spared us all a lot of pain. Intervention is always steroidal. Major League Baseball has made the determination that steroids are not worth using even if records are broken. Congress, which spent a great deal of time investigating Roger Clemens in 2009, seems to agree. But if Congress can indict Roger Clemens for using steroids, the government should not turbocharge any other markets. Enormous booms are almost always followed by enormous busts. Obviously, the data sample here is extremely small, as there are just two impeachments of a president during

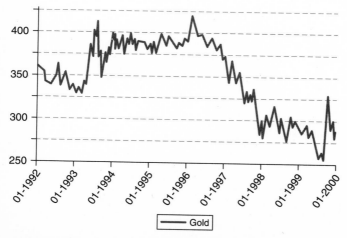

FIGURE 10.4   Gold Prices, 1992–2000. Source: Kitco

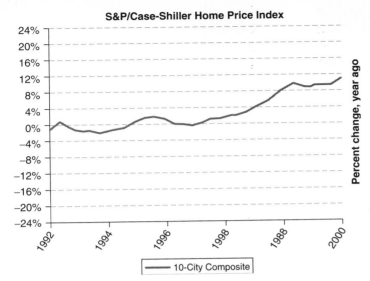

FIGURE 10.5 S&P/Case-Shiller Home Price Index, 1992–2000.
Source: Standard & Poor's

the course of the American experiment in the past 200 years. Perhaps the most confirming piece of data regarding the benefits of impeachment is that after five years of fabulous insider trading, Ziobrowski and his fellow researchers found in 1998 that the congressmen who had been world-beating traders from 1993 through 1997 were simply average in 1998.[1] Five hundred thirty-five congressmen without a meaningful legislative agenda could no longer beat the market on average by 10 percent, and in fact they were quite ordinary that year. Without any legislation to shoot at, a congressman didn't have the same informational advantage and didn't have the same set of favors to trade in exchange for information.

PRESIDENT ANDREW JOHNSON

President Clinton's impeachment was actually the second one of a sitting president. The first was President Johnson, the 17th president of the United States, in 1868. He had been the only southern senator to stay in office in the Union during the Civil War, and when he rose to the presidency after the assassination of President Lincoln, he was at odds with the radical Republicans who imposed Reconstruction on the South. During the 1866 elections, the Republicans got veto-proof majorities in both houses of Congress, and they passed civil rights legislation. They also took back control of Reconstruction and limited the number of representatives and senators from the South who could be seated in Congress. To obstruct the radical Republicans or to frustrate the Republicans, Johnson used his command of the military as president. Unfortunately for Johnson, the Secretary of War, Edwin Stanton, was a very powerful and committed radical Republican who was also committed to Reconstruction.

In 1867, Congress passed the Tenure of Office Act to make sure that Secretary Stanton would stay in office and thereby keep the Reconstruction process in force through the military districts that had been set up in the Confederacy. The Tenure of Office Act allowed the president to suspend officials when Congress was out of session, and Johnson suspended Stanton without his formal resignation on August 15, 1867. Thereafter, he instead appointed Ulysses S. Grant as the commanding General of the Army and the Secretary of War. By the fall of 1867, there was talk of impeachment. Meanwhile, Secretary Stanton, who had been suspended, had never recognized the president's power to dismiss him, and when General Grant resigned, Secretary Stanton refused to vacate his office to the successor appointed by President Johnson. Things came to a head on February 24, 1868, when the House of Representatives voted 106 to 47 to impeach the president of high crimes and misdemeanors. The trial of President Andrew Johnson started on March 13, 1868, and ended on April 9. On all three Senate votes taken over the course of the impeachment process 35 senators voted guilty and 19 voted not guilty. Since a two-thirds majority was required to impeach, he was not convicted and he served out his term. One point worth noting is that there is some evidence that the impeachment process was derailed by bookmakers, who had a vested interest in the impeachment's failing.

During this entire impeachment process, Congress was preoccupied with its own internal power struggle, and while we do not have daily data for that period, there was a rise in the market that started in June 1867 and was widely reported to have continued with very little volatility and just generally rising from June 1867 through 1872. Perhaps it was because in those days the congressional politics itself played a much smaller role in the economy of the country, but it's clear that the impeachment process did not adversely affect a bull market that was under way. Whether impeachments fail because the bookmakers enjoy betting against them or because good economies make for unsuccessful impeachments, the fact remains that in noncrisis times, impeachment prevents Congress from undertaking much legislative initiative, and therefore generally contributes to a better stock market.

RESIGNATIONS

The title of this small section is resignations, although there has been in fact only one resignation, that of President Richard Nixon. In 1974, President Nixon was undone by the Watergate scandal. The House Judiciary Committee charged him with "high crimes and misdemeanors" in anticipation of impeaching him. On August 8, 1974, he resigned. It is clear in hindsight that his resignation, coming in the middle of a deep recession, aggravated market uncertainty. From the date he resigned through the end of 1974, the Dow Jones Industrial Average (DJIA) fell another 24.6 percent, even adjusting for dividends. While President Nixon was not formally impeached, there was little doubt he was going to be impeached—and probably convicted—if he had not resigned. His resignation came during the worst recession at that time since the Great Depression.

Having pointed out that impeachments can be good for the market and resignations can be bad, I think the bigger message is that the government tends to act as an amplifier of the economy even though it is trying to be a counterweight. In good times, impeachment can help the market and therefore the economy. In bad times, dysfunctional government makes the economy worse. Resignations to head off an impeachment fall under that category.

LAME DUCK SESSIONS

By now the reader should suspect that the concept of the Congressional Effect is that less government is generally better for the market. So out-of-session days are historically better because there is less risk of government action. In each election cycle, there is a period after the new Congress has been elected, but the old one is still in session. That period, commonly referred to as the lame duck session of Congress, is a particularly good time to invest. Very little major legislation is likely to get done during these sessions because the members who are returning want any new laws to be attributable to their next term. You might as well call it vacation. Not surprisingly, then, the lame duck returns of the market are several times the average return of the market. On an annualized basis, using the DJIA, since 1928 the market has returned an arithmetic average annualized gain of 19.48 percent during this little less than two-month period. No doubt, part of the return may be accounted for by year-end efforts to mark up stocks, but it is a statistical outlier for another two months out of every four years to be so much higher than the market average.

In general, when there is a new president, the lame duck period averages an annualized 16.47 percent, while the same president reelected averages 20.82 percent. The market likes the lack of surprise, although this is not a very big difference. This is confirmed by the fact that when the political party of the president does not change, the lame duck period on average does even better, averaging a 23.28 percent annualized return. However, when the party of the president changes, the lame duck session annualized average return is 5.54 percent, in line with an average day in market, although still better than an average in-session day.

This same pattern is repeated in the Senate. When the Senate stays in the hands of the same party, the average lame duck annualized price return is 21.94 percent. However, if the Senate changes hands, the return is 12.55 percent—still on vacation but not as much. There is no meaningful difference is this sample between the average for the House staying the same or changing.

Table 10-1 shows lame duck periods going back to 1928. As you can see from the table, for our recent presidents, the lame duck session in loss of an annualized −44.63 percent in 2008 was exceeded only by the lame duck session of 1930, and was exactly tied (to the second decimal place) with the lame duck session of 1974, which took place after President Nixon resigned, and was not the result of a four-year election cycle. The sample size on these data is small so it has to be taken with a large grain of salt, but it is helpful for thinking about the markets. It is worth noting that some presidents commonly associated with robust markets, like Presidents Reagan and Clinton, had at least one poor lame duck session.

LITIGATED ELECTIONS

Like resignations and modern-day impeachments, there is only one recent example of a litigated election, although there have been several close calls. In 1960, President Kennedy had 10 states where the margin of victory was less than 10,000 votes, including Illinois and Texas. In the aftermath of that close election, using former President Hoover as an intermediary, a meeting was arranged between Vice President Nixon and President-elect Kennedy. Nixon was offered the chance to play a prominent role in the Kennedy Administration, but he declined. After that meeting, it was clear that Nixon would not contest the election. In subsequent years, he would describe himself as "at peace" with the decision not to contest it. As can be seen from Table 10-1, in the lame duck session of 1960, the stock market rose at an annualized rate of 23.03 percent, slightly better than the historical average of those periods.

TABLE 10-1 Annualized Returns and Lame Duck Sessions

Year	Annualized Return	President Changes	Party of President Changes	House Changes	Senate Changes
1928	175.03%	Change	Same	Same	Same
1930	−53.35%	Same	Same	Change	Same
1932	−37.92%	Change	Change	Same	Change
1934	69.82%	Same	Same	Same	Same
1936	12.08%	Same	Same	Same	Same
1938	−2.42%	Same	Same	Same	Same
1940	−18.10%	Same	Same	Same	Same
1942	28.89%	Same	Same	Same	Same
1944	19.82%	Change	Same	Same	Same
1946	10.94%	Same	Same	Change	Change
1948	−34.31%	Same	Same	Change	Change
1950	46.36%	Same	Same	Same	Same
1952	63.88%	Change	Change	Change	Change
1954	127.96%	Same	Same	Change	Change
1956	5.62%	Same	Same	Same	Same
1958	54.78%	Same	Same	Same	Same
1960	23.03%	Change	Change	Same	Same
1962	54.91%	Same	Same	Same	Same
1964	−0.99%	Same	Same	Same	Same
1966	−13.36%	Same	Same	Same	Same
1968	−1.70%	Change	Change	Same	Same
1970	74.24%	Same	Same	Same	Same
1972	26.81%	Same	Same	Same	Same
1974	−44.63%	Change	Same	Same	Same
1976	27.39%	Change	Change	Same	Same
1978	4.25%	Same	Same	Same	Same
1980	19.78%	Change	Change	Same	Change
1982	15.76%	Same	Same	Same	Same
1984	−16.15%	Same	Same	Same	Same
1986	1.19%	Same	Same	Same	Change
1988	14.08%	Change	Same	Same	Same
1990	46.99%	Same	Same	Same	Same
1992	9.79%	Change	Change	Same	Same
1994	0.67%	Same	Same	Change	Change
1996	46.52%	Same	Same	Same	Same
1998	39.72%	Same	Same	Same	Same
2000	−9.77%	Change	Change	Same	Change
2002	−22.73%	Same	Same	Same	Change
2004	55.94%	Same	Same	Same	Same
2006	18.32%	Same	Same	Change	Change
2008	−44.63%	Change	Change	Same	Same
2010	23.53%	Same	Same	Change	Same

Source: Congressional Effect Management, LLC

The only actually litigated election was the Bush/Gore election of 2000. In the event the state of Florida was subject to an election recount and numerous legal appeals to Florida courts, federal courts, and ultimately the United States Supreme Court. Because an election had never been litigated before, there was a great deal of uncertainty surrounding what the final outcome would be. From the date of the election, November 7, 2000, until the date that the Supreme Court made an administrative ruling indicating it was moving to take control of the case on December 4, the DJIA fell at an annualized rate of 25.63 percent. If the total market capitalization of all U.S. companies was $15 trillion, as estimated by the World Bank at the end of 2000, the unrealized loss in the market was $540 billion. How much of that was attributable to the decision to contest the election? $50 billion? $100 billion? Again, as was the case with MasterCard and Visa, a reasonable directional answer is "some," whether 10 percent, or 20 percent, or half. In fact, after the Supreme Court decided the election, the market did rally a little but still wound up losing value at a 9.77 percent annualized rate, almost 30 percent below the annualized performance typically associated with lame duck sessions.

VETOES

Going back to 1965, there have been exactly 200 vetoes of congressional legislation by the president that were not pocket vetoes. Of the vetoes requiring an active decision to sustain or override a veto, 97 were unchallenged, meaning that the proposed law was rejected by the president. Seventy-three vetoes were sustained, again resulting in the law's being rejected. Thirty were overturned, with the legislation failing. The market reaction to these vetoes is consistent with the Congressional Effect. You can think of the vetoes as individual moments of gridlock or filibuster-proof majorities. On an average day, the Standard & Poor's (S&P) 500 Index has gone up in price by about 2 basis points since 1965. Using the market reaction on the day of the veto, it turns out that for the days when a veto is unchallenged, the market on average goes down 9 basis points. An unchallenged veto has the appearance of political posturing, and the public probably views Congress as grandstanding when they pass legislation and then do not try to override a veto. When a veto is sustained, the market rallies, albeit slightly. On average, the S&P 500 Index rose 13 basis points on the 73 days a veto was sustained since 1965. This is the version that is similar to a gridlocked Congress. Finally, on the 30 successful veto overrides, the market went up 3 points on average, probably largely reflecting that the news on any highly popular legislation (which is what veto-proof legislation tends to be) was already widely discounted.

SUMMARY

What common theme is there to these disparate instances of government grinding to a halt? It is that whenever the government is preoccupied with itself, it is better for the market, and therefore for the private economy.

All in all, looking back, President Clinton's impeachment successfully distracted Congress during a period in which the highest and best use of Congress was to have it be distracted. It enabled President Clinton to focus on how to make the economy accelerate even faster, to which he contributed by promoting the housing industry. The unintended consequence of his impeachment was to contribute to an extra year or so of the 1990s' bull market run. This bull market took the average investor experience from simply being a good one in the stock market to being a once-in-a-lifetime run in the stock market.

I believe what the extremely limited data show is that impeachment, in a good economy, can, as counterintuitive as it seems, be good for the stock market, and that in a bad economy, it can be bad for the stock market.

Of much greater concern to me as a practical matter is that litigated elections clearly are bad for the market, and there is a good chance that in the next several election cycles we will see more litigated elections affecting both the presidency and the composition of Congress.

Unlike impeachments or litigated elections or resignations, lame duck sessions and vetoes are a more regular part of the fabric of governing. Lame duck sessions, which usually amount to paid vacations for our congressmen, have a lot of evidence of being as benign as out-of-session days for Congress.

NOTE

1. Alan J. Ziobrowski, Ping Cheng, James W. Boyd, and Brigitte Ziobrowski, "Abnormal Returns from the Common Stock Investments of the U.S. Senate," *Journal of Financial and Quantitative Analysis* 39(4), December 2004.

CHAPTER 11

More Ways to Dodge Congress's Stray Bullets

As discussed in Chapter 7, the Congressional Effect approach offers a systematic, tactical approach to reducing legislative risk. It involves consistently avoiding the times when Congress is most likely to create headline risk for your portfolio. The core of this risk is that Congress is relentlessly incented to act with an extremely short-term bias. To the extent that Congress aggravates the short-term volatility of the market, the goal of advisers seeking to reduce legislative risk for a portfolio is to use strategies that have genuinely long time horizons. The Congressional Effect approach of avoiding market risk when Congress is in session is executed daily, but it is actually based on long-term data and is best used in a long-term consistent approach.

The key to minimizing legislative risk is first to identify it and appreciate its significance, and then to choose strategies that minimize that risk. Most strategies that help to reduce this risk effectively are long-term strategies that are good strategies in their own right.

To avoid some of Wall Street's natural short-term bias, the investment styles of value investing, resource investing, and international investing all have elements that when applied with long time horizons can reduce the short-term risks created by Congress and reduce investment correlation with the broad equity market. We examine each of these in this chapter.

VALUE FUNDS: LONGER TIME HORIZONS THAN CONGRESS OR THE SOMALI PIRATES

We saw in Chapter 4 that Congress and the Somali pirates both have very short time frames for their business cycle planning. True value investing has a long time horizon, or perhaps more accurately, is time indifferent. Value investing probably has the purest approach to time of all the investment styles. Ben Graham and David Dodd, the fathers of value investing, said investors should "look for values with a significant margin of safety relative to prices." Ben Graham also famously said in his book *Securities Analysis*, "In the short term the stock market is a voting machine, but in the long term it is a weighing machine."[1] I think the best way to explain what he meant is that in the short term, a stock might be very popular or unpopular and not objectively valued, but in the long term, at its moment of truth, it would be mechanically, and therefore accurately, weighed or valued. That is to say, it would have an objectively undeniable value. A good example of an undeniable objective value is an acquisition price. He was relatively indifferent to the time frame of realizing value as long as he knew he had purchased a company for half or less than its fair value as an ongoing business. He did not know when his purchase would pay off, but he knew it eventually would. He focused on metrics for buying companies for their overall value as private entities and purchasing their stocks only if they were trading at significant discounts to their fair enterprise values.

There have been many disciples of Ben Graham, and as a crude generalization, over long periods of time they generally have outperformed other styles in most markets, with the exception being highly frothy markets like the late 1990s. Because value investing emphasizes the long-term view, it should, in theory at least, provide investors with a discipline that carries them past the short-term biases of both Congress and the gremlins of behavioral finance discussed in Chapter 4. Warren Buffett, the only student in Graham's investment seminar to earn an A+, made billions of dollars by methodically and rationally implementing the tenets of Graham and Dodd's book.

Another one of the foremost practitioners of value investing is Jean-Marie Eveillard, who was a portfolio manager with the First Eagle Family of Funds for many years and still serves as a senior adviser. Contrary to most advisers who are concerned about career risk, he identified a particular risk of the investment community which is finance professionals managing other people's money to reduce career risk as opposed to reducing investment risk. The first rule of not being fired is to "do what everyone else is doing." If you are in the herd, you will at least be able to say you preserved your clients' relative purchasing power but if you are taking too much risk for average returns, you are not serving your client well. That is why, as we know from Chapter 5 and the discussion of behavioral finance, "groupthink" can be very dangerous. (Just look at what happened in 2008.) So Mr. Eveillard prides himself on an approach that at times may have been painful for his clients, but advantageous for shareholders focused on overall long-term returns. He states his investment philosophy simply; "I would rather lose half my clients than half my clients' money."[2] The consistent emphasis of First Eagle Family of Funds is an authentic commitment to the long term. As a portfolio manager at First Eagle Investment Management put it when asked about investing in the United States:

> *It's a matter of price. Investors spend a lot of time on these macro issues, and it's scary. The fiscal situation is certainly poor, but that creates opportunities for value investors like us. We [attempt] to thrive when there's a lot of uncertainty, which creates volatility. The value of a business is a function of the cash flows generated over its entire life, not over the next year or two. With Wall Street focused on the next three to six months that [may create] an arbitrage opportunity for ... long-term investors.*[3]

Robert Kleinschmidt, managing director of the Tocqueville Fund (TOCQX) calls himself a contrarian investor, within a framework of having an overall value orientation as well. "The analysts look at this information in real time, deciphering which news actually affects the fundamental value and what is just noise." One way to think of the Congressional Effect is that Congress systematically creates noise that obscures the value of portfolio companies. But sometimes that noise can be deafening. *Forbes* magazine asked Kleinschmidt what lessons he learned in 2008 and 2009 from owning Fannie Mae and Freddie Mac after they were nationalized. He commented:

> *So what I learned is that the power of bad government policy to do great damage to asset values is something that I had historically underestimated. And that I had to pay more attention to what was going on politically—not on a case by case, stock by stock basis, but just in terms of the general, overall investor perception or investor environment. And I think that was a very painful lesson to learn. But it's a lesson that we need to pay attention to today.*[4]

One key to this fund's very successful performance appears to be the willingness of the portfolio manager, Kleinschmidt, to admit error and make adjustments accordingly. This fund has significantly outperformed both its category and the Standard & Poor's (S&P) 500 Index since 2002—$10,000 invested in 2002 would have compounded into $17,690.42 by the end of 2011 as compared with $14,522.94 for the S&P 500 Index.

Sometimes, as we have seen earlier, you can use awareness of Congressional Effect to invest in industries where their stocks have overreacted to the damage created by Congress, and this is how the Congressional Effect can be integrated into a value approach. The Fairholme Fund (FAIRX), run by Bruce Berkowitz, is an outstanding example of an extremely well run value approach that looks for companies with "fixable problems" [5] and has had some of its biggest successes by buying stocks and industries that had their biggest sell-off attributable in part to the Congressional Effect and waited for it to dissipate. For example, when the market was most discounting the Congressional Effect of health care reform at the end of 2008 and the beginning of 2009, Fairholme committed disproportionately to the health care industry and tremendously outperformed. Recently, the fund reduced its health care position and invested more heavily in financials, in part because Berkowitz felt that the market was discounting the impact of financial regulation too heavily and that bank values were greater than their stock prices. In hindsight, he acknowledges that he probably made that switch too early, but he believes he is very well positioned for the future. Asked about the pain of 2011, he recently said "[j]ust because you are right does not mean you are going to be immediately right, and the value investor suffers from being a bit early, and we shall see. If it is anything like a replay of the 1990s it will be quite good." [6]

The Turquoise Fund (TURQX) is also a good example of a value manager looking beyond the short-term impact of congressional action, and waiting for the value of the long-term franchise to reemerge. After the Durbin amendment to Dodd-Frank, Visa was devastated. As we saw earlier, both Visa and MasterCard fell roughly 15 percent in the week or so following the first announcement of regulations under the Durbin amendment in December 2010. However, Cohen looked at Visa as having a worldwide franchise in over 160 countries. He was not very bothered by new regulations in one country. Using a discounted cash flow model, he determined that Visa has a value today of over $200 per share and he committed heavily to Visa. The Turquoise Fund bought Visa at prices in the $72- to $77-per-share range after the Durbin Amendment was announced. As of April 2012, Visa was as high as $123 per share.

GOLD FUNDS: AVOIDING CONGRESSIONAL DEBASEMENT

As central banks get bigger and place more strain on the public balance sheets of their countries, it is essential to have some gold. The question is, how much? Jean-Marie Eveillard compares owning gold to having insurance. It protects you from outlier events. A different way to say it is that you hope the gold you own does not appreciate or depreciate very much. If that is the case, then you are likely to be living in normal times, where the rest of your portfolio can do its job of preserving your purchasing power.

One way to have exposure to gold is to own a mutual fund focused on gold and gold related investments. Many of the funds in the First Eagle Family of Funds have historically had some exposure to gold. When a portfolio manager at First Eagle was asked to comment about gold's price, the portfolio manager responded:

We have no view on the future direction of the price of gold. Gold ETFs, such as GLD (GLD), have risen [in price recently]. GLD may be the fifth-largest holder of gold in the world, after the central banks of the world. So people from the ground up have chosen to put some of their reserves in gold as a hedge against the currency. To me, it doesn't feel like speculation like in the late 1990s with Internet stocks, or the credit bubble. This seems to be rational behavior. Whether we're ahead of ourselves temporarily or not, I have no clue. What we've said ... is [many investor should consider keeping a portion] of [their] assets in gold, just in case.[7]

Another fund worth considering is the Permanent Portfolio (PRPFX). At all times, the fund has a strict formula of asset exposure including 20 percent in gold, 5 percent in silver, 35 percent in Treasuries, 10 percent in Swiss franc assets, 15 percent in U.S. stocks, and 15 percent in real estate stocks. It has been included in this section because it must explicitly have gold in the fund. The purpose of this fund is to help investors fight inflation. Over the past 10 years ended December 31, 2011, $10,000 invested in this fund would have grown to $28,250 as compared to $12,017 for the S&P 500 Index. A by-product of fighting inflation is that the Congressional Effect is reduced. The Swiss franc asset exposure has no congressional input, and the Swiss constitution, which requires a balanced budget more stringently than ours does, is helpful for limiting government damage. Michael Cuggino, who joined the fund in 1991, has been managing the fund with this adherence to his highly disciplined approach since he took over from the founder, Terry Coxon, in 1995. The goal of the Permanent Portfolio is that it always has some portion of its assets that protect against inflation and debasement of the dollar.

The Tocqueville Fund is another gold-oriented fund that has achieved good long-term results. Its manager, John Hathaway, has been with the fund since 1997. His 2012 outlook for gold and gold-mining companies includes this passage:

> *We are bullish on the price of gold and the appreciation potential of mining companies. Given the increasing appetite for gold, we believe that the price may top $2,000 per ounce in 2012. Mining companies may also fare well. Investors are returning to the equity markets and are often looking for opportunities that have the potential to outperform the market as defined by the S&P 500 Index with lower overall correlation. Gold mining equities should accomplish that objective.*[8]

Funds that have the underlying physical asset of precious metal, like the Sprott Physical Silver Trust (PSLV) or the Central Fund of Canada (CEF), are also good ways to own gold and silver.

The election of 2012 poses some very major cross-currents for gold. As we saw in Chapter 9, there is some statistical evidence that Democratic Congresses, and particularly Senates, tend to be better for gold appreciation. In fact, a disproportionate amount of the price gain in gold has historically fallen on days Congress is in session. While a Republican Congress might initially be less relatively bullish, this time there is a chance that the laws will change, favoring gold and most other commodities. In the New Deal, to prevent speculation in commodities in general and gold in particular, mutual funds were assessed a second layer of tax at the 35 percent corporate rate if more than 10 percent of their profits came from gains in commodities including gold. This rule makes it very difficult for most funds to commit to gold or other commodities now because it is hard to predict which part of your portfolio will result in 10 percent of your realized gains.

As I have said consistently throughout this book, I believe that the government has set into motion both massive deflationary and massive inflationary forces that may overwhelm the natural forces of the economy. If I had to pick today which force will prevail, I'd pick inflation. It is important to note that gold is a store of value in crisis, not just in inflation. In a deflationary environment, unleveraged gold can still act as a superior store of value because it does not require a counterparty to redeem it. To the extent a deflationary crisis happens, it will be recognized to have happened because of government interference in the markets, and the demand for a store of value unaffected by government action is likely to remain a significant source of demand for gold. In fact, gold is being considered by central bankers as an asset that qualifies as a reserve asset for banks, which would be a very bullish development if it happens.

There is one other very important consideration regarding the demand for gold. In the long run, if more countries decide to simply reduce their exposure to the dollar by doing more trading and barter in non-dollar-denominated transactions, it will be good for gold and bad for the dollar. For example, in the winter of 2012, both China and India were rumored to be purchasing oil from Iran with gold, circumventing the sanctions placed on Iran by the West. While the terms are not disclosed, it is clear that bilateral arrangements like this provide a floor on the demand for gold.

So where does that put us with respect to gold as the fall 2012 elections approach? If the Democrats keep control of the Senate, it will likely be good for gold because there been no budget discipline in the Senate in the past three years. If the Republicans win Congress and the presidency, I think there is a good chance that this law will be revisited on a bipartisan basis to allow investors to participate in commodities through their mutual funds. Congressman Rangel (D) was apparently willing to visit this subject last year, and he is a good barometer of potential bipartisan sentiment. The United States is holding enormous gold reserves, and financial repression has the apparently intended consequence of driving investors into the stock market in the absence of yields. A tax policy that created an additional class of buyers for commodities and gold would help the government tilt the playing field toward inflation, which is what it appears it wants to do because that would be a way to default on our debt without formally defaulting. If this double taxation is reduced, it would be enormously bullish for gold on a long-term basis because it would effectively add another $10 trillion of new potential buyers of gold into the market. If 2 percent decided to convert their holdings into gold, it could create several hundred billion dollars of additional demand for gold. By way of comparison, the largest exchange-traded fund (ETF) for gold, GLD, recently had a market capitalization of $70 billion. In short, a change of policy on this issue would probably result in a sharply higher price for gold.

BEYOND CONGRESS: INTERNATIONAL FUNDS

The investor who sees the impact of the Congressional Effect should also be wary of investing in international funds with holdings in countries whose government plays an even larger role in the economy than the United States, or where the government's role is growing on a relative basis compared to other countries. Here is a list of the 2012 top 10 economically free countries from the Heritage Foundation:

1. Hong Kong
2. Singapore
3. Australia
4. New Zealand
5. Switzerland
6. Canada
7. Chile
8. Mauritius
9. Ireland
10. United States

Since the Heritage Foundation created this index in 1995, the United States has dropped from 4th to 10th place, now surpassed by Hong Kong, Singapore, Australia, New Zealand, Switzerland, Canada, Chile, Mauritius, and Ireland. It is no accident that countries with more freedom tend to do better on the acceptance of their credit in the market. In September 2011, for example, the BlackRock Sovereign Risk Index ranked 13 countries ahead of the United States in the quality of their sovereign risk. It is no coincidence that during this period the United States fell from AAA to AA+ with Standard & Poor's.

It is worth noting that some of the countries on this list, like Canada and Chile, have rising credit ratings as they have reduced the relative size of their government, expanded their trading relationships, and increased their relative freedom. Chile, which is now rated A+ by Standard & Poor's, has been put on credit watch for an upgrade to AA, in part because its citizens have reinvested so much productive capital through their terrific approach to privatized Social Security. In fact, the average Chilean, relative to their fixed costs, is in fact wealthier than the average American. This is evidenced by the average house cost and their savings rate—they are able to save a much higher proportion of their income. Canada, which was AA+ in 2000 and upgraded to AAA in 2002, has seen its stock market sharply outperform the United States since 2000 (see Figure 11.1).

Canada has an economy very similar to the United States, but with a totally market-driven mortgage and housing market, they have experienced less housing volatility than we have. When coupled with their greater exposure to natural resources and the fact that they spend only 10 percent of their gross domestic product (GDP) on health care while we spend

FIGURE 11.1 S&P 500 Index vs. TSE Index, 2000–2011. Source: Yahoo! Finance

16 percent (in part because they get to take advantage of our health care research and development at wholesale prices), they have been sharply outpacing the United States in wealth creation since 2000. The Congressional Effect approach to investing internationally would be to choose markets where freedom is rising, and overweight these markets. That is to say, see where government is likely to play a *smaller* role in the national economy over time. Canada and Chile are good examples of this effect.

REDUCING GLOBAL SECURITY RISK

One remaining fund worth mentioning in conjunction with the Congressional Effect has its own unique approach that can be used to either reduce risk attributable to governments or attacks on government. The Patriot Fund (TRFAX), managed by Mark Langerman and Paul Wigdor, has a strategy aimed at reducing global security risk. They identify 33 companies out of the S&P 500 Index, plus hundreds of additional publicly traded companies that do business with nations and institutions that are on the U.S. State Department's list of "State Sponsors of Terror." Beyond just a moral and patriotic stance against funding terror, they believe investing in these corporations makes a portfolio unnecessarily vulnerable to instability and political changes abroad. This undoubtedly increases risk and unpredictability in the world market, potentially damaging your portfolio's value. Just like many public entities have ceased the funding of those who support terrorist organizations, this fund offers a means for the individual to divest his portfolio of terror-supporting agencies.

One corollary of the Congressional Effect approach is that risk is increased for an investor when a company invests in a business plan that is unsustainable in the absence of government support and that, at some point, the government support will be reduced. The example given for this was the ethanol industry, where the stocks associated with this business ran up hard and ran down quicker. In the same vein, if a company has a material portion of its business in states that sponsor terrorism, arguably that company is working too hard to keep the top line growing. The Patriot Fund offers the individual the opportunity to divest their portfolio of volatility and risk from toxic externalities. The Patriot Fund mimics the public sector's "terror-free" policy, and is offering up the same strategy for private-sector investors.

SUMMARY

The key to avoiding wealth destruction by Congress is to have investing time horizons that take you past Congress's relentless dysfunction in the moment. You can do this using the Congressional Effect approach on a sustained basis. You can also do it by adopting strategies such as value investing, which looks to buy companies at prices in the stock market that are trading at a significant discount to their long-term value. Contrarian investing is another way of identifying out-of-favor values.

Congress has shown itself to be innumerate and incontinent in dealing with our budgetary dynamics, so much so that the Senate has not produced a budget as required by law for the past three years. The impact of this has been that the dollar has weakened steadily as a store of value over the past 10 years. Investors should have some portion of their assets in gold and gold-related funds as insurance against further deterioration in the dollar's value and role as the world's reserve currency.

International funds obviously are much less directly impacted by Congress's actions and allow diversification away from legislative risk. In seeking to reduce risk exposure, it is also a good idea to focus on funds that reduce global security risk.

Finally, the government has intruded into the marketplace with conflicting impacts on the economy. On the one hand, the government is trying to create inflation by printing more money. On the other, the avalanche of new regulations in health care, finance, employment, and the environmental area have paralyzed businesses, and this paralysis creates deflation. The government has no real idea which of these forces will prevail, although the odds probably favor inflation. Even if that plan succeeds, what is the likelihood that we will get only a modest amount of inflation and not too much? It is a good idea for investors in general to still defend against extreme scenarios that would have been considered highly improbable just a few years ago.

NOTES

1. http://dailyreckoning.com/emerging-markets-walk-a-fine-line/
2. CNN Money Roundtable Interview with Abhay Deshpande, December 13, 2010, http://features.blogs.fortune.cnn.com/tag/abhay-deshpande/
3. Ibid.
4. *Forbes* magazine interview with Robert Kleinschmidt, August 23, 2011, www.forbes.com/sites/steveforbes/2011/08/23/steve-forbes-interview-robert-kleinschmidt-contrarian-investor/4/
5. www.reuters.com/article/2012/04/04/us-funds-fairholme-idUSBRE83312 B20120404
6. www.valuewalk.com/2012/02/bruce-berkowitz-sears-intrinsic-value-is-the-64-question/
7. CNN Money Roundtable Interview with Abhay Deshpande, December 13, 2010, http://features.blogs.fortune.cnn.com/tag/abhay-deshpande/
8. Tocqeville Fund Manager Q&A (Question Five), www.tocqueville.com/sites/default/files/TGLDX_2012–03_ManagerQA.pdf

CHAPTER 12

"That Government Is Best that Governs Least"

Thomas Paine was right when he said it in 1776, and it is still valuable advice for governing and for understanding Congress's impact on the stock market today. We have seen in earlier chapters how Congress is relentlessly short-sighted. I do not mean to suggest that all congressmen are bad actors, especially intentionally bad actors. In fact, the ones I have met are predominantly intelligent, articulate leaders, many of whom clearly went to Washington with a motive of trying to make the world a better place. But once they drink that Washington water, something happens. When they are in that Washington crowd, doing what they see everyone else do to get reelected, the natural outcome of the forces that drive them harms your investments.

This chapter reviews the impact that the drift toward partisan politics is likely to have on investing, the aggravating impact government has on the business and investing cycle, and the conflicting and cumulative, mostly harmful, impact Congress has on the market. In passing, it deals with whether there are some things we can do to start to change the adverse incentives Congress has to intervene in the broad markets.

PROGNOSIS: INCREASINGLY PARTISAN POLITICS IS NOT GOOD FOR THE MARKET

It is the nature of all politics that there will be factions. Henry Adams identified the nature of the beast when he said, "*Politics*, as a practice, whatever its professions, has always been the systematic organization of *hatreds.*"[1] It is one thing to systematically organize hatreds in the agrarian economy that existed in 1791, or in Henry Adams's time of the late 1800s. It is quite another to organize hatreds with all the tools of modern targeted communication available today. This in large part accounts for our general feeling that political discourse is getting out of hand.

The age of the Internet has accelerated the channeling of America in an echo chamber of reverberating opinion, leaving us all more partisan than ever. It is manifested both physically and in our self-censored news and culture diets. In *The Big Sort: Why the Clustering of Like-Minded America Is Tearing Us Apart* (New York: Houghton Mifflin, 2008) by Bill Bishop and Robert Cushing, the authors found that America is increasingly physically dividing into micro neighborhoods of homogenous political views. The nature of social targeting in advertising allows politicians to micro-target as never before. President Bush, for example, had a mailing campaign that reached almost every house in the country with a letter on the single most important issue to that household. President Obama had a legendary effort on the Internet to target his supporters, and it is expected that his next campaign will be even more advanced from a data management and targeted communication point of view.

When these sophisticated marketing and targeting techniques are combined with the political tradition of gerrymandering to create mostly safe congressional districts, the result is an *increasingly* partisan political process, even as the professional political class works harder and more successfully to entrench its clients. As commentator Joe Scarborough noted in his book *Rome Wasn't Burnt in a Day*:

> *[B]ecause Republicans and Democrats conspire to gerrymander one another's districts so incumbents are rarely challenged at the polls, the turnover rate on Capitol Hill is lower than in the old Soviet Politburo. This means reckless politicians rarely have to pay the price for their misdeeds.*[2]

As a result of these disparate forces, even though there are many more voices on the Web and traditional media is fracturing, each community hears a greater conformity of opinion. So we have the paradox of the Internet making many more sources available to people to investigate, but in practical effect faced with almost overwhelming choices, people actually rely more on political branding than ever.

As our democracy expanded and we became less of a republic, this ratcheting of partisan politics has in turn enabled the federal government to relentlessly capture more of the economy. But the state economy does not run efficiently. As the government has taken control of more and more of the economy over the past 100 years and used the leverage of power to promote its agenda, there has been a greater and greater disconnect between the productive private economy and the parasitic government economy.

This process, repeated with increasing intensity over the past several generations, and especially over the past decade, has brought us to the brink of disaster. In 1929, the federal government accounted for 3 percent of the economy. Today, it is 25 percent and growing. In every area of policy, our nation's encrusted, barnacled hull is barely scraping by. In almost every industry, to a greater or lesser extent, Congress has created so much red tape and distortion of the natural market that we no longer know the price of many of the most important things in our lives. In medicine, there are at least three prices for every visit with a doctor: your copayment of $20, the $270 bill he sends the insurance company, and the $137 reimbursement he actually receives beyond the copayment. In housing, after years of tax breaks and Fannie Mae and Freddie Mac subsidies and misallocation of credit, the entire housing market became completely overdone, creating an astonishing multigenerational bubble and collapse. At the end of 2011, 29 percent of all homes with mortgages were estimated to be underwater—with mortgages in excess of their fair value—because the average home collapsed by more than a third in value from its 2006 peak just as millions were encouraged to overborrow to "own" a home. In retirement resources, in 2010, 43 percent of all workers had less than $10,000 of any kind of savings, including retirement savings. Our deficit of $1.299 trillion in 2011 *exceeded* the $1.272 trillion we raised from federal income taxes. Our main entitlement programs, Social Security, Medicaid, and Medicare, are growing much faster than the official inflation rate and faster than our economy. The entitlement programs are unsustainable because under current benefit formulas, they have all tipped and are now increasingly paying out more than they take in. Because of such growth, mathematically there is no difference between these programs as they stand now and a Ponzi scheme. Like other Ponzi schemes, the participants will be stiffed compared to their expectations. The only question that remains is how much.

We have reached a moment when 130 million Americans out of 310 million rely on the government for a material portion of their daily sustenance.[3] They are dependents of the government. For example, there are now 46 million Americans receiving food stamps. Over 10 million are on Social Security disability.[4] Dozens and dozens of millions more are receiving transfer payments of some sort, including Social Security, Earned Income Tax Credit (EITC), unemployment benefits, college tuition, Medicare, Medicaid, and so on. The official number of federal, state, and local employees is over 22 million, more than double the number of Americans employed in manufacturing. During any one year, an additional 20 to 40 million Americans are employed delivering goods and services to the government as well.

From reviewing behavioral finance as it applies to Congress, we know that Congress perceives taking away a benefit to be at least twice as painful as the perceived pleasure of providing a benefit. In votes, this means that taking away something may result in losing two or three or four times as many votes as providing a benefit gains. As a result, Congress lives in a universe where at every step it feels it is about to touch a third rail and get electrocuted. So both parties are now in paralysis, and engage in comprehensive posturing designed to give the impression of resolving differences, but not resolving meaningful differences. Having defaulted into a role of simply preserving their power, Congress is rightfully worried that the people understand how unwisely we have been governed. According to a recent Rasmussen poll, 59 percent of Americans would replace *every single* member of Congress today if they had the chance.

Not that the American public is wrong in its thinking. For that matter, even Congress doesn't trust Congress. For sheer mismanagement, it is difficult to outdo Congress's performance in August 2011, when it failed to reach a meaningful compromise on reducing our budget deficit, with the awful result that the debt of the United States was downgraded. Faced with that imminent downgrade, and spending other people's money without any budget for over two years, in violation of the Budget Act of 1974, Congress reached a dysfunctional "compromise" of assigning the task to a congressional super-committee of 12 senators and congressmen. To force the super-committee to identify cuts, the law provided that if there was no compromise, the budget would be cut across the board in defense and health care. But no deal was struck. In the event, the compromise default cut that actually took effect had less than $1/2$ percent of its cuts take place in the first two years following the compromise. For all of 2011, it would be fair to characterize the entire legislative session as one long game of hot potato. With over $5 trillion added to the debt of the federal government in the past four years, we have reached the point where our budget is simply incomprehensible. Congress has become completely innumerate and irresponsible.

Congressional incontinence on the budget has also made it mathematically inevitable that we will suffer further credit downgrades. So far, there has been a willing suspension of disbelief. The Federal Reserve Bank, nominally independent but with its leaders chosen by the government, in recent auctions has purchased over 60 percent of the offered Treasury bonds and notes, directly from a branch of the government, our Treasury. No doubt, a big portion of the remaining 40 percent is other central banks scratching our back so we will scratch theirs. We no longer know what the price of our debt used to fund our country on a daily basis really is. The real price is that price that the market will take to clear the amount we have to raise without having the Fed as the lead buyer. Italy is now paying over 5 percent and so is Spain. Our finances, on the pure numbers of debt as a percentage of gross domestic product (GDP), are not in very different shape. At some point, it is likely the bond vigilantes will be seen on the horizon and the market will ask us to pay the same amount in interest as other countries with more than 100 percent debt to GDP coverage, and we could find ourselves dedicating between a third and a half of the income taxes we raise just to service interest on our debt. Remember federal income tax receipts were $1.27 trillion in 2011,[5] and our interest expense was $454 billion,[6] or 35 percent. And that is with interest rates averaging under 3 percent on our debt.[7] At 5 percent, the average rate that prevailed for most of the past 50 years, we would have to pay more than half of the money we raise from income taxes just to pay interest on our debt. What happens if rates go that high? Or higher, as they were when inflation nearly got out of control in the late 1970s?

These mathematical facts, coupled with the August 2011 downgrade call into question the patience of the ratings agencies. In April 2012, Egan Jones, which had been the first to downgrade the United States, further downgraded our country's debt. And the dollar, which until now has acted as the world's reserve currency is slowly being undermined in that role as many countries reach bilateral agreements to start trading in their own currencies without translation into dollars. And rating agencies don't have to move one rating at a time. If conditions warrant, there can be multiple downgrades. Certainly, the 500 percent march of gold from under $300 per ounce at the end of 1990s to over $1,600 today lets us know the dollar is in grave peril. A similar logarithmic move of 500 percent would place gold at $8,000 per ounce. This is a pretty conceivable move over the next 10 years given that we are now borrowing 43 cents of every dollar we spend.

CONFLICTING GOVERNMENT MANDATES PROMOTE MARKET INSTABILITY

One of the observations in this book has been that the government is working at cross purposes with itself in order to try to manage the economy when what the economy really needs is to be left alone. The left hand really does not know what the right hand is doing, and sometimes is much stronger and sometimes much weaker than the other hand, so they do not know how to coordinate. The government has set in play giant forces, some of which are extraordinarily inflationary, and some of which are extraordinarily deflationary, and the one thing you know for sure from the track record of the government is that, triumphant appearances on TV notwithstanding, the government is essentially like the little man who played the wizard in *The Wizard of Oz*. Even though the government would tell you, "Do not pay any attention to that little man," like Dorothy, we all know that it is just a little man behind a screen who is really pulling the strings, a little man who knows less than the market. If you catch him alone and ask him, "Do you really know what the outcome is going to be here?," in a moment of honesty he would be forced to say, "I do not."

The right hand of the government is the inflation side of the government's "reptilian brain." The reptilian brain is that part of the brain we have in common with lizards and dinosaurs. The inflation lobe of the government's network is led by the Fed. That little man behind the curtain is Fed chairman Ben Bernanke. The Federal Reserve has essentially tripled its balance sheet in the past three years and has printed trillions of new dollars. They do not like to actually call it "printing money," but instead prefer obfuscating terms like *quantitative easing* and *operation twist*. He's given it as much stimulus as he can and he's used quantitative easing and he's printed money as fast as he can, but he doesn't know if the investing public will really believe the economy has recovered. Certainly, the net flows of money out of domestic equity mutual funds as discussed by TrimTabs and the extraordinarily low volumes that accompanied the rallies in the spring of 2012 suggest the broad public is still skeptical about the state of the economy. The Fed has also adopted a zero interest rate policy (ZIRP) to force investors to take on risk and buy into equities, if they do not like the "financial repression," as Bill Gross of PIMCO puts it,[8] of receiving little or no interest on their savings. Nevertheless, Fed chairman Bernanke is determined to create inflation and tells us not to worry, we can handle inflation. That is the one economic force we think we can manage.

The left side of the government's reptilian brain is the fiscal and regulatory side. This is the side that taxes, and regulates, and depresses economic activity, leading directly to deflation and credit defaults. Its primary means of creating deflation is the paralysis caused by the relentless blizzard of regulation emanating out of Congress and the presidency. Dodd-Frank alone has 243 new regulations (as compared to the 16 in Sarbanes-Oxley that were sufficient to effectively shut down the initial public offering [IPO] market). Between the 5,000 new pages of laws passed for financial and health care reform in the past two years, and thousands more regulatory pages for things like new rules for energy and pollution, the rest of the government is promoting regulatory paralysis, which is deflationary. The banks are being turned into utilities that can lend very little to business. There is talk of the banks having to have 17 percent reserves. The regulators want the banks to have virtually no risk on their balance sheet. But the banks are supposed to lend to vibrant businesses, projects, and people. How can they have no risk? The wealth advisory firms have been guided by regulators to commoditize their advice, and securities firms increasingly no longer effectively make markets because it might be proprietary trading in the eyes of the regulators. Only the largest firms will survive in the law's current format. The Environmental Protection Agency (EPA) is passing regulations that seem to be aimed at bankrupting most coal companies without any useful risk-reward calculation from the benefits of the regulation. Dodd-Frank has so many sources of liability associated with offering consumer finance products that it is likely that if the law is not modified, that the average consumer will be strapped for years, even if there is a nominal recovery. We have reached a point where the regulatory burden in the country has been estimated at $2 trillion a year.

THE CUMULATIVE EFFECT OF UNINTENDED CONSEQUENCES IS CONGRESSIONAL WEALTH DESTRUCTION

Why do I think the government has no clue about all the unintended consequences of its uncoordinated activities? Because the actual motive of people in government is to expand the power of the government, which each administrator measures in the size of their department, not to help the private sector. They do not have their own money at stake, so they can be very unconcerned and incoherent about the outcomes. From what I have seen, Fed Chairman Bernanke takes his job quite seriously, but even he was caught utterly speechless when JP Morgan Chase CEO Jamie Dimon asked him "whether anyone had considered the cumulative impact of all these regulations."[9] If the Fed Chairman cannot tell what the impact of all these regulations is going to be, how is the average citizen supposed to figure it out?

We have reached a point where the out-of-pocket costs to comply with new regulations is likely *exceeded* by the wealth destroyed by Congress as reflected in lower stock market prices. Earlier in the book we described the many different times that Congress considered laws, considered issues, and on a structural basis just had their own basic job description that drove them to do some things that were utterly dysfunctional. We have seen how each industry is depressed while Congress goes through a consideration of what additional regulations need to be implemented or threatened as a means of extorting and seeking rents. In very rough numbers, we showed in Chapter 5 that health care reform penalized the stock market $350 billion in market capitalization, and Dodd-Frank as much as $500 billion; the coal industry, which currently supplies over half the fuel we use to generate electricity, lost another $10 to $30 billion in market capitalization. It is like this for almost every industry caught in Congress's legislative focus. In big, round, order-of-magnitude numbers, the housing market at first probably created what seemed like an extra five trillion dollars in excess wealth in its steroid-induced bipartisan boom into 2006. That represents 70 million homes peaking at a median price of $240,000, or $70,000 above their sustainable affordable price. In hindsight, the superheating of the housing market probably wiped out $10 trillion of wealth between 2006 and 2012 if you count both the collapse of housing prices, which has in turn deeply damaged housing as a store of value for the average American, and the follow-on effects on the rest of the economy from losing housing as a source of financing for so many other things in life.

These numbers are obviously order-of-magnitude numbers. While the damage caused by Congress may not all be permanent, it is damage, and it affects the economy's opportunity to take advantage of other opportunities. We saw from William Bernstein in the Introduction that all of the material progress we have made from the beginning of the Industrial Revolution amounts to 2 percent real growth per year, compounded over 200 years. Yet now, we are only hoping for 2 percent real growth in good times. Why can't we be as free as Hong Kong, and go back to growing at a greater rate, like 4 percent real growth? We should be able to have policies that allow that. After all, we grew faster than that in the 1980s. Just the three industries cited above accounted for depressed values of nearly $900 billion in the last stock market downturn. On a total U.S. equity market capitalization of $15 trillion, this represents a 6 percent loss, even apart from the much larger loss in housing.

But even that loss does not reflect the full impact of the regulatory burden imposed by Congress. Losing $2 trillion in value every year just to regulatory burden alone represents lost wealth that is enormously deflationary. For example, we now have a patent backlog of over 1 million patent applications pending,[10] as against approximately 10 million patents issued through 2010.[11] But the value of our intellectual property is a significant portion of our wealth, representing at least $5 trillion or more, and our most important exports.[12] What happens if Hong Kong or Britain or Estonia starts processing patents quicker so inventors flock to their shores instead of ours? Congress has played a key role in ignoring this sort of wealth destruction, and this is damage that is becoming increasingly irreversible.

The best way to think about it is that in economies that are freer and are growing as we once did when we were freer, their stock markets are in a virtuous cycle where they find themselves adding to their net worth. We find ourselves depleting our net worth. In industry after industry, we shoot ourselves in various parts of our anatomy and then blithely expect the rest of the world to patiently wait while we toy around with nonsense. The Chinese must be laughing uncontrollably at our antics on projects like the Keystone Pipeline. Energy that is at our doorstep, where we could make the money from processing it and have more secure supplies, is about to be routed to and dedicated to China. The rejection of this project alone is proof that we have entered the fourth stage that Ray Dalio has identified in the progress of nations when a country is no longer rich but thinks it is rich.

CONGRESS'S DYSFUNCTIONALITY AND THE 2012 ELECTION

So we find ourselves with highly partisan politics on the eve of the election of 2012. As this book goes to press, it is clear that the 2012 federal elections will be the most viciously fought in the memory of anybody alive. To make matters worse, Congress's utter dysfunctionality will be on full display in the fall. In August 2011, having had more than half a year to negotiate a bipartisan debt ceiling, Congress found itself unable to make any meaningful short-term cuts in the budget, and instead delegated its power to a "super-committee" consisting of 12 selected senators and congressmen. The super-committee was charged with reaching a bipartisan solution by Thanksgiving. Unable to compromise by Thanksgiving, the super-committee lapsed into allowing the "default" cuts in the budget agreement to fall solely on Medicare and the defense budgets to trigger automatic cuts beginning in 2013. The *only* thing the budget agreement promised is that we had bought enough time to get the budget issue past the 2012 elections. You would think that was the one thing neither political party wanted to have happen. But just as the Cash for Clunkers program was designed to last for four months but ran out of capacity in six days, Congress has likely managed to put itself in the position of having to lift the debt capacity. In January 2012, the debt ceiling was quietly lifted an additional $1.2 trillion based on Congress's failure to object to President Obama's request for a further increase. So here is Congress, about to give an instant replay of its single most humiliating performance ever. Sometime soon, likely before 2013, we will run out of money again. But this will take place against the background of the elections, the continued unraveling of the Eurozone, and the declining status of the dollar as the world's reserve currency. Watching the dysfunctionality of Congress, in 2011 Standard & Poor's rating agency concluded that the United States had so degraded its political decision-making capability that it downgraded the U.S. debt for the first time in history. What will they think if they have to watch the same movie with worse numbers and worse timing?

Making it even more appalling, many of the nation's most significant tax cuts will be set to expire at the end of 2012. The Bush tax cuts, the patch to the alternative minimum tax, the corporate tax, the estate tax, and the payroll tax all have had temporary reductions set to expire at the end of this Congress's term. Rough estimates are that $500 billion in additional taxes will hit the economy starting in January 2013 if nothing changes. Even the *New York Times* has embraced the term *Taxmageddon* to describe it.[13] Others call it the "fiscal cliff." Personally, I prefer the term "fiscal abyss." Not knowing what the new tax rates will be, many long term owners may choose to sell their assets in the second half of 2012 just to avoid the uncertainty of the "fiscal abyss." The uncertainty created for business from the budget and the tax contingencies suggest that extreme caution is warranted for the fall and beyond, and may well negatively impact the market.

As this book goes to print, it also seems that this hotly contested election will be a close election. If it is close, it may well be seriously litigated. As we saw in Chapter 10, litigated elections cause additional market sell-offs because they add to uncertainty. Coming against a background of a shaky world economy (especially in Europe), an international order in upheaval, and the most important aspects of our federal budget and tax regimes unsettled, it may not be a good idea to take a full measure of exposure to the equity markets.

So what should an investor do to minimize the damage caused by Congress? Well, one way to systematically avoid the damage posed by Congress is simply recognize when your portfolio is exposed to damage that Congress might cause and consider reducing your exposure to equities when they are in session, as discussed in Chapter 7. The main idea in reducing the impact of legislative risk created by Congress is to understand how short-term Congress is in its thinking and to do the opposite by thinking long term and contrarian whenever possible. As discussed in Chapter 11, the styles of investing that I think most capture this are value investing, contrarian investing, and international value investing. When looking for countries to invest in, it is best to focus on countries having rising amounts of freedom. You can find a list of these countries every year in the studies done by the Heritage Foundation.

This book has gone to some effort to emphasize that we have left the era of "normal" investing, when the government was not as much of a factor in evaluating prospects. In the good old days, the chances of meaningful inflation were not very great, and the chances of deflation appeared *de minimus*. Today, given the government's overreach into our economy, the chances of either of those extreme forces becoming the dominant factor are much greater than ever before. So investors have to be defensive and have a mix of assets, at least some of which will hopefully outperform in extreme environments. To the extent the government continues to print money, I think it is a good idea to have some gold in your portfolio, and some other inflation hedges. It is also a good idea to have some cash and other securities that thrive in a deflationary environment like utilities. It may seem strange to try to play defense against two opposite outcomes, but the nature of good asset allocation is playing it safe. If it turns out we go back to having a more normal economy, and we know it and believe in it, there will be plenty of opportunities to make money.

There will be occasional opportunities to look at something the government is doing and, if you think it is insane, to do the opposite and make money. Many years ago, there was talk of an apocryphal memo listing indicators, entitled "The Fidelity 100" that was circulated to the Fidelity fund managers. In those days, to identify a piece of news that was fully discounted, one indicator they reportedly used was the Sunday *New York Times* indicator. They felt that if a business story was on the front page of a widely circulated news source like the Sunday *New York Times*, there was no one who had not heard the news, and the market was set to go in the opposite direction. The most prominent example of this was the cover of *Time*, which in 1980 proclaimed the death of equities at the beginning of a 20-year record breaking bull market.

WHAT HAPPENS WHEN CONGRESS DOES NOT KNOW THE PRICE?

One other thing profoundly concerns me about reducing the damage that Congress sporadically inflicts on our investments. At the very beginning of the book, I expressed a concern that Congress does not know the cost or price of its actions. The CBO uses only static scoring to estimate the impact of a law on our budget. Many people have advocated dynamic scoring, which would allow for higher revenues being estimated for certain lower tax rates. It should be about optimizing revenues, especially in an internationally competitive world. In addition, I think the CBO process should be supplemented to assess the capital markets impact of what Congress does. Perhaps some committee should have the responsibility for estimating that the health care stocks' market capitalization will decline by $500 billion if we pass this law, or the retail sector will decline by $100 billion in market capitalization if we pass that law.

Let's call that committee the Capital Markets Impact Committee or CMIM for short. It has long been accepted in Washington that the presence of an acronym makes a prediction credible. Scoring by the CMIM could be used in the political arena to help weigh whether a bill was good or bad for the country, and it is highly unlikely that it could be less accurate than the scorings currently produced by the CBO. In hindsight, if a CMIM had scored the Patient Protection and Affordable Care Act as eliminating $500 billion of wealth in the stock market, there might have been a different outcome regarding that law.

As Congress spends other people's money, it has lost track of the price. Whole sectors of our economy have been shunted away from being market economies where the feedback of price and demand exert relentless discipline to sectors being driven in large part by government interference and price setting and massive regulation. The health care sector, the banking sector, the food sector, and the energy sector, to name just a few, have all been subject to rising government intervention over the past 10 years. Even the Internet sector, our one unequivocal growth sector, is now threatened with new, comprehensive legislation. All of this has been aggravated by a decline in market information. The JOBS Act, well intentioned for small businesses, mostly favors the plugged-in private investor. It does relax SarbOx and research restrictions, but I doubt it will add enough to the attractiveness of small company IPOs to achieve its purpose of "jump-starting" the IPO market back to 1990s levels. And the private placements that will result from the it will not deliver a daily stock price, and will not encourage the feedback that a daily stock price gives to a small company about whether they are doing the right things. For example, the valuations of small companies in the private venture market still often exceed those available to small public companies that suffer from the regulatory burden of being public. In that sense, an inverted equity curve still exists for many sectors, and the regulatory burden is too high. While it remains high, we can expect to remain in this subpar "recovery" that has brought so many families to their knees. We might even have a double-dip recession. If we see instead a significant reduction of taxes or regulation hampering business formation, that would be a contrary indicator, as it was when Presidents Kennedy, Reagan, Clinton, and Bush cut taxes.

This fundamental innumeracy of Congress is starting to interfere with our ability as a nation to understand the price and even the function of a market, let alone the data that the market is telling us. In industry after industry, thanks to the involvement of Congress, we no longer know the price. When the government is subsidizing your lifestyle, you no longer know the true price of your lifestyle. One hundred thirty million people in America have government help. It's clear that no one in Washington knows the price. When you visit Washington, everyone in Washington is to a greater or lesser degree a member of a cost center. If they're directly in the government, they're a a cost center. If they're with a large litigating firm as lawyers, they're a cost center. If they're with a lobbying center, they're a cost center. The only people that I can think of in Washington who are genuine entrepreneurs are people who are basically selling food or music or have restaurants, cleaning supplies, and tourist gifts.

CONGRESS NEEDS TO ATTRACT THE BEST TALENT

I cannot resist asking whether there are other things we could do to make Congress more effective. Well, given that they could hardly be less effective than they are now, the answer has to be yes, although it is mostly beyond the scope of this book. I will just mention a few random thoughts on this subject. First, the rest of America travels for business, sometimes a lot. I think congressmen should mostly work out of their districts. Why do they have to be in Washington, D.C., to vote? A CEO doesn't have to be at the office in this day and age to get a sales report, or to tell marketing to launch the ad campaign with the lizard. Congressmen who lived primarily in their districts would be better informed by their constituents, less subject to lobbying, and get divorced less. Everyone would be better off.

Second, I think Congress should work smarter, not harder, by which I really mean they should work less. Their very presence in Washington creates uncertainty. If they stayed on vacation longer, the stock market would benefit. We would be particularly better off if they could start to reduce the size of government the same way the average American household has deleveraged. Article I, Section 4 of the Constitution states:

The Congress shall assemble at least once in every Year . . .

It is unrealistic to think Congress could meet so little, but aspirationally, there is no difference between understanding that all congressional meetings have a cost in uncertainty that impacts our markets, and understanding that every trip to the hospital carries risk.

Third, while I doubt you can get congressmen to agree to forego gerrymandering, I am certain you could get them to agree to give themselves a raise. A giant raise. I want every congressman to be rich *if they do a good job*. It is bad business for the stewards of our economy to think that the only way they can get wealthy is to earmark a road next to their property or short mortgages after a briefing by Bernanke. In Singapore, the legislators are paid the average of the highest paid professionals in other fields. If our top business and professional private sector talent didn't think they were taking a giant pay cut, more of them would show up in Congress, and we would all be better off for attracting better talent. Congressmen should get rich from their day jobs. Tying their bonus income to successful governing, and perhaps even real returns for the overall economy has its own problems, but at least their incentives would be aligned with ours.

I think we need to pay enough to attract top talent even though that does not sound like the citizen-legislators the founders had in mind. If we are going to have a professional political class, let's get the best available people at least thinking about it.

Finally, I would embrace Warren Buffett's quip on managing the budget. Having given Congress a chance to be wealthy, if in any year they permitted a deficit in excess of 3 percent, they should be ineligible for reelection.[14] If they can't save the country, they can at least save their own skins.

IN CONCLUSION

This book has tried to make investors more aware of the damage Congress causes to our investments. In industry after industry, there has been too much emphasis by the government on almost completely eliminating risk when in fact the biggest creator of risk is the government itself. Documented impacts of the effect of legislation show that some of our most important industries, including health care, finance, and energy, have their stocks suffer when government changes or even just threatens to change the rules. As we have seen, just the recent damage caused primarily by the government to the stocks of those industries has totaled hundreds of billions of dollars or more over the past several years.

On a cumulative basis, over very long periods of time, this Congressional Effect has caused a great deal of daily damage to our stock market. Unfortunately, the structural weaknesses of our political system incent each member of Congress to "do something" to further entrench their position and avoid the accusation of being part of a "do-nothing Congress." But when they do something, they get more power and we get less success because it is we who pay the price in our businesses and in our investment returns. Congress uses behavioral finance principles to make us fear that what we already have will be taken away. But with more freedom, we could all have so much more than we do now. The missing hundreds of billions mentioned earlier could have helped to fuel a stock market rising the way it did for the 50 years after World War II at long-term rates of return of 9 percent or better. Instead of those kinds of results, the last decade has been a lost decade.

George Santayana taught us all that "those who cannot remember the past are condemned to repeat it." Congress has for a very long time been dysfunctional, it is currently dysfunctional, and unfortunately it will likely continue to be dysfunctional no matter who is in office. As investors, as long as the markets are hostage to Congress, it is up to us to minimize the harm they do to our investments. Congressional wealth destruction is just a fact of life, but like most chronic conditions, it can be reduced and mitigated if you are aware of it. Investors are well advised to use an understanding of the Congressional Effect to further protect and reduce the risk to their portfolios from the impact of relentless government activity.

NOTES

1. Henry Adams, *The Education of Henry Adams* (Boston: Houghton Mifflin, 1918).

2. Joe Scarborough, *Rome Wasn't Burnt in a Day: The Real Deal on How Politicians, Bureaucrats, and Other Washington Barbarians Are Bankrupting America* (New York: HarperCollins, 2005).

3. Conservative Byte, "1 in 5 Americans Are Dependent on Government," February 3, 2012, http://conservativebyte.com/2012/02/1-in-5-americans-are-dependent-on-government/

4. www.ssa.gov/policy/docs/quickfacts/stat_snapshot/

5. www.usgovernmentrevenue.com/yearrev2011_0.html

6. www.treasurydirect.gov/govt/reports/ir/ir_expense.htm

7. www.treasurydirect.gov/govt/rates/pd/avg/2011/2011_01.htm

8. Jim Fink, "Federal Reserve Extends Zero Interest Rate Policy (ZIRP) to 2014," February 3, 2012, www.investingdaily.com/14714/federal-reserve-extends-zero-interest-rate-policy-zirp-to-2014

9. Courtney Comstock, "Jamie Dimon Stunningly Confronts Ben Bernanke, Suggests Excessive Financial Regulations Are Slowing the Recovery," June 7, 2007, http://articles.businessinsider.com/2011–06–07/wall_street/30061911_1_job-growth-big-bank-lending

10. www.cbsnews.com/8301–503544_162–20029731–503544.html

11. www.inventionstatistics.http://www.inventionstatistics.com/Number_of_New_Patents_Issued.htmlcom/Number_of_New_Patents_Issued.html

12. http://dcipattorney.com/2010/12/the-us173–4b-global-intellectual-property-marketplace/

13. David Leonhardt, "Coming Soon: 'Taxmaggedon,'" *New York Times*, April 3, 2012, www.nytimes.com/2012/04/15/sunday-review/coming-soon-taxmageddon.html?_r=3&ref=opinion&pagewanted=all

14. "Warren Buffett Says Congress Is Playing Russian Roulette," *New York Post*, July 8, 2011, www.nypost.com/p/news/business/warren_buffett_says_congress_is_fE02GYJiEgmzPy7MjWxVaN

About the Author

Eric Singer manages the Congressional Effect Fund, a public mutual fund launched in 2008 (www.congressionaleffect.com). Before starting this mutual fund, his practice focused on raising funds for—and investing in—small-cap public companies. During the 1990s, he was head of Corporate Finance at Gerard Klauer Mattison & Co., a research-oriented brokerage firm. In the 1980s, he launched a corporate finance new products group at Smith Barney, and headed a similar group at PaineWebber. He also practiced law for several years and developed the Empire Hotel in New York City.

He is a frequent op-ed contributor in *Investor's Business Daily* as well as *Forbes, American Spectator, American Thinker, Townhall, Seeking Alpha, The Future of Capitalism* and *Newsmax*, and has appeared on national radio and TV programs, including *Fox & Friends, Fox Business News*, CNN, and Bloomberg TV.

He graduated from the Bronx High School of Science; SUNY at Stony Brook, where he was Phi Beta Kappa; and Cornell Law School, where he was on Law Review. He is married to Aet Paaro Singer, whom he met in college, and has two children.

Index

Stay in touch!

Subscribe to our free Finance and Accounting eNewsletters at
www.wiley.com/enewsletters

Visit our blog: **www.capitalexchangeblog.com**

 Follow us on Twitter
@wiley_finance

 "Like" us on Facebook
www.facebook.com/wileyglobalfinance

 Find us on LinkedIn
Wiley Global Finance Group

WILEY Global Finance
WHERE DATA FINDS DIRECTION